"READY
FOR THE
PEOPLE"

"READY FOR THE PEOPLE"

MY MOST CHILLING CASES
AS A PROSECUTOR

MARISSA N. BATT

Introduction by Johnnie L. Cochran, Jr.

Arcade Publishing · New York

Copyright © 2004 by Marissa N. Batt
Introduction copyright © 2004 by Johnnie L. Cochran, Jr.

FIRST EDITION

"Mr. Pitiful" (words and music by Otis Redding and Steve Cropper) copyright
© 1965 by Irving Music, Inc. Copyright renewed. All rights reserved. Used by
permission.

Library of Congress Cataloging-in-Publication Data

   Batt, Marissa N.
      "Ready for the people" : my most chilling cases as a prosecutor /
   Marissa N. Batt ; introduction by Johnnie L. Cochran, Jr. —1st ed.
         p. cm.
      ISBN 1-55970-705-4
         1. Batt, Marissa N. 2. Public prosecutors—California—Los
   Angeles—Biography. 3. Criminal justice, Administration of—
   California—Los Angeles. I. Title.
      KF373.B346A3 2004
      345.794'9401—dc22   2003061752

Published in the United States by Arcade Publishing, Inc., New York
Distributed by AOL Time Warner Book Group

Visit our Web site at www.arcadepub.com

10 9 8 7 6 5 4 3 2 1

Designed by API

EB

PRINTED IN THE UNITED STATES OF AMERICA

For Ollie

CONTENTS

AUTHOR'S NOTE

In the world of big-city crime, the parlance of the streets has crept into the police station and made itself at home in the courthouse. The cops sound like crooks and the lawyers sound like cops. Sometimes our harsh language is filtered a bit before it finds its way onto the court record, but not always. Some crimes are so brutal that they can only be described in brutal terms. To pretty it up or water it down would be less than honest. The Buddha teaches that "even though one may resort to harsh words, if such words help the person to whom they are addressed, then they are worthy to be regarded as truthful words and gentle words."

ACKNOWLEDGMENTS

I owe a debt of gratitude to several people who offered me encouragement, criticism, and help during the writing and editing of this book. Thanks to Preston A. Whitmore II, who literally ordered me to write and presented me with a lovely fountain pen to underscore his point. Thanks to Cousin Lillian, Cousin Barbara, Brother Dan, Rachel Brown, and Ken Rotcop for their thoughtful comments. Thanks to the best agent on the planet, Mike Hamilburg. Thanks to the sweetest, smartest, fastest judge, Wayne Denton, for his friendship and support. Thanks to Mr. B., who teaches me about the Buddha's strength and compassion every day. And *mahalo nui loa* to Florence, *no ka oi*.

INTRODUCTION

I began my law career as a deputy city attorney in Los Angeles, where I gained firsthand knowledge of the daily challenges that prosecutors and district attorneys face. In fact, knowing how to effectively represent "the People" was one of the most critical and influential chapters in my legal education. Representing "the People" is an enormous task and an immense responsibility that prosecutors in this country take very seriously. They are acutely aware that they are sworn to uphold the law and that they bear the burden of proof.

Los Angeles Deputy District Attorney Marissa Batt is a prosecutor's prosecutor. She is full of zeal for her profession and possesses an insider's knowledge of the workings of the criminal justice system. She understands that from the moment a case is presented until a verdict is rendered, the public seldom gets an unfiltered view of what happens in and around the courtroom. Marissa sets out to balance the scales of justice with *"Ready for the People": My Most Chilling Cases as a Prosecutor.*

In a straightforward and compelling writing style that closely mirrors the way she speaks, Marissa takes a penetrating look at three of the most disturbing of the thousands of cases she has prosecuted in her twenty-five years in the Los Angeles district attorney's office. Each case illustrates the various manipulations and repercussions of our remarkable justice system. They involve crimes ranging from arson, rape, and attempted murder to same-sex rape and the bludgeoning of an unarmed man. She introduces us to lowlife criminals, to modest, unsung heroes, and, most important, to LaShon, Patrice, Sheldon, and Jesús, the real people whose lives were so cruelly and permanently changed by crime.

The cases Marissa chose were selected less for their "shock and awe" value and more for the way they struck a chord in the fundamental human nature of this passionate prosecutor. Each case exhibits how crime comes a-callin'—sometimes in the most unlikely neighborhood setting and sometimes on victims who, at least on the surface, appear to be the least vulnerable to its whims.

In analyzing the details of these cases Marissa offers a seamless study in how the wheels of justice turn and sheds a penetrating human light into the minds of the victims and the perpetrators. She takes us to the crime as it is being committed and brings us along with her on the unpredictable route to the trial and jury selection. She explains the case that the defense attorney and prosecutor must make before the jury, and she explores the invisible dynamic behind the final verdict and its immediate aftermath. Finally, she reveals things we rarely see on TV courtroom dramas, like why there are times both parties would prefer a plea agreement rather than the strain of a lengthy trial.

The reader, in effect, becomes a member of Marissa's prosecution team, as she shares her thought processes, her work with police and investigators, her assessment and presentation of the evidence, her opening statement, and as she mulls over and delivers the most effective closing—the one that will best illustrate her case in the minds of the jury.

Some of the details Marissa shares are gritty and gruesome and difficult to absorb. But crime is never pretty or easy to digest. There are always victims, and those victims and the lives of their loved ones are forever altered by the brutality and senselessness of crime. Prosecutors are more aware than most members of society of the painful effects of crime, and they often identify and sympathize with the victims. Marissa succeeds in making us feel their pain, as well.

On occasion, prosecutors are fortunate enough to have the case at hand played out in the courtroom of a judge who believes in justice for all. Unfortunately, that is not always the case. In *"Ready for the People"* we see that sometimes the victims are able to describe the brutality of the crime in great detail, which helps the prosecutor build a solid case, but not always. And, sadly, sometimes the victim is victimized again by the trial itself. No matter what the outcome, as Marissa notes, these cases are about the "strength of the human spirit and my faith that justice is always done," whether or not it is on display in the courtroom.

Two of the featured cases in *"Ready for the People"* do not end with the results Marissa would have preferred, but she is not bitter or burdened by feelings of defeat because she knows that *the system works*. No prosecutor wins every case, and at the end of the day, this extraordinary prosecutor does her best by "the People" who put their trust in her. I congratulate Marissa not only for her outstanding skill as a prosecutor but equally for her dedication to her craft and for turning the courtroom into a classroom for readers everywhere. Marissa has sworn to give readers "the truth, the whole truth, and nothing but . . ." And because she delivers, our understanding of criminal justice will never be the same.

Johnnie L. Cochran, Jr.

"READY FOR THE PEOPLE"

PROLOGUE

I am what the media call a "veteran prosecutor." At one time or another over the past twenty-five years I have stood up and answered "Ready for the People" in each of the thirty-five courtrooms in the CCB. That's our shorthand for the Criminal Courts Building at 210 West Temple Street in downtown Los Angeles. I have prosecuted thousands of violent felonies, from armed robbery and hot prowl burglary to rape and sodomy, mayhem and murder. I have, quite literally, seen and heard it all.

You might assume that a quarter century spent immersed in violence and its concomitant pain and suffering would leave one jaded and hardened, perhaps with a more jaundiced view of one's fellow man and woman than someone not involved in The System. That is not how I feel. While the life of a trial deputy in the D.A.'s office is frequently frustrating and demoralizing, it can also be gratifying and inspiring.

The courtroom is the stage on which real-life dramas are played out. The audience is usually few in number—smaller than at any equity-waiver theater. And it isn't like they bought tickets and want to be there. Most jurors would rather be visiting the dentist than performing their civic duty. The witnesses are typically just as thrilled to be there: the exhausted police officer who has just come off the graveyard shift, the Latino or Asian victim who is obliged to relate everything through an interpreter, the humiliated prey of a violent sexual predator.

The prosecutor is the director and producer, and usually the prop manager and the scenic designer—but never, ever, one of the actors.

Perhaps you will recall how this cardinal rule of trial advocacy was broken many times during the internationally televised "trial of the century." It wasn't a pretty sight. The audience's attention should not be diverted from the facts of the case by the prosecutor's hairstyle or any other "incompetent, irrelevant, and immaterial" bit of stage business.

Among the myriad cases I have handled over the years, there are three that will always remain engraved in my memory. Although each of these cases received some media attention, I have not chosen to recount them for that reason.

You may think you know about crime and the criminal justice system because you pay attention. You read the paper—maybe more than one—listen to the radio, and watch television. The trouble is, you can read ten newspapers and you will still be left with information that is filtered, distorted, and incomplete. You deserve better.

If you'll join me, I'll give you "the truth, the whole truth, and nothing but." All except for a few names, which have been changed—not to protect the innocent, but to protect me, from possible recrimination, retribution, or worse.

So, come along. We'll lift the sheet, peel back the skin, and shine a penetrating light into the darkest corners of the criminal justice system. Let's get off the elevator on the eighteenth floor. . . .

ROAST TURKEY

GOOD NEIGHBOR

They might have gotten away with the whole thing if they had just stopped after the raping, pillaging, and burning. There had been five men originally involved in the offenses, but the other two had had enough and had gone home. They were never apprehended. Not so for our trio of criminals—they had to pull that one last purse-snatch robbery.

There was Dora Woods, bundled up in a long coat and muffler, her purse hanging over her shoulder, waiting for the 5:45 bus on Central Avenue. This was the way every weekday morning started for Dora. First a quick breakfast of oatmeal and black coffee with her husband, Henry. Then remember to put out fresh food and water for Sparky, their terrier. Then the hurried walk to the bus stop. Henry took the car to his job as a parking lot attendant downtown while Dora transferred three times from one of the MTA's graffiti-embellished chariots to another on her somewhat circuitous trek to the Westside, where she worked as a domestic.

Dora wasn't thinking about much of anything. It was a blustery morning, the stars were still out, she was glad she had remembered the muffler, it would be nice to get on a warm bus. . . .

She didn't see them coming up behind her until it was too late to run. One of the three, the little dark-skinned fellow with the oddly shaped head, grabbed the muffler and yanked her off her feet while the tall, light-complected one wrenched her purse away from her so violently that she could feel her shoulder pull out of the socket. She screamed in pain and terror while the third man, whose distinguishing feature was a set of very prominent and badly discolored teeth, told her to shut the fuck up. She screamed anyway, Dora couldn't stop herself. She couldn't seem to get up off the pavement, her purse was gone, her shoulder was throbbing. Bad Teeth repeated his order to shut up and kicked Dora in the stomach for emphasis. The three men then casually walked off in the direction of 128th Street.

Dora's screams had been heard by her neighbor, Toby Tyler, a body builder and trainer who was out walking his three Dobermans. You can imagine what happened next. Toby told me later that he thought one or more of them might have a gun, or at least a knife, but he was a good neighbor and a good citizen and the bad guys were going to be apprehended, there weren't no two ways about it. Another neighbor had heard screams and had dialed 911. Within minutes, a patrol unit was at the scene. There were the three punks, cowering in the dead end of an alleyway, the Dobermans on the verge of breakfast. If any crooks were ever happy to see the cops, it was those three thugs. An arrest for purse-snatch was a hell of a lot better than being torn to ribbons by Toby's Dobies.

Discipline

Of course, the part with Dora and Toby was just the beginning, or just the end, depending on your point of view. It was the beginning of the criminal case and it was the end of a vicious night of crime. Johnson, Houston, and Logan, along with their two still unidentified crime partners, had started out early in the evening the night before. The whole thing had been Johnson's idea. As Johnson explained to his homies, it was time to discipline his ho. A man should not have to tolerate an uppity ho who thought she could get by without her man. She had been holding out on him, he knew that. Her profitability had seriously diminished since she had taken up with that little dyke girlfriend of hers, that fuckin' LaShon. Patrice was his woman and she needed to be taught a lesson. This shit with LaShon was getting out of hand. LaShon telling Patrice she don't need no pimp. Fuck that shit. Come to think of it, LaShon needed a little correction herself. Both those bitches were getting on his last nerve.

Johnson mapped it out for Houston and Logan and his other two associates. You could always find LaShon and Patrice hanging out at the Hole in the Wall on Sunday evenings. Then they'd spend the night over at old Mr. Parsons's. Shit, Johnson speculated, that old muthafucka probably paid to watch them lick each other's pussy. Just thinking about it made him even madder. Fuck Mr. Parsons too, that sorry old broken-down nigger. Fuck him too. Yeah, Logan was up for this kind of a caper. Didn't Parsons have a color TV? His wife was in a nursing home—didn't he still have all her jewelry and shit at the house? Oh yeah, this will be good, Houston agreed.

The folks who hung out at the Hole in the Wall called the place a club, but you would take it for just another dilapidated, abandoned building, nestled between other dilapidated, abandoned buildings and trash-strewn, empty, burnt-out lots in a part of town that once was the hub of African-American culture. Back in the thirties, the long, grand stretch of Central Avenue was the center of the Black Renaissance in Los Angeles. In addition to the ubiquitous beauty parlors, barbershops, and small churches, Central Avenue was home to some of the swankiest restaurants and hippest nightclubs in the city. Even in the early forties, the gloss had yet to tarnish. But things were different now. Times had sure changed.

For Patrice and LaShon the place was perfect: cheap booze, readily available smack, and a clientele of like-minded individuals who had no problem with two lesbian hooker hypes who just wanted to have some fun. LaShon really loved Patrice; she'd liked her right off. They'd met about six months before at a needle exchange program. It made LaShon laugh—not the kind of place where you'd expect to find romance. But there was Patrice with that pretty golden skin and just a couple of freckles across her nose and those beautiful light eyes, those shiny eyes. And they had a lot in common: they'd both been raised by their grandmothers, they both had brothers in the joint, and they both had tried braiding hair before turning to prostitution as a more lucrative endeavor.

The feelings were mutual. Patrice was immediately impressed with LaShon. Here was a chick who could take care of herself. She didn't need no pimp to beat her up and take her money. It inspired Patrice. She had been with Johnson so long she could hardly imagine any other way until she hooked up with LaShon. LaShon was smart and fearless. Patrice adored her.

The crowd was thinning out at the Hole in the Wall and LaShon and Patrice were just fixing to leave out to Mr. Parsons's when Johnson and some of his buddies showed up. As soon as he saw Patrice and LaShon, Johnson went off on them. He grabbed Patrice by the wrist and started dragging her out the door, but LaShon jumped on his back and tried to stop him. Then a shot rang out. Everyone's attention was now riveted on Miz Calvinia, the proprietress of the establishment, who had just cracked off a round into the rafters. It had become so quiet you could almost hear the plaster dust falling from the ceiling.

"This is a peaceable club," Miz Calvinia advised, "and we'll have none of this violence shit here. Do I make myself clear?" With the gun now pointed directly at his head, Johnson acknowledged that the message was clear indeed. He released his hold on Patrice and the two women slipped out the door.

A Walk through the Penal Code

Mr. Parsons's place was just a few blocks away on 130th. He was a great old guy. As soon as they walked in, he offered them some soup he had made himself. An old movie was on TV and the three of them had just made themselves comfortable on the sofa, each with a mug of soup, when there was a knock on the door. Before LaShon could stop him, Parsons had opened the door wide. There were Johnson, Houston, Logan, and the other two crime partners, looking even angrier than they had minutes before at the club. LaShon knew they were outnumbered and cornered in that house. Years ago Parsons had boarded up the back door after a burglar had broken the lock.

Patrice was doing some fast talking, telling Johnson to be cool, that she'd do whatever he wanted, just be cool. Mr. Parsons was still standing in the doorway, mug in hand. The whole situation had yet to completely register with him. LaShon stood up and moved toward the front door. Without any warning, Logan punched Mr. Parsons hard in the face, breaking his spectacles and cracking his dentures. He punched him a second time. Mr. Parsons went down. There was blood everywhere. Johnson grabbed Patrice by the hair, pulling her head back until she felt her neck would snap. Houston and a big man who smelled like sweat and malt liquor had LaShon on the floor. The fifth man, who was wearing a Raiders jacket, had come prepared with a length of rope.

Parsons felt blood leaking out of his mouth and more blood coming from a cut below his right eye. Someone snatched his watch off his wrist. Someone else pulled his pants off. "Pockets is empty. Where the fuck is the money?" he heard one of them ask. He tried to tell them to take the TV, take anything but leave his wife's belongings alone. Every week when he visited her, he would tell her how nice the house looked. How all her clothes and jewelry were waiting for her when she was well enough to come home. Soon she'd be able to get dressed up again and go out. She loved to hear that. It pleased her to know that all her things were safe and sound.

He tried to tell them again to take the TV, but then someone put a bunched-up rag in his mouth. He felt he was choking on his own blood. The pain in his mouth was awful. He thought he might pass out. Now they were tying him up with some rope, arms behind his back, legs secured at the ankles. He was being dragged into the closet.

Once the perpetrators had Parsons out of the way, all their attention was focused on the women. Then, as I sometimes say, they "took a walk through the Penal Code," in this case concentrating on the two hundreds: Section 245(a), assault with a deadly weapon and with force likely to produce great bodily injury; Section 261, rape; Section 286, sodomy;

Section 288, forcible oral copulation; and Section 289, rape by instrumentality or foreign object. This was real teamwork. One would hold a victim down while another would assault her. Then they'd trade places. Then they'd trade victims. No orifice was left unsullied. Broom handles and Coke bottles were used. It went on for hours.

Parsons could hear Patrice and LaShon moaning, he could hear the men making graphic comments. He knew what was happening and he couldn't do a thing to stop it. Those young women were like daughters to him, or maybe granddaughters. They were the children he and Angela were never able to have. Oh, he had few illusions about LaShon and Patrice, but, despite their circumstances, Mr. Parsons was fond of them.

He had first met Patrice years ago when her grandmother brought a sulky ten-year-old to their gospel study. For some reason, the old man and this golden little girl had hit it off, and Patrice had become a frequent caller at his house. Although she was never formally invited, her unannounced visits were always welcome, especially after Angela was forced to move into the home. Now, LaShon, that girl took a little getting used to. But Parsons saw how happy Patrice had become since meeting LaShon, and his attitude softened. Now he couldn't do a thing to help either of them. The cords binding his wrists and ankles were so tight that his hands and feet were getting numb.

Then it seemed to end. The raucous male voices subsided. He couldn't hear LaShon or Patrice. Oh God. Were they dead? Had the monsters left? Had they forgotten him in the closet or were they going to kill him too? After all, even without his glasses, he could identify them. Then he heard some conversation:

"I say we cut 'em. Then we know they be dead."

"No need. Just hog-tie the bitches and torch the place."

"Check it out, me and Jerome got Patrice trussed up like a turkey."

Now it was LaShon's turn. They'd already literally hog-tied Patrice—her hands and feet bound together behind her back, lying on the floor naked and bloody. LaShon quickly put her hands together in front of her chest, and Johnson lashed them together. The guy in the

Raiders jacket tied her feet and then pushed her down on the floor next to Patrice. Logan lit a match and held it up to the curtains in the front room.

"What you doin', Jerome?" Johnson barked. "We still lookin' fo' the money."

"Shit. They ain't no money here," Logan replied and let the curtains erupt into flames.

He and Houston struck a few more matches and dropped them in what they felt were strategic places. The small structure was soon ablaze and the men were forced by the sudden heat to run from the house. The guy with the distinctive body odor grabbed the TV on his way out and headed in the same direction as the dude with the Raiders jacket. Our three suspects headed toward the bus stop on Central.

LaShon told me later that she knew if they had hog-tied her like Patrice, they'd all have died in that fire. She consciously put her hands together in front of her with the hope that Johnson would tie her up that way. It worked. As soon as the men ran out, she was able to untie her feet, open the closet door, and untie Mr. Parsons's feet. There was no time to untie their hands. There was no time to untie Patrice at all. There was no time to find their clothes. Parsons was in a daze. She pushed him out the door and then went back and dragged Patrice out, still hog-tied. The ropes on her hands were burning. She rolled on the front lawn to put out the fire and screamed at Patrice to do the same.

Just then the firemen arrived, followed almost immediately by the police. Folks had come out of their houses and were watching the fire being put out. LaShon wanted to go with the police and make a report, but the paramedics said she needed to go to the hospital first. They wrapped her in a blanket. Oh, man. She had forgotten that she was butt-naked! Patrice had to go to the hospital first, too. An officer explained that they both had to be examined because they'd been raped.

Mr. Parsons was going to be taken directly to the police station. Everything would be all right. Mr. Parsons wondered if that was possible. His home was gone. Everything was gone. All that was left was the fire-place and some of the wood frame. It looked like the skeleton of a strange animal outlined against the sky. He'd never tell his wife. It would break her heart.

ACTING CRAZY

Southwest Station is always crowded. There simply isn't enough space for all the cops, crooks, and victims who need to be there at the same time. The drab hallways are too narrow, the equally drab conference rooms are small and cramped. Every desk is covered with too much stuff: computer monitors and keyboards, stacks of files, photographs, mug books, the odd personal item left to adorn and personalize an otherwise unadorned and impersonal work space.

So it came about that old Mr. Parsons found himself at one end of a very crowded bench in a hallway at Southwest Station. At the other end of the same bench, and handcuffed thereto, was a purse-snatch suspect who told the cops his name was Willie Logan but who later came to be identified as Jerome Montgomery.

Parsons thought he would crap his pants when he saw Jerome. That is, if he were wearing pants. But, actually, all he had on was a blanket, his trousers having been burnt up along with everything else in the fire. As soon as he could, he got the attention of one of the detectives who had asked him to sit down and wait to be interviewed. It had been a busy weekend; there had been several homicides that took precedence over a mere arson, rape, robbery, burglary, attempt-murder case. Nothing personal.

When Mr. Parsons got Detective Wheeler's attention, he could only stutter, "That's one of 'em. The one with the bumpy head." With no teeth and a cut lip, Mr. Parsons's excited whisper would have been unintelligible to most folks, but Wheeler got the message right away.

Glenn Wheeler was just two years shy of retirement, and the time spent with the LAPD had taken a toll on him physically. His thin, sandy hair had become a gray fringe, and what was once a robust physique had turned to paunch. But his detective's mind was as sharp as ever. Detective Wheeler never missed an opportunity.

Johnson and Houston were already in a cell together. Logan had been acting incoherent and was therefore being held for transportation to the jail ward at County-USC Medical Center so a shrink could take a look at him. Wheeler didn't waste any time. The holding tank was wired for sound. He turned on the tape recorder. Then he unhooked Logan from the bench and put him in the same cell with his homeboys. As he was being escorted down the hall, Logan noticed Mr. Parsons still seated on the bench. He couldn't believe his eyes. Shit, that muthafucka should've been roast turkey by now!

"Where you been, homes?" Johnson wanted to know when Logan was reunited with them.

"You know I always acts crazy when they hooks me up. Metro be better than county. Any fool know that." Some experienced inmates would agree that the menu and accommodations at Metropolitan State Mental Hospital are superior to those at Men's Central Jail.

"Hey, them fuckas be crispy critters by now," Houston cackled.

"That old man be alive. I just seen him here!"

"Nigger, you all fucked up," Johnson advised warmly. "I believe Metro be the place fo' you." He and Houston cracked themselves up on this one. When they finally stopped laughing, Logan reiterated that he had seen Parsons right here at Southwest and very much alive.

"I tol' you we should'a cut 'em," Houston snarled.

"Bitches be dead," Johnson offered hopefully. And quickly the conversation segued from rancorous recriminations for not cutting everyone's throat to vivid and detailed recollections of their shared sexual escapades. The men were soon laughing again.

"I fuck Patrice up the ass. She be screamin' fo' mercy. 'Oh, please, stop! Stop!'" Houston related in a high-pitched falsetto to the relish of his cohorts.

"Both those ho's suck my dick," Johnson bragged. "I say, 'Suck it good, bitch.'"

Detective Wheeler and his partner, Tom Pritchard, were in an adjoining room, listening to the conversation as it was being taped. Pritchard was shaking his head in disbelief, disgust, and satisfaction.

These suspects were convicting themselves out of their own mouths. This tape would be like gold in a courtroom. No juror could fail to convict after hearing this stuff.

GOOD NEWS AND BAD

When Wheeler and Pritchard presented the case to me two days later for filing, Wheeler was like a desperate writer pitching a script.

"This is a great case. Everyone in it's black, so you won't have to deal with any cross-racial IDs. And this tape locks it up."

Of course, I smelled a rat. I'd been regaled with the "good news" and now I needed to hear the bad. Wheeler hesitated and then confessed that there were some serious problems with the victims.

Mr. Parsons was in the hospital. After he gave his report to the police, he returned to the place where his home had been in order to see if he could salvage anything. Apparently he had fallen in the rubble and badly cut his leg. He had left it untreated and it had become infected. It turned out he was diabetic, and now there was a real possibility he might lose the leg. He was under heavy sedation for the pain.

I made a mental note that I'd have to interview him at the hospital and schedule a "bedside hearing." When essential witnesses are unable to attend court proceedings because of some physical infirmity, we bring the courtroom to the hospital or to the witness's home if necessary. This is always an expensive and dangerous procedure, especially when the accused is in custody. Here we would have three custodies for the sheriff's department to transport. Add their attorneys, the judge, the clerk, the court reporter, the bailiff, numerous backup deputies, my investigating officers, and myself, and you get a picture of the caravan of vehicles that would make the trip to County-USC Medical Center and the horde that would gather around Parsons's bedside.

Okay, there was a problem with Parsons. If we couldn't get him off the painkillers, he'd be no good as a witness anyway. A bedside hearing would be a waste of effort. But the women could make the entire case.

Wheeler and Pritchard looked abashed, and Pritchard spoke. "We may not find them. They're transient. They each have fairly lengthy rap sheets—mostly 484s [petty thefts] and B cases [soliciting for prostitution]—and they don't like cops very much."

How could I ethically file a case when I didn't know if I could produce witnesses at a preliminary hearing, let alone at a trial? I couldn't.

"All right." I was thinking out loud. "I'll start the paperwork for filing the complaint. We don't want these scumbags back on the street."

The detectives looked relieved. Suspects must be released from custody within a reasonable time unless charges are filed. In California, this means within forty-eight hours, barring weekends and holidays.

"It's 9 A.M.," I noted. "Have the victims in my office by 3 P.M. and I'll make sure the defendants are arraigned in a timely fashion."

Wheeler and Pritchard were real gentlemen. They didn't look happy but there was no argument.

A PROMISE

Most cases are filed without the prosecutor meeting the witnesses, but sex crimes are a notable exception. And for good reason: frequently the credibility of the victim is the deciding factor in a sexual assault case. If a case cannot be won in front of a jury, it should not be filed. That is the test. It would be unethical to file a case in the hope that a defendant will plead guilty.

Well before 3 P.M., the detectives were back in my office with Patrice and LaShon in tow. Reading the police reports was inadequate preparation for meeting my two victims. I was shocked at the extent of their injuries. They were both covered with bruises and abrasions. Patrice's eyes were swollen shut, and LaShon's lip was split open. She had lost at least two teeth.

"Ain't no big thang," LaShon mumbled in response to what must have been a look of horror on my face.

"Fuck," Patrice added in a matter-of-fact tone, the comment addressed to no one in particular.

The initial interview with the victim of a violent crime is crucial to the successful prosecution of the case. There are many goals: establishing rapport with the witness, explaining the criminal justice process, getting a commitment from the victim to see the case through to a conclusion, helping the victim to deal with the trauma of the attack, protecting the victim's testimony from accidental or inadvertent impeachment, and, of course, extracting pertinent information about the case.

Some prosecutors take a Joe Friday approach to witness interrogation: "Just the facts, ma'am." And then they wonder why their witnesses are not particularly forthcoming. You don't want to learn about your case during the defense's cross-examination of your witness. I've found that the best way to get all the necessary details is to start, not by asking questions, but by supplying information.

"First thing," I told LaShon and Patrice, "from this moment until the case is over, you two cannot talk to each other about what happened during the attack."

They looked confused but I let the words sink in.

"When you are on the witness stand, the defense attorneys will ask you a bunch of questions. One of the questions will be who y'all talked to about the case. If you say you talked to each other, they will accuse you of getting together and making this stuff up."

"Fuck," Patrice commented. I was starting to wonder if that was the extent of her vocabulary.

"Okay," I went on, "there are several things we can cover first before I speak with you each separately about the facts of the case." I then proceeded to explain the process: there would be a preliminary hearing in a couple of weeks, followed by a trial which would take place within weeks or months of the prelim. I promised to do what I could to make the process move along as swiftly as possible.

With three defendants, each with his own attorney, this case could drag out for more than a year. It had happened before. Just coordinating everyone's trial calendar could be problematic. And the defense generally likes to "age" a case as long as possible. Unlike a fine wine, a criminal case usually gets weaker over time: memories fade, witnesses die or disappear, evidence gets lost, cops have other cases to investigate and lose interest in working on a case that's already been "solved." In this case I figured the defense attorneys would do everything in their power to delay the process in the hope that I would lose my witnesses.

"I promise that I will be your prosecutor from start to finish," I told my two battered lumps of humanity. Not only was this our office's protocol for handling such cases, it was my personal ethos. No rape victim should be shuttled from prosecutor to prosecutor over the course of the case, forced with each new D.A. to retell and relive the details of the attack.

"We need to make a commitment to each other to see this case through and make sure that justice is done."

I was sounding a little preachy, and I heard another "Fuck" escape Patrice's swollen lips.

"In other words," I quickly amended, "we need to teach these sorry fools a lesson they will never forget."

"I'm down," LaShon promised.

"Me, too," echoed Patrice.

SLIGHT EVIDENCE

The importance of the preliminary hearing is frequently overlooked or minimized by lawyers. All the prosecution has to do is prove a prima facie case, that is, demonstrate by "slight evidence" that a crime has been committed and that there is reason to believe the accused did it. Some prosecutors believe that putting on a bare-bones prelim is therefore the way to go. Why show all your cards to the defense before you have to?

While the defense is entitled to every bit of evidence—police reports, lab results, photographs, et cetera—as soon as the D.A. has it, that doesn't mean you're going to slap every last witness on the stand at the prelim and ask every nitpicking question. The more detail elicited at the prelim, the more chance of contradiction at the trial.

Of course, as with most aspects of the law, a contrary position can also be supported. A demonstration of strength at a preliminary hearing could result in pleas of guilty and the avoidance of a trial altogether. If a defendant feels he is likely to be convicted and given the maximum sentence, he's going to be receptive to plea bargaining.

In this case I felt a plea negotiation would be in the best interest of the People. My witnesses, although viciously attacked, were not the kind of folks with whom your typical jury empathizes. Jurors would have some sympathy for Parsons, but I knew a lot of jurors would feel Patrice and LaShon had put themselves in harm's way by virtue of their lifestyle.

A much bigger problem would be finding them again for the trial. That, and keeping them straight. Junkies tend to make lousy witnesses. So I delivered my standard pep talk for such situations to Patrice and LaShon about the importance of strong testimony at the prelim. Then I separated them and interviewed each, alone, about the facts of the case.

To my relief, they both were able to give detailed accounts of what occurred and, remarkably for any victim of a gang rape, to recall clearly who did what to whom and when. Their accounts were consistent in most respects but not in every detail, which, in my opinion, is the hallmark of truthful testimony. If the detectives could just keep tabs on them until the prelim, we'd be in good shape.

It was time to check in on Mr. Parsons. It had been a week since the attack and he was still hospitalized. The prelim was set for a week hence, and the defense attorneys had all indicated they were ready to go. I took a trip over to County-USC in order to interview Parsons and check out the physical layout for a bedside hearing. Parsons was doing better. The doctors said he would not lose the leg, but he was not going anywhere soon, either.

I sat down at his bedside and introduced myself again. We had spoken briefly by phone, but Parsons had sounded groggy and I wasn't sure if he would remember me or my purpose for being there. He did, and immediately burst into tears. It wasn't so much the physical pain as the emotional trauma; this man had lost everything. I held his hand, and it was like a thin piece of brown leather, dry and light as a wafer. I imagined that it would crumble to dust under the force of a robust handshake. What comfort could I offer? Only the comfort that comes from retribution. Sometimes payback can be pretty darn satisfying.

Parsons turned out to be a much stronger person than my initial observations suggested. At the mere mention of painkillers interfering with his testimony, he declared that he would forgo further medication. Having a bedside hearing was okay with Parsons, his only issue was his lack of dentures; he took pride in his appearance and didn't like folks seeing him without his teeth. I told him he looked fine and the main thing was for people to understand what he was saying, so he'd have to speak as clearly as he could. A bigger problem was getting him a new pair of glasses so that he could actually identify the culprits from a safe distance.

Things were coming together for the preliminary hearing. Every day Parsons got stronger and more determined. We located a spare pair of glasses at his sister's house, so that problem was solved. The preliminary serology reports came back on the rape kit evidence, and the results were consistent with a gang rape. The next step would be to get blood samples from our defendants for further analysis.

Every day the detectives drove by the locations frequented by Patrice and LaShon to make sure they were still in the picture. Most days they were able to find at least one of the girls. I say "girls" not because they were prostitutes. Patrice and LaShon were both only seventeen when this happened.

It was a relief to finally put on the preliminary hearing and memorialize everyone's testimony. If Parsons died and if Patrice and LaShon disappeared, at least the transcript could be read to a jury. Of course, this is a futile and desperate way to put on a case and has never, to my knowledge, resulted in a conviction. But getting the testimony on the record made me feel better, anyway.

Both girls did okay and Parsons was terrific. Everybody identified the three crooks, and their descriptions of the two who were still in the wind were vivid and detailed. All three defense attorneys were relatively restrained—it seemed like they, too, were appalled by the viciousness of the attack.

No Plea Bargain

I couldn't have asked for three more gentlemanly, intelligent, and decent lawyers to populate the other side of the table. First there was the deputy public defender appointed to represent Johnson's interests. Typically, in a multidefendant case, the public defender will represent the heavy, or the suspect against whom the State has the strongest evidence. Here, although Johnson was the instigator, there had been no shrinking violets on board. Johnson's lawyer was Edward Doyle, a brilliant tactician with a close to encyclopedic knowledge of the law and an ability to reason clearly and speak eloquently while registering a .20. That's blood alcohol level. Even in those freewheeling days, the legal presumption of "under the influence" kicked in at .10. Ed was the first, and only, truly functioning alcoholic I have ever met.

On behalf of Houston, Mr. Donald Henderson had been appointed. He was one of the "panel" attorneys, a group of prescreened private practitioners who routinely are appointed in conflict cases. Anytime there are multiple defendants, an inherent conflict of interest exists because antagonistic defenses may be presented. One defendant's best argument may be at the expense of another's best interests. Donald was a straight shooter, a no-nonsense kind of lawyer who frequently would refer to his client as "that asshole." Trust me, this can be very endearing to a prosecutor.

Last, but in no way least, we had Peter Angelini on behalf of Logan. Another private defense lawyer who occasionally took appointments, Peter (never Pete) didn't need this case or any other to make ends meet. He was independently wealthy, having the benefit of birth into a famous banking family. Practicing law was fun, and Peter was a great courtroom performer. His stunning good looks and dazzling smile always helped him mesmerize a jury, and a few prosecutors, along the way.

I had the distinct feeling that these three attorneys were saving themselves for the trial. They had certainly been guarded at the prelim, and no one was asking me for an offer to negotiate a plea. None of the homeboys was going to roll over on the others. My hopes for a three-way plea bargain began to fade.

The pretrial motions were all handled decorously and professionally. Bail reduction motions were heard and promptly denied—these miscreants were staying put. Discovery motions were filed and heard without issue or acrimony. As is ethically, legally, and morally mandated, I gave everything remotely related to the case to defense counsel. Everything I had was reproduced in triplicate.

The defendants were required to submit blood samples for testing. The subsequent serology results corroborated the victims' statements. Seminal fluid attributable to these defendants was found on each victim, along with genetic material not identifiable to these defendants or to the victims but indicative of two other perpetrators. The victims' blood was found on the clothing of the defendants. Gruesome photographs, graphically showing the victims' injuries, were blown up to courtroom size and shown to the defense prior to trial, along with heartbreaking pictures of what was once Mr. Parsons's home. A copy of the tape recording of the defendants' odious and highly incriminating statements was given to each lawyer. Still no suggestion by any defense attorney that they might accept a plea bargain.

"My asshole wants his trial," Donald commented to me after one of our pretrial conferences.

"You know he's looking at a chunk of time in the joint if he's convicted," I advised in my warmest tone.

This was 1979, and the Uniform Determinate Sentencing Law had been enacted three years earlier. During subsequent terms the legislature had seen fit to increase the penalties for sex crimes, particularly for "in-concert" (a polite way of saying group or gang) offenses. These defendants were facing longer state prison sentences than had ever been imposed for such crimes in the history of California. "Chunk of time" was putting it mildly.

"Well, yeah, that's true," Donald averred, "but he wants his trial."

Peter and Ed made similar comments, Peter at one point sounding almost apologetic: "I really shouldn't be taking a case like this to trial. I know you'll destroy me."

Peter always cracked me up—the fact that his client might spend the rest of his unnatural life in prison was secondary to Peter looking less than marvelous in court.

Ed, who had been practicing law before I had graduated from grade school, took the most philosophical approach:

"I've lost a lot of trials over the years. One more won't make any difference to me. It's the nature of the job. If you don't like losing, you shouldn't be a public defender."

WORRY

All this commentary failed to buoy my spirits as the weeks turned into months and the trial date loomed large on the horizon. What did they know that I was missing? We had been assigned for trial to one of my favorite judges, Julius Leetham, known to his admirers (mostly prosecutors, I might add) as Julius the Just and to his detractors (predominately from the defense bar) as Lethal Leetham. Still no suggestion of a plea bargain from the defense, and although I had broached the subject obliquely on a couple of occasions, I didn't want to do so again. I had nothing to worry about, so why act less than confident?

Still, I was worried. I made Wheeler and Pritchard crazy keeping tabs on LaShon and Patrice. If a couple of days passed and the detectives were unable to locate the girls on the street, I was apoplectic.

Dora Woods had become a high-maintenance witness herself. Compared to LaShon and Patrice, she had gotten off easy, but the emotional trauma associated with being a crime victim defies logical measurement. Dora had become agoraphobic. She was terrified to leave the house. As a result, she had lost her job. There was tremendous pressure on Henry to work additional shifts in order to pay the bills. But leaving Dora alone for long periods was not good either. Dora had started drinking.

On more than one occasion, I got an anxious call from Henry at work. Would I go over to the house on my lunch hour and check on Dora? She'd stopped answering the phone, and Henry couldn't leave work. Just check and let him know that everything was okay. On one of these quick trips to the Woods house, I ended up spending a couple of hours trying to console and comfort Dora. She would sit for hours with Sparky on her lap, the drapes pulled tight, the lights off, overcome with fear. I reminded her that her good neighbor Toby was just a couple of houses away and that, if anything happened, she could call 911 as well. I had no idea how Dora would perform on the witness stand, or even if I would be able to get her to court at all.

And poor Mr. Parsons had aged a decade during the intervening months. He had moved in with his sister but, without his own place and his own things, he seemed to have become somewhat disconnected from real life. He continued to visit his bedridden wife and continued to report to her that all was well at home. Perhaps these frequent fabrications were becoming his own reality as well.

"Back in the day," Parsons informed me during one of my after-work visits, "all the women were as beautiful as Dorothy Dandridge and all the men had the wit and elegance of Duke Ellington . . . or at least we aspired to it!"

It pleased me to see a smile on Mr. Parsons's face for a change. I nodded encouragingly and he continued.

"In point of fact, it was Duke Ellington hisself was responsible for me and my lovely wife, Angela, getting married! You see," Parsons went on, despite what must have been a dubious look on my face, "Angela and I both worked at the Dunbar Hotel up on 42nd Place. It was a grand establishment. I was the doorman and Angela worked as one of the housekeepers. The year was 1941, but I remember it like it were yesterday. The great Mr. Ellington and his entourage was in town to put on a stage show. The whole orchestra stayed at the Dunbar. You understand, the Dunbar was the finest colored hotel in the entire city. A man of Mr. Ellington's stature would not have considered staying elsewhere.

"Anyway, the first night he's there, Mr. Ellington comes over to me and asks me to recommend a nightclub in the vicinity. He and Mr. Strayhorn and some of the others had put in such a hard day working on their own show, they felt like being entertained themselves for a change. Well, I commended the Club Alabam, it being right across the way on Central Avenue and having a very good reputation. When Mr. Ellington inquired had I frequented the establishment, I had to admit that I never had. That was all it took—he invited me to be his guest and, as my shift was just up, I accepted.

"Now here's the uncanny part. Before we'd finished our first drink, Mr. Ellington is asking me about Angela. Had I noticed how pretty she was? Did I ever think about taking her out on a date? I was dumbstruck. Was it that obvious or did Mr. Ellington have powers of perception as remarkable as his musical genius? I confessed that I was quite smitten with Angela but was simply too shy to do anything about it.

"I could not believe I was talking that freely, and in such company. Mr. Blanton was there, and Mr. Webster, and that handsome young Jewish actor, John Garfield, was at our table. They all seemed amused by my predicament. After all, I was not a young man even back then. Mr. Ellington announced that he had the solution to my problem. Right then and there he hands me two tickets to his show!

"Angela and I, we had the time of our lives. And you know what? We got married two months later! So you see, it was Mr. Ellington who got me and Angela together. I still remember the name of the show. It was called 'Jump for Joy.'"

I left Parsons in a better mood than I had found him, but I was still worried about how he'd hold up in front of a jury. If only his recollection of the crimes were as sharp as these older but fonder memories.

But whenever I started to stew over the problems with my case, there was one sure way to cheer myself up and restore my confidence. I just had to play the tape. The detectives had been right all along—all the witnesses might falter but, after hearing that tape, no jury could fail to convict.

In the Jury Box

The trial was now at hand. I was surprised that none of the defense attorneys was seeking a continuance. They usually do, and in this case I felt that the longer things dragged out, the more problems I could anticipate with my witnesses. Dora and Mr. Parsons were not getting better. Patrice and LaShon kept disappearing. If the defense had asked for a continuance, I would have opposed it, but it never came to that.

These lawyers were true professionals. They had cleared their respective calendars and were prepared for what was estimated to be a monthlong jury trial. Leetham was known as an efficient judge, and he had already indicated that he hoped the case could be given to the jury within three weeks. I wasn't sure. In addition to Dora, Toby, Patrice, La-Shon, and Mr. Parsons, I had forensic and serology evidence to put before the jury. There would be an arson expert. The paramedics and several doctors would be called as witnesses.

Depending on how well the women did on the stand, I was prepared to call an expert on rape trauma syndrome and another on posttraumatic stress disorder. With three defense lawyers, each cross-examining every prosecution witness and each potentially calling his own succession of witnesses, I thought a monthlong estimate was optimistic.

Jury selection, or voir dire, began promptly at 10 A.M. in Judge Leetham's court. He would press through his other calendar matters with his typical energy and forcefulness. Some of his favorite expressions were "I have ruled, counsel" and "I have a jury waiting, counsel." Another, which never failed to amuse as long as it was not directed at oneself, was "I have read that case, counsel, and it does not and never will stand for that proposition."

The prosecutor always sits closest to the jury box in any courtroom. I don't know who made up that rule, but it's fine with me. These are my people, the ones who will decide my case. I need to get close to them so that I might find the most appropriate words, the most compelling phrases, and the most suitable tone with which to reach not only their ears but their hearts. If the law permitted it, I'd ensconce myself right in the jury box.

I turned around in my chair and eyed the venire, the potential jurors, as they filed into the courtroom and took their places on the wooden benches behind the bar. There have been many manuals and treatises published on the Art of Jury Selection. Everything—from age, race, and occupation to body language and other nonverbal cues—has been discussed by the alleged experts. I'd read my share of the literature in this area and had, over the years, attended several seminars on jury selection. Some of my colleagues had adopted rigid rules that governed them in every case: no postal workers, no social workers, no engineers, no young black men.

My luck with jury trials had been very good, and I had been asked on many occasions how I went about the task of deciding whom to accept and whom to challenge. I would usually answer somewhat flippantly that I employed the science of phrenology and based my decision wholly on the shape of a potential juror's head. That would usually stop the curious in their tracks. When they realized I was kidding, they usually got my point—there is no sure-fire answer. Jury selection is a highly personal endeavor. My method for selecting a good jury is a combination of common sense and instinct, with emphasis on the latter.

A Good Juror

The judge had called for a large panel of prospective jurors, and every seat in the courtroom was now occupied. I ran my eyes over the rows of faces, careful not to stare at anyone in particular. As a group, they looked good to me. The gestalt I got was well dressed, alert, and reasonably happy. I figured they were probably pleased to be in a courtroom rather than stuck in the jury assembly room with its uncomfortable furniture, flickering TV sets, and loud but muffled PA system.

There was some commotion on the other side of counsel table, and it was not coming from the defendants. They were all sitting quietly, dressed in street clothes rather than the usual jail garb they had worn until now. The buzz was coming from their lawyers, who had suddenly huddled together in animated conversation. I strained to overhear what they were saying, but to no avail. I looked at the judge and he had an odd smile on his face. I allowed myself to scan the audience again and then I saw him—an older white man, appearing to be in his sixties, tastefully attired in a suit and tie, with refined features and a look of intelligence on his face. Why did this guy look so familiar to me?

Leetham had embarked upon his usual introductory remarks. This was the case of the People of the State of California versus Clarence Washington also known as Charles Johnson, Tyrone Jackson also known as Maurice Houston, and Jerome Montgomery also known as Willie Logan. Leetham then recited the charges that the People had brought against these defendants. He next introduced the lawyers, and when our names were announced, we each stood and faced the audience. When my name was called, I took that opportunity to once again steal a look at the distinguished gentleman who looked so familiar. Was he smiling at me? Did I know him?

Next Leetham read from a list of names I had provided. These were the prosecution's prospective witnesses. Finally, he asked those in the audience an all-encompassing question. Did any prospective juror know anyone associated with the case? I wondered if the distinguished-looking guy would respond. He did!

"Well," he offered with a broad smile, "I am acquainted with you, Your Honor." He scrutinized the defense attorneys and then gave me a piercing look.

"To my knowledge," he continued, "I do not believe I have had the pleasure of meeting counsel before and I am not acquainted with the facts of this case nor any witness involved in this prosecution." This guy was well-spoken. Who on earth was he?

Judge Leetham asked counsel to approach the bench, with the court reporter.

"Perhaps you have recognized Donald Wright," Leetham said, "retired chief justice of the California Supreme Court." I was in the presence of one of the finest jurists our state had ever produced.

"It occurs to me," our judge went on, "that you all may wish to stipulate that he be excused from jury service on this case. If so, we need not wait to see if he is called to sit in the box. I could excuse him right now and avoid wasting his time." Leetham seemed to be urging this on us. I wondered if there might be some history between the two of them. Perhaps Wright had overturned some of Leetham's rulings in the past.

"I would stipulate on behalf of my client that Justice Wright be excused," Doyle stated without hesitation.

"I join in that stipulation on behalf of Mr. Montgomery," Angelini added.

"Mr. Jackson would join in that stipulation," Henderson offered.

Leetham turned his steely gaze on me.

"Well, Ms. Batt, shall we bid our illustrious visitor adieu?" It was one of those situations where the desired answer was obvious, but I hesitated.

"If you don't stipulate, I'll just have to kick him," Henderson hissed at me, referring to his ability to exercise a peremptory challenge against the chief justice.

"You will address yourself to the court," Leetham admonished Henderson while fastening a look of some irritation on me.

"Your Honor," Doyle interjected, "I understand Mr. Henderson's point. If one of us were going to use a peremptory on Justice Wright, we might as well let him go right now."

My mind had been racing as we stood there clustered around the reporter at sidebar. I had read all of Wright's opinions in the area of criminal law. Wasn't he responsible for the historic opinion in *People v. Rincon-Pineda*? Before that case was decided in 1975, jurors in rape cases were routinely instructed that "rape was a charge easily made and difficult to disprove." It was Justice Wright who, in abolishing that instruction, recognized what all sexual assault victims already knew. Rape is the most difficult crime to report and prosecute.

For decades, our society had sent an unambiguous message to women. If you are the victim of a sexual assault, it is because you brought it on yourself. You asked for it by the clothing you wore, by being out late at night, by doing whatever you had been doing. That "common wisdom" had been so infused into our collective consciousness that this outrageous jury instruction had never been challenged until the trial of Mr. Rincon-Piñeda. The trial judge refused to give this instruction. The defendant was convicted, but he appealed, citing the refusal as reversible error. When the case reached the Supreme Court, it was Chief Justice Wright who recognized the truth and had the courage and wisdom to uphold the trial judge's decision. I wanted this man on my jury.

"Your Honor," I said, "the defense will have to use a peremptory if the justice is called as a juror. The People will not stipulate."

"Very well," Judge Leetham responded, and invited us to return to counsel table. Twelve individuals from the audience were asked to take seats in the jury box and the voir dire process was under way.

THE OLD WAY

Over the years, many state court judges have come to follow the federal model and strictly limit counsel's questioning of prospective jurors. Some judges will permit no direct questioning at all and conduct the entire voir dire process themselves, occasionally, and usually reluctantly, incorporating questions suggested by counsel. Others prefer to rely heavily on the most impersonal method of all—printed juror questionnaires.

But back when I was prosecuting Johnson, Houston, and Logan, counsel in the state courts were given great latitude in questioning prospective jurors. The judge would typically begin the voir dire process by posing a series of general questions regarding prior jury experience, employment, and contact with law enforcement—either as a victim or a suspect—and then turn the questioning over to counsel.

As a trial lawyer, I believe that the old way is much better, and I am always grateful today when a judge permits me to directly question my prospective jurors. Voir dire is the only time during a trial when a lawyer is permitted to converse directly with a juror. This is an opportunity not to be missed. It is my one chance to establish a connection that needs to last throughout the trial. I'm not just going to ask a few questions and sit down—I'm going to sell myself to these folks.

By the time the jury is selected, I want each juror to view me as the voice of reason in the courtroom. Let opposing counsel bark out questions and scream objections. I will strive to express myself in a measured tone. When I ask a question, I want the jurors to know that the answer is something important, something they should remember. When I register an objection, I want the jurors to understand it is because defense counsel's question was improper, not because I want to keep anything from them. When the judge becomes exasperated or angry during the trial (and they all do), I want the jurors to look at me in order to gauge what the appropriate reaction should be. Voir dire is the way I create that bond with my jury.

Typically the defense questions the jury first, and Leetham adhered to this convention. I like it this way; it allows me to ask probing follow-up questions to the defense's more general inquiries, and it gives me time to make some preliminary decisions regarding whom I intend to have excused before I even ask my first question. Back then, it also afforded me the opportunity to memorize the jurors' names. Believe me, this was a very good thing to do, and most attorneys never even tried. Sadly, owing to security concerns, today's jurors are cloaked in numerical anonymity. Somehow, memorizing a series of numbers doesn't have the same effect.

As the three defense attorneys were questioning the venire, I was sizing them up. An older black woman who had worked for years in a factory: very good for me. She would relate well to Dora Woods and Mr. Parsons and, with some luck, her positive feelings for them would spill over on LaShon and Patrice.

A young, athletic-looking black man: again, good for me. He would identify with Toby Tyler. I had already decided that Toby would be my first witness. I always put a lot of thought into the order of testimony, and Toby was a glorious way to start this case. Most cases don't come complete with a real hero.

An older, pinched-looking white woman who had never worked "outside the home": probably bad for me. She would be disgusted by

Patrice and LaShon and probably wouldn't have much concern for Dora or Parsons.

And so it went for the next couple of hours, with the defense questioning and then exercising their peremptory challenges. They were afforded a significant number of challenges under the law: ten that must be exercised jointly and an additional five each to be exercised independently. The prosecution is entitled to an equal number. If you do the math, you come up with a grand total of fifty peremptory challenges.

Finally, it was my turn. I posed the kinds of questions that would help to inform the jury about the case without actually asking them to prejudge it, which would be inappropriate. I wanted to know what they thought about lesbians, about prostitutes, about drug usage. I wanted to make sure I was left with twelve people who realized that Patrice and LaShon were human beings, entitled to the protections of the law just like everyone else. This would be a theme I would revisit in my closing argument.

Jury selection continued into the afternoon. I was feeling pretty good about how the panel was shaping up, but Justice Wright remained in the audience. It looked like the defense attorneys were winding down and would soon each "accept the jury as presently constituted." I had a couple of peremptories left, but I didn't want to use them indiscriminately just in the hope that I could get Justice Wright in the box.

It was Doyle's turn. He asked the court to "thank and excuse Juror Number Eight" and, to my joy, Justice Wright was called to fill that seat. I fastened what I hoped was an impassive look on my face in an attempt to conceal my glee. My notes told me that the defense had a number of challenges left. Would they use them as they had previously threatened? Either way, it would be good for me. If Justice Wright remained on the jury, the prosecution could only benefit from his intelligence and bona fides. If any defense attorney had the temerity to excuse the justice, the remaining jurors would think less of them all and would wonder what was so wrong with their case that they couldn't risk having a real brainy fellow on the jury.

I saw Leetham look at the wall clock. It was 4:30 P.M. and court was adjourned for the day. The prospective jurors were admonished not to discuss anything they may have learned about this case with anyone and not to form or express any opinion about the case. I stood respectfully while the jurors filed out of the courtroom. No sooner had they gone than Doyle was all over me like a bad case of the flu.

"You've got to kick him, Marissa," Doyle urged in his sincerest tone. "I'm sure you've read some of his opinions. He's so liberal. He has a real defense orientation."

"Ed's right," Peter added while Donald nodded sympathetically.

"I was going to stipulate to excuse him," Doyle continued, "but, upon reflection, I think he'll be a real gift to the defense." This dude was good, he was actually saying this with a straight face.

"I have just one word for you guys," I retorted, repressing a smirk that was about to become a full-blown grin. "Actually, it's a hyphenated word—*Rincon-Pineda!*"

The next day, I awoke with a sense of elation. We would have our jury and alternates sworn by midmorning, I would make my opening statement, and then we would finally get to some testimony. I was eager to get the show on the road, but not at the expense of attending to all the necessary details. I had learned as a young deputy that you can have the charisma of a Johnnie Cochran and the legal scholarship of a Lawrence Tribe and still look like a sorry fool in court without adequate preparation.

Although I had no intention of excusing the chief justice, I was not about to relinquish the opportunity to question him. The defense attorneys had been restrained and deferential, each asking a couple of questions of the most generic sort. Not me. I had all sorts of questions for the Honorable Donald Wright. I inquired if he would keep a tally of how many objections were sustained against the prosecution and, if they outnumbered the defense's, think less of the prosecution's case as a whole. Of course not, he quickly responded, and proceeded to issue a brief lecture on the purpose of evidentiary objections and the role of the jury as contrasted with the role of the judge. A few more questions from me elicited mini-sermons on a variety of pertinent topics. I was using the chief justice to preinstruct the other jurors in certain areas of the law.

Even Leetham couldn't resist asking Wright a few questions. The judge wanted to know what the chief justice would do if he, the trial judge, made an erroneous ruling. The justice replied that he would keep his legal opinions to himself and would rely on the appellate courts to correct matters, if necessary. He fully understood his role was one of fact finder and not judge. He appreciated that there was only one judge in this courtroom and that was Judge Julius Leetham. That answer sat well with Leetham.

THE EXPECTATION OF PRIVACY

After all their collective bluster, not one of the defense attorneys had the nerve to challenge the chief justice. Both sides finally accepted the jury—with Donald Wright on the panel—just as the hands on the court-room clock registered the noon hour. The jurors and alternates were sworn and then promptly excused for lunch with the traditional admonition.

Commencing one's opening statement right after lunch is not ideal. But I was determined that, no matter how much greasy food my jurors had consumed, I would still be able to hold their attention. Court resumed promptly at 1:30 P.M. and I was about to step to the podium to begin my opening statement. But Ed Doyle was on his feet, asking that we all approach the bench.

Judge Leetham didn't even attempt to mask his irritation. "What is it now, counsel?" he snapped in a gravelly tone that passed for a whisper. We had all assembled at sidebar with the court reporter. Everyone spoke quietly so the jurors would not overhear something not meant for their ears.

"I apologize to court and counsel for bringing this matter up now, but we may need a 402 hearing on this issue." Ed was referring to an evidentiary hearing outside the presence of the jury to determine the admissibility of a particular piece of evidence.

What piece of evidence, I was about to ask.

"It's the jailhouse tape recording," Ed went on, as if in response to my unspoken question.

Oh shit, I thought with such celerity that the words almost popped out of my mouth and onto the permanent court record. Had smart-guy Ed figured out a way to keep my best piece of evidence away from the jury?

"Your Honor," I ventured, "I am aware of no legal authority, either statutory or case law, that precludes that tape from coming into evidence. All three defendants were present during the course of the taping and each can be clearly identified by his voice. There are no *Aranda-Bruton* issues, and I will lay a sufficient foundation before I ask that the tape be admitted into evidence."

I was referring to the two seminal cases in the area of codefendant admissions and confessions. Generally speaking, if only one defendant makes a statement, it can be used only against him and not against another defendant who was not present at the time the statement was uttered. The reasoning is that the first defendant is under no obligation to take the stand; he has a right to remain silent. Thus the second defendant would be necessarily precluded from exercising his equally important right to confront and cross-examine the first defendant.

No such problem existed in my case. Because the three defendants were together when all the statements were made, everything said can be imputed to everyone present unless there were disclaimers. It's what we lawyers call an adoptive admission. I love this stuff.

"Ms. Batt is correct, of course," replied Judge Leetham in his most beatific tone. I was about to turn on my heel and head back to counsel table when the judge continued.

"However, that may no longer be the case after the Supreme Court's next term. If memory serves"—and it always did where Judge Leetham was concerned—"they will be deciding the case of *People v. Delancie,* which is factually on all fours with this case. It involves the expectation of privacy in a jail facility."

"Your Honor," I implored, "could we not try this case under the current state of the law?" I tried not to sound impertinent but Leetham was starting to piss me off.

"A good jurist, and a good lawyer, I might add, always strives to appreciate where the law is going and is sensitive to these important trends," Leetham stated. "You wouldn't want to be reversed on appeal when you could have tried the case without some gimmicky tape."

The judge was ruling against me. Angelini, Doyle, and Henderson were astonished by their good fortune. Frequently defense attorneys will spew out numerous objections to the prosecution's evidence with the hope that if repeated challenges are registered, something will stick. Baffle 'Em with Bullshit is like a mantra to most criminal defense attorneys.

Ed was smiling and shaking his head at the same time. I couldn't believe it. The jury was not going to hear my best piece of evidence!

"If I don't secure a conviction, any appellate issues will be a moot point," I complained. "How about this," I went on. "I'll make no mention of the tape in my opening statement and I'll brief this issue for the court if Your Honor will reserve ruling."

Leetham agreed, but I knew no amount of briefing would change his mind. I had the uncomfortable feeling that this ruling was the direct result of the chief justice sitting on the jury. Leetham wanted to impress the guy with his appellate erudition.

My opening statement went well, I thought. The facts were compelling, and the jury seemed alert and serious about their task. They even took notes during my remarks. A good sign. The defense reserved their opening remarks, a sensible strategy in such a case.

SPLIT THE BABY

Toby was splendid as my first witness. It was now summertime, and he showed up for court in a tank top, a garment well suited to show off his burnished, rippling muscles. He was gorgeous and had everyone's attention. His testimony was clear, coherent, and filled with compassion for Dora, a good lead-in for what might be a less than lucid witness.

I had spent many hours at the Woods house, trying to get Dora in shape for the trial. My efforts were close to fruitless. It seemed that every time I tried to get Dora to relate the events surrounding the robbery, her responses became more garbled, her demeanor more querulous.

Although I had decided to put LaShon and Patrice on near the end of the trial, I had scheduled a meeting with them after the first day of testimony. It was partly to check up on them and partly to prepare them for their testimony. To my relief, Wheeler and Pritchard and the two women were waiting for me when I got off the elevator on the eighteenth floor.

LaShon quickly assured us that she and Patrice could find their own way back to the 'hood, so the cops took off. I escorted the women into my office. Typical of the offices in the CCB, mine was small, poorly lit, and crowded with files, books, and mismatched furniture. The good news was that it had a window, and I had done what I could to give it an inviting air. Many of the cases I handled in those days involved child victims, and I had a bookshelf filled with dolls and coloring books for their entertainment while waiting to testify.

I had duplicated separate portions of the preliminary hearing transcript for each of my witnesses, and I was careful to give LaShon and Patrice each the correct section containing only her own respective pages. As I handed them their individual packets, I advised them, as I do all witnesses I am preparing for trial, that the preliminary hearing transcript should not be viewed as a script for the trial. It should be used merely to refresh one's recollection and identify any prior misstatements.

"One should never feel obliged to conform one's testimony to what has been recorded," I continued. I was about to say more about dealing with the small, inevitable inconsistencies between the police reports, prelim transcripts, and trial testimony, but the looks on their faces stopped me. LaShon had a particularly stony, sullen look, and Patrice was just staring at me.

"Fuck," Patrice commented. This time there was a world of meaning in her favorite expletive. What was wrong with me? Why had I presumed that these women could read?

"You know," I stumbled, "on second thought, I have a better idea. The defense attorneys always ask witnesses if they have read the preliminary hearing transcript. If y'all just say no, that is a fine answer. Listen, you two don't need to refresh your memories. I think you both remember what happened."

Patrice looked relieved and LaShon was nodding in agreement. I took back the copies of the transcript and unceremoniously dropped them in the wastebasket.

"You guys can go now, if you like," I said, "and we'll get together in a couple of weeks when it's time for your testimony."

I had decided to devote the evening to briefing the issues surrounding the jailhouse tape. The sooner I had that task out of the way, the better. And who knows, I thought, maybe I could get Leetham to change his mind.

"Could we stay and color?" Patrice had noticed the stack of coloring books on my bookshelf. I was dumbfounded, but Patrice and LaShon both had eager looks on their faces.

"Sure," I said. "It'll be nice to have some company tonight. I'm going to be here a while working on a memo for our judge. He doesn't want the jury to hear a tape I have of the defendants talking about their crimes."

"Why not?" LaShon wanted to know.

"He thinks it might be too prejudicial," I explained. "But I'm going to try to change his mind. But if I don't get to use the tape, it's not the end of the world. I mean, I have you guys. You will be great witnesses. The tape was just a little insurance. We're going to be successful either way."

I was saying this to encourage myself as much as anyone else. I knew only too well that without that tape, the success of the entire case rested on Patrice and LaShon.

I started typing the first draft of my brief—probably an exercise in futility but I was still determined to do the best job I could. The jury needed to hear the tape. They needed to know what monsters these men were. I glanced over at my star witnesses. They were both sprawled out on the floor, each with her own coloring book, each intent on the task at hand, keeping the selected color inside the lines. LaShon was a study in concentration, her tongue tightly sandwiched between her lips. Patrice was actually smiling to herself. I felt my eyes fill with tears.

As I expected, my motion to play the tape to the jury and present them with transcripts of pertinent portions was summarily denied by Julius the Just. The jury was not going to hear any part of the tape nor read a single transcribed word. Of course, like many courteous judges, Leetham said no in the nicest possible way. After filling the record with praises for my exhaustive research, brilliant legal reasoning, and elegant writing style, Leetham invited my response. Patrice's favorite word was in my mind but there was only one thing to say.

"Thank you, Your Honor," I responded in what I hoped was a respectful tone. Some of you may wonder why lawyers routinely thank judges for ruling against them. This is actually a no-brainer. A response is expected, and if you say what is really on your mind, you'll probably be held in contempt.

"However," Leetham continued, "I will not have my ruling interpreted as granting license to the defense to be overly creative in their testimony." This was the judge's polite way of saying perjury.

"If any defendant takes the stand and opens the door," the judge went on, "then that tape may very well come into evidence as part of the People's rebuttal case. It certainly is not coming in as part of their case in chief. But if it comes in at all, it will be because the defense opened the door."

Leetham had ruled. And, with a Solomon-like wisdom, he had, in effect, split the baby while keeping it very much alive.

Heart and Soul

Dora Woods had followed Toby on the witness stand and had, to my profound relief, acquitted herself well. Her frail frame and hesitant voice served to underscore one of the dominant themes in the case: these defendants were predators; they targeted the old, the infirm, the weak.

The prosecution's case continued with a series of noncivilian witnesses, as we call them. Police officers, firefighters, lab technicians, and forensic experts. I got them on and off the stand as quickly as I could. The last thing I wanted to do was bore my jurors with technical terminology and scientific minutiae.

Mr. Parsons was the lead-in witness for my two female victims. The determined look on his face when he was sworn in as a witness allayed most of my concern about him. I started my direct examination gently, with questions about the layout of his house and background on his relationship with the other victims. Then we moved into the more painful testimony about "the date in question."

I should never have doubted Mr. Parsons; he had always been a dedicated and hardworking man. This was a job, albeit a difficult one, and he was up to the task. His testimony held the jury's attention, and he did not waver once during cross-examination. No need for redirect, I decided as Leetham noted that it was approaching 4:30. It's nice when you can end the day on a strong note.

It was now time for the grand finale. The heart and soul of my case. It was time to put Patrice and LaShon on the stand. It had been a little over a week since they had been in my office, docilely coloring while I pounded away on my brilliant, but losing, brief. The detectives claimed they could produce the girls at a moment's notice. Were they saying this just to keep me mollified?

The girls were supposed to be in my office at eight in the morning, ready to go when court convened for our trial at 10:30. I intended to put first Patrice and then LaShon on the stand. I wanted to end the case with LaShon because she was clearly the stronger and more articulate of the two. It was 8 A.M. So where on earth were they? I could feel my guts tying themselves into a tight knot. The phone rang, and I snatched it off the hook before the second ring.

"Don't panic." It was Pritchard. "We don't have them right now, but we'll get 'em in your office within an hour."

They must have flipped a coin to determine who would call me with this choice news. I could feel Tom cringing at the other end of the line.

I repressed an expletive. There was no point in screaming at my cops. They had been terrific throughout the entire case. I knew they did much more than just "keep an eye" on Patrice and LaShon. They had bought them more than one lunch and supplied them with fresh clothes before the prelim. Their compassion for our victims was real.

"Okay," I replied, "but if you guys don't find them in time for the morning session, I think we're screwed. I don't see Leetham cutting me a whole lot of slack. He'll ask me to call my next witness or rest my case. If you can't find them soon, I'll ask for a hearing outside the presence of the jury to demonstrate your due diligence and we'll read in their testimony from the prelim. God, I hope it doesn't come down to that after all."

"Me too," Pritchard said and hung up.

"Due diligence" is legal shorthand for proving that the prosecution has made a "due and diligent effort" to keep in touch with important witnesses who cannot be found at the time of trial. This is an essential element in proving that they are legally unavailable. Unavailability is a legal prerequisite to reading prior testimony into the record at a subsequent trial. Far from ending my case in chief on a strong note, this would be the weakest possible way to conclude the People's case.

It was 9 A.M. Then it was 9:15. No Patrice and LaShon. No cops. Not in the foyer, not in the reception area, not in my office. I checked for phone messages. None. I put my head down on my desk. I felt disappointed in myself. I thought I had established enough trust with my victims that they would see it through. They had been great witnesses at the preliminary hearing. Maybe it was my faux pas with the transcript that had caused this.

There was a knock on my already open door. It was Glenn Wheeler.

"We got 'em," he reported. But he looked worried rather than relieved. What was going on?

Pritchard rounded the corner with both girls in tow and quickly deposited them in the two chairs I had facing my desk. His pale face was pink and I noticed beads of sweat on his forehead. LaShon looked a little more disheveled than usual, but nothing a little soap and water and a comb couldn't straighten out. Patrice, on the other hand, looked completely wasted. Her eyes were half shut and her mouth was half open. She almost slid out of the chair.

"I tol' her, don' do it," LaShon protested, "but she felt real sick. I say, just skin pop a li'l bit but she don' listen when she sick."

"Sorry, Marissa," Patrice slurred and then, to my horror, vomited all over herself.

I was stunned but I was in motion. We had less than an hour and a half to be back in court with a witness on the stand.

"Let's get her to the restroom," I said while I propelled Patrice out of my office and down the hall. A few fellow deputies who were still sipping coffee in their offices looked up from their desks with mild interest, but no one lent a hand. I'm sure they had their own problems to worry about. LaShon was right behind me as we entered the ladies' room. No one else was there. A definite benefit.

I gingerly peeled off Patrice's soiled garments and handed them to LaShon, who immediately started washing them in the sink.

"Use lots of soap," I suggested, and LaShon nodded.

"You gonna throw up some more?" I asked Patrice, who shook her head vehemently in response.

"Let's get you as clean and as straight as possible," I said in what I hoped was an encouraging tone. LaShon finished washing Patrice's clothes and we wrung them out and put them on her, still damp. Then I took her by the hand and we walked out of the restroom. The detectives were right outside the door, looking worried.

"Everything okay?" Wheeler wanted to know.

"Much better," I said. "I'd appreciate it if you guys would take Patrice for a walk around the block. It's a nice sunny day. That should help dry her clothes and maybe tighten up her mind a little too." I knew from my own experience, in a hospital setting, that narcotics are more quickly metabolized when an individual exerts physical effort.

"One brisk walk coming up," Pritchard responded.

"We'll be back in your office before 10:30," Wheeler assured me without my saying a word.

CLEAN

Where was LaShon? She must still be in the restroom, I realized, and hurried back there. When I opened the door, there was LaShon all right. Completely naked.

"I been clean since that day. The day of the rapes. I don' use no mo'," LaShon declared with pride. "Check it out," she encouraged. "I don' have no fresh marks. Just ol' tracks."

LaShon bent over and assumed what I considered a degrading position—no doubt a position she had assumed many times in the past at the request of jailhouse matrons.

"No need for me to check any part of you, baby," I said. "I know you been clean."

"You do?" LaShon's surprise and happiness were instantaneous. "How you know?" she wanted to hear.

Her prodigious consumption of sweets during the intervening months had been a clue. There had been other, less agreeable indications. But why elaborate?

"I just knew," I said. "Now put on your clothes and give me a hug before we go to court and take care of business."

"I'm glad you're our lawyer," LaShon declared on our way out of the restroom.

"Thank you. I'm glad to be the prosecutor on this case and I'm honored to know you and Patrice."

"You are?"

"Very much so. I know how difficult it is to be a witness. It takes less effort to be the one asking the questions. I have the easy job. I think you both are very brave, and I think you, LaShon, are incredibly smart. If you had let them hog-tie you like Patrice, I'd be trying a triple murder case right now. And on top of that, to quit cold turkey . . . I admire you very much."

LaShon gave me a wide smile, displaying the gaps where her teeth had been. "We're partners!" she announced. We marched back to my office arm in arm.

We had a few minutes to review her testimony. I was concerned if LaShon would still be able to relate who had done what to whom in the same order as she had described it to the police and then to the judge at the prelim. I asked her to rap it down to me again, and she did, in a real matter-of-fact tone.

"You know," I felt compelled to say, "when we go over it in court, in front of the jury, I'll ask you to describe it with a lot more detail."

"I know," LaShon replied. "I can do it."

And she did. Her testimony was powerful and raw and unflinching. LaShon's lexicon didn't include polite euphemisms like "private parts" or legal terms like "sodomy." Our jury heard about what happened to LaShon in LaShon's own words. At first, I noticed a few raised eyebrows when I quickly stole a glance at the jurors during LaShon's direct testimony. After a while all I saw was rapt attention. By the end of my direct examination, the jurors had become involved in the events of the case. One of the jurors dabbed at the corners of her eyes. Another held a hand over her mouth. A male juror kept shaking his head, not in disbelief but, I felt, in sympathy.

On cross-examination, LaShon continued to control the courtroom. Whenever she was asked a confusing question, she told the particular defense attorney she did not understand, thereby forcing him to rephrase the question in her terms. "You claim Mr. Montgomery allegedly sodomized you" became "You say Jerome fucked you up the ass." The more the defense tried to push her, the stronger LaShon got.

At one point Henderson took issue with what LaShon stated she saw happen to Patrice. LaShon stood her ground.

"I know what I seen. I seen what happened to Patrice. She'll never be the same." Then LaShon did something I had never seen her do before — she started to cry.

At that instant I knew how I would present Patrice to my jury. Far from being my weakest witness, she would be my strongest exhibit. I had checked on her over the lunch hour and she seemed better, although far from completely straight. But it wouldn't matter if she couldn't remember the details of the attack the way LaShon did. It wouldn't matter if she was obviously under the influence of narcotics. She was a mess and she was living proof of the truth of the charges. She would never be the same.

LaShon had done a great job; she'd been on the stand all morning and most of the afternoon. The defense attorneys had concluded their cross-examination. If she hadn't been such a strong witness, the defense probably would have dragged out its cross-examination for a couple of days.

HALF A SPOON

I had a decision to make. I could ask LaShon some questions on redirect and hope to stretch out her testimony for the rest of the afternoon. Then I could call Patrice as a witness the next day, when she might be in better shape. But there was no legitimate reason to question LaShon any further. And there was no guarantee Patrice would be in any better condition tomorrow. And I wasn't going to rest my case without calling Patrice to the stand. Patrice was going to testify today. But first, I asked to approach the bench. When we were all assembled and out of earshot of the jury, I told the court and counsel what had happened.

"I have reason to believe that my next witness may have ingested a narcotic this morning. I believe that she is competent to testify, and I want to call her as my next and last witness. Of course, I understand that her current state of sobriety is a matter the defense may go into in order to test her credibility."

"Your Honor," Doyle said, "I would suggest that we be allowed to question this witness outside the presence of the jury in order to determine if she is even competent to give testimony."

"I agree with Mr. Doyle," I said. "Although I believe she is competent, it's a call Your Honor should make."

"Thank you, Ms. Batt. It's always a pleasure to have a prosecutor who understands the role of the court," Leetham responded with a smile. "We'll give the jury a fifteen-minute break. As soon as they're safely back in the jury room, bring your final witness in. I'll conduct the examination myself."

With the jury out of the courtroom, Patrice was brought in and put under oath. Leetham can be intimidating, to both witnesses and attorneys alike. His voice can be gruff and his manner stern even when he's in a good mood. It seemed to me that the judge was aware of this and was trying very hard to be kind and encouraging to Patrice.

"Now, Miss Williams," he began, "no one will have you arrested for being under the influence. I just need to know the truth. Did you use some type of drug earlier today?"

"Yeah," Patrice readily admitted.

"What drug was that?" Leetham inquired.

"Hero'n."

"What was that?"

"HER-O'N!" Patrice said louder, emphasizing the two syllables.

"Oh, HER-O-IN," Leetham repeated, carefully pronouncing all three syllables.

"That's what I said," Patrice responded, looking a little confused.

After further colloquy relative to when ("this morning"), how much ("about half a spoon"), and how frequently ("whenever I can score"), Judge Leetham had heard enough and, without permitting additional inquiry from either side, ruled that Patrice was a competent, albeit not entirely sober, witness.

The jury was asked to return to the courtroom and Patrice was resworn as a witness. My initial questions to her mirrored those the judge had asked. Might as well get it out of the way. If I didn't elicit the evidence of my witness's addiction, the defense certainly would, and it would look like I was hiding something. I didn't want to leave anything for the defense. I'd rather break down my own witness.

"Did you know you would be called as a witness today?" I asked.

"Yes."

"And knowing that, you still decided to inject a narcotic this morning?"

"Yes."

"Why did you do this?"

"I was feeling sick and scared. I needed to fix."

"What were you scared of?"

"Of seeing them again. Those mu—those defendants."

What an excellent segue into the facts of the case. The defense didn't even register an objection. I smoothly moved from Patrice's drug problem into her recollections of the attack. Her memories were somewhat imprecise, but it was a matter of inaccuracy, not dishonesty. On cross-examination all the defense was able to show was that Patrice's drug usage had helped her to block out some of the more horrific details of the attack. Her credibility remained intact.

And then it was over.

"No further questions," each defense attorney informed the court.

"No redirect, thank you, Your Honor," I added, and Patrice slowly stood up and walked off the witness stand, relief and exhaustion etched in every feature.

"The People ask that all exhibits previously marked for identification be received into evidence at this time," I asked.

"No objection," the defense attorneys chorused. All their objections had been heard and ruled upon weeks ago, outside the presence of the jury. Nothing had been marked as an exhibit that was not going to be admitted into evidence.

"Then they will be received as previously marked," Judge Leetham stated.

"The People rest," I stated and then sat down.

It was 4:15 P.M. Ordinarily, Judge Leetham would continue until 4:30, squeezing every second of court time out of every day. But I heard Leetham advising the jury that we had reached a good stopping point and that they were being excused until 10:30 the next morning. I took another look at the jurors. Leetham had made the right call. They looked as worn out as Patrice. It had been a long day for all of us.

The Last Word

I was grateful to get back to my office a little early. I needed to do some more work on my closing argument. If the defense rested without calling any witnesses, as I expected they might, I would be arguing to the jury tomorrow morning. Other than the defendants, I couldn't imagine who the defense witnesses might be. The defense had not indicated that they would call any alibi witnesses. You know, the mother who says her son was home helping her prepare for some cousin's birthday party. Of course, that type of thing doesn't work so well when the crimes take place at 2 A.M.!

My guess was that the defense would not run the risk of putting any defendant on the stand. These guys would be hard to control, and it would be impossible for them not to "open the door" to the jailhouse tape. The defense could recall some of the prosecution witnesses, but what for? They had vigorously cross-examined them during my case in chief.

I spent the night polishing my closing argument. I had written the first draft prior to jury selection and had revised it as the case progressed. Now was the time to put on the finishing touches and to make sure that I included all the points that I felt were important. I take copious notes during testimony. Whenever a point is made that I feel should be woven into my final argument, I put a big star in the margin. I needed to check my margins one last time.

My assessment proved to be correct. At 10:30 A.M. the next day the defense promptly rested its case without calling a single witness and I was on my feet making the first of my two closing arguments to the jury. The prosecution is given the opportunity to argue twice to the jury in final summation because we bear the burden of proof. The People give an "opening-closing" argument and then a final or "closing-closing" argument in rebuttal to the defense argument. We get the last word. I like this very much.

When I sat down after concluding my initial closing argument to the jury, I felt satisfied that I had accomplished my task. I had explained the elements of each offense and had demonstrated how the prosecution had proved each element of each charge beyond a reasonable doubt. I felt I had been clear and concise. No one was asleep, so I assumed that I had done the job without boring them into a complete stupor.

Some attorneys think their job during closing argument is to entertain as well as inform the jury. To that end some lawyers adopt the mannerisms of preachers or politicians or movie stars during closing argument. While one obviously does not want to put the jury on the nod, I don't think entertainment value should be the hallmark of a good closing argument.

The lawyer should resist the impulse to become a character in the trial and should remember his true role as a conduit for information to flow to the jury. What is convoluted should be straightened, what is obscure should be clarified, what is complex should be simplified. That is the job. And if it can be performed with flair and finesse, so much the better. But showmanship without substance is just plain garbage.

Having said all that, I must tell you about Peter Angelini's closing argument. He went last, after Doyle and Henderson had both done workmanlike jobs of pointing out small (and I felt meaningless) inconsistencies in the testimony of the People's witnesses. Then Peter stood and addressed the panel. He was magnificent. He told a fascinating tale about a conspiracy between Patrice, LaShon, and Parsons to implicate the defendants in these ghastly crimes.

He started by readily acknowledging their culpability in the Dora Woods purse-snatch robbery. But then Mr. Angelini stated boldly that that was the only crime the defendants committed. He spun a tale involving a plot by Parsons to recover insurance funds by torching his own property, coupled with a devious scheme to accuse the defendants not only of the arson but also of a series of revolting sexual crimes. Who better to concoct something like that than a couple of drugged-out hookers? The physical injuries the victims suffered? The result of surviving the arson fire they set themselves. Note that the defendants did not have any injuries. Nothing to prove they were in that house other than the word of the three conspirators. The rape kit evidence? Nothing more than you would expect to find if you examined any street prostitute.

Peter went on and on. He reminded the jurors that Parsons had "admitted" that he had a homeowner's policy. He made it sound so sinister. Patrice and LaShon had both acknowledged their hatred of defendant

Washington. He made it sound like a motive. He was on a roll. The jury was hypnotized.

Peter concluded his comments with a flourish and sat down. It was my turn again. My heart was pounding. What should I say? One can prepare exhaustively for one's opening argument but the rebuttal argument is, perforce, mostly extemporaneous. I stood and approached the podium for the last time on this case.

"Wow," I gushed, "that was fantastic!" The jurors stared at me in amazement. Why was the prosecutor complimenting a defense attorney? Leetham looked impassive. The defense attorneys looked concerned. What was I up to?

"That was one of the best closing arguments I have ever heard," I continued. "Too bad it had nothing whatever to do with the facts of this case." I then started pawing through a sheaf of papers I had brought up to the podium.

"I'm sorry, ladies and gentlemen of the jury, I can't seem to find what I'm looking for. I'm looking for the verdict form that says, 'We loved your lawyer but you are still guilty as sin'!"

More than half of the jurors laughed out loud. The defense attorneys were too stunned by my behavior to object.

"So I guess you'll have to use this verdict form," I continued. "It's the one that says 'guilty as charged,' for that is certainly the only just verdict in this case." There was nothing more to say. I sat down.

THE VERDICT

Leetham always instructed the jury on the law after closing arguments. After he informed the jury of the law applicable to the case, the jurors were entrusted to the bailiff and their deliberations began.

No matter how long it takes to get a verdict, it always seems too long. And while you're waiting, it's difficult not to second-guess everything you did during the course of the trial. Perhaps I was too flippant in my closing argument? Maybe putting Patrice on the stand was a poor call? Did I spend enough time explaining the rape kit evidence?

Then the phone rang. We had a verdict. It had only been a day and a half. A respectable length of time, given the number of defendants and the multiplicity of charges and special allegations. There was no time to try to find Patrice and LaShon. I'd telephone the Woodses and Mr. Parsons with the results when I got back from court.

The jury found the defendants guilty on all charges. They found every special allegation to be true. It was a complete victory.

The defense attorneys requested that the judge "poll" the jury. This is a routine procedure where the court clerk asks each juror individually the following question: "Is this your true and correct verdict?" Each juror answered affirmatively, and when Chief Justice Wright said "yes" he looked right at me and nodded.

The jury was then thanked and excused by Judge Leetham. We attorneys all rose as the jurors filed out of the courtroom. After a few ministerial matters were handled, including fixing the date for sentencing, Doyle, Henderson, Angelini, and I walked out together. We had been friends before the trial and we would continue to be friends thereafter. We each had fought hard, but it had been a very fair fight. Even if I didn't get to use The Tape.

Most of the jurors had remained in the hallway in order to speak with the lawyers. Once the case is over, this is permissible, and I find it to be beneficial. Invariably I learn something that I can apply to the next jury trial.

The chief justice had waited for us along with the other jurors. Angelini, Doyle, and Henderson made a beeline for him and I observed much handshaking. I kept a respectable distance and waited my turn. Soon the defense attorneys were walking away and Chief Justice Wright was approaching me with a hand outstretched. We shook hands and I found myself—perhaps for the first time in my life—speechless.

"You did a superb job on this case," the chief justice told me, "and perhaps we should consider revising our verdict forms! I loved your final argument!"

"Thank you, sir," I managed in response, and then blurted out, "and I loved your opinion in *Rincon-Pineda!*"

A Pair of Shoes

Sentencing was put over for two weeks. I asked the detectives for one last favor: find Patrice and LaShon one last time and invite them to be present at the sentencing. Dora and Mr. Parsons were invited but politely declined. They'd had their fill of the criminal courts, thank you very much.

When the day for sentencing the defendants arrived, I was ready. This was going to be an historic occasion. Even if Leetham did not impose the maximum sentences, he could saddle these hoodlums with more time for these crimes than had ever been imposed in our state. My sentencing brief was a small tome with lengthy sections devoted to each individual defendant. The press was on hand. Some of my fellow prosecutors had slipped away from their own courtrooms in order to witness what was about to happen.

Even my favorite court watchers were in the audience. This was a group of five older gentlemen who devoted their retirement years to watching criminal cases. They were like members of a very exclusive club. I assumed that they always reached a consensus on which case they would follow, because you never saw one without the other four. There was Carl with the perpetually florid face and ready smile, the distinguished, silver-haired Ernest, Alfred with the slight tremor, Milt with the thick spectacles and thicker accent, and Joe with the two canes. These men were knowledgeable and opinionated. They knew good lawyering from bad and were never shy about sharing their collective opinion on how a case was going. Some lawyers found them annoying, but I always felt honored when they decided to follow one of my cases.

But most important, Patrice and LaShon were there to witness the court's final judgment against their assailants. It is the right of every crime victim to be present and speak at the sentencing hearing. Patrice said she wanted LaShon to speak for both of them.

Leetham took the bench and invited argument from both sides. The defense attorneys spoke first, arguing that the law was too harsh, that their clients were too young, that the crimes, while serious, were not so bad that the clients should be locked up forever. A lengthy determinate sentence is tantamount to a life term.

The enormity of the situation was finally dawning on Johnson, Houston, and Logan. They fidgeted in their seats and mumbled to each other under their breath. I was relieved to see that there were backup bailiffs everywhere. These guys might go crazy when they heard their sentences. It was unlikely Leetham would disappoint us. I knew he would hit them hard. The only question was how hard.

After the defense attorneys put their comments on the record, Judge Leetham turned to me.

"The People's position is stated fully in my sentencing brief, Your Honor," I began. There were a couple of snickers from the cognoscenti in the courtroom. My brief was anything but—it was the longest document I would ever write as a courtroom lawyer.

"However, one of the victims in the case, Miss LaShon Brown, would like to address the court."

"Come forward," Leetham encouraged.

LaShon stood at the podium. For a moment it looked like she was not going to say a word. She stared at the defendants. Montgomery started to come out of his chair, but one of the bailiffs forcefully replanted him. Angelini immediately whispered something in his client's ear. I could imagine what it was. Jerome seemed to calm down. Finally LaShon turned her attention from her tormentors to the judge.

"They hurt us bad," LaShon said simply. "I trust you. Do what's right."

And Leetham did just that. He sentenced each defendant to nearly one hundred years in the state prison. He actually could have imposed a few more years on each of our felons, but this was more than enough. They would never be released. They would die in the joint. These were life sentences.

Before it had time to sink in, the defendants were whisked into the lockup. The courtroom soon emptied. The reporters had deadlines to make. The lawyers had other cases. So did I, but I lingered. LaShon and Patrice were waiting for me on the other side of the bar.

"We did it," I said. "You guys did it. You were both wonderful."

"You did it," LaShon replied. "You really worked fo' us."

"Yeah," Patrice agreed.

"Uh, can I ax you a personal question?" LaShon wanted to know.

"Sure."

"Uh, what size shoe you wear?"

"Five and a half. Why?"

"Well, we really appreciate what you done fo' us," LaShon explained, "and I'm fixin' to boost you a pair o' shoes."

"Oh, baby, don't do that. I don't want you going to no trouble on my account. Remember, it's the thought that matters."

"You helped me do something I didn't think I could do."

"I love you, LaShon."

"I love you, too."

OBSTACLES

Life has the capacity, like flames reaching toward heaven, to transform suffering and pain into the energy needed for value creation, into light that illuminates darkness. Like wind traversing vast spaces unhindered, life has the power to uproot and overturn all obstacles and difficulties. Like clear flowing water, it can wash away all stains and impurities. And finally, life, like the great earth that sustains all vegetation, impartially protects all people with its compassionate, nurturing force.

— Daisaku Ikeda, *Faith into Action*

A BIG SURPRISE

THE GAY LIFE

Sheldon Silverman had been in Los Angeles for over a year and the "gay life" was still eluding him. He'd figured things would change dramatically for him when he moved here from Grand Rapids, but this was ridiculous. Sure, he'd met a few gay men at work, but nothing had turned into a relationship. Everyone at the accounting firm seemed intent on blending into the overall heterosexual corporate culture. His tentative overtures to his gay coworkers had been politely rebuffed. It was smarter to keep your private life private, he was cautioned.

Sheldon had located a gay roommate through an advertisement in the *Advocate* and this man, Jacques, had turned out to be Sheldon's best friend in L.A. They'd go hunting for art deco treasures at the Rose Bowl swap meet, they'd dine at Mark's in Hollywood or go to Silverlake for Mexican food at Casitas. But they were just buddies, not lovers. Jacques was not seeking a committed relationship; he preferred the excitement of brief encounters with strangers at the baths or at various bars. He tried to encourage Sheldon to get out and "live a little."

This was something very foreign to Sheldon. Until he'd moved to Los Angeles, Sheldon had been in the closet—in the back of a very large, deep closet. After he'd met Jacques and moved into the apartment, he finally wrote to his mother, outing himself. It had taken him a month

to mail the damn letter. And even after this written confession of his gay-
ness, Sheldon remained gay only in a theoretical sort of way.

He couldn't bring himself to tell Jacques the awful truth. It was just
too mortifying. But here he was, a college-educated, twenty-six-year-old,
not bad-looking—in a bookish sort of way—gay guy who was technically
a virgin. He had a real job and most of his hair. He worked out at the
gym at least three times a week. All right, so he wasn't real muscular, but
he wasn't a lard-ass either. So, what was the problem?

Jacques, who had surmised the full extent of the problem, felt the issue was Sheldon's basic shyness. All Sheldon needed to do was to get out
and meet some people. How tough is that? *Merde alors,* Jacques did that
every night of the week when he was in the mood.

Sheldon had found a roommate by answering an ad in a gay publi-
cation; why not find a lover the same way? Jacques was forever clipping
out advertisements and leaving them in conspicuous places around the
apartment.

> Buffed and cut cowboy
> from Montana ISO
> dark-haired man under 30
> who likes leather. You
> wear the chaps, I'll
> handle the whip.

> Young, straight-looking
> executive likes travel,
> cooking, opera, and
> serious ass-play. If
> you do too, let's party.
> NO FEMS PLEASE!!

> ME: Richly endowed,
> very affectionate Black

> man who likes dining
> out, dancing, theater.
> YOU: Very smooth white
> or Asian nonsmoker.
> Prefer shaved body hair.

Sheldon was more confused than intrigued. Who were these guys? Did they have real jobs and families? Of course, Jacques explained, and then disclosed what Sheldon had suspected: most of the ads were outright lies.

"I once answered an ad where the man claimed he went to the gym every day," Jacques confided, "but when we met I knew it could not be so. He was a fat pig." Jacques always pronounced the word "peeg," something guaranteed to evoke a laugh from his roommate. "Perhaps he drove by a gym every day!"

Jacques's amusement at the recollection dissipated when he saw the look of dismay on his friend's face. All right, then. Perhaps the more direct approach should be taken.

"Go to any gay bar," Jacques advised. "You don't have to jump into bed with the first guy you meet."

Jacques had a point. After all, why had Sheldon moved to L.A. in the first place? To meet someone. For all the good it had done, he might just as well have stayed in Michigan. L.A. was one of the gay capitals of the world: there was Hollywood, West Hollywood, Silverlake, and Los Feliz. There was the art scene, the theater scene. The place was chock-full of fairies. Sheldon laughed to himself. There was someone here for him and tonight was the night. It was Friday, a balmy April night, and it was his birthday, for God's sake. Twenty-seven. It was time to take action.

CRUISING

Right after work Sheldon made his way to the Westside to check out a few places on Santa Monica Boulevard. The Sidecar, Daddy's, Rampage —

he'd driven by these places many times but had been too timid to go in. Not tonight. Rampage—that sounded a little too aggressive. Daddy's—perhaps an allusion to some unsavory fantasy. Oh hell. Sheldon was talking himself out of this. What about the Sidecar? A wholesome reference to an old-fashioned mixed drink. What is wrong with that? Nothing, nothing at all.

Sheldon parked his BMW and walked in. He'd dressed with care that morning. A light gray shirt that looked even better once he removed the obligatory tie. His slacks fit perfectly and flattered what he felt was a cute little tush. He found an empty stool at the bar, ordered a gin and tonic tall, and waited for something wonderful to happen.

But it seemed like he'd wandered into someone's private party. The men all appeared to know each other. They were addressing each other by their first names. And they were gorgeous, too. Most of them looked like they lived at the gym. They were dressed in tank tops and skintight T-shirts with pressed jeans. They all seemed to have short hair and earrings. Sheldon felt overdressed. And for all the attention he was getting, he might as well have been invisible. Even the bartender seemed remote. Sheldon sipped his drink and looked around the room.

There were some men engaged in a lively game of pool. He'd have considered challenging the winner, but that would be stupid. He was a poor pool player. These guys seemed like a bunch of arrogant snobs. His glass was only half empty but it was time to go.

It was a little after 7 P.M. This was only the first bar. No need to panic or lose confidence. He'd make his way slowly east toward his apartment in Los Feliz and stop at a few "gentlemen's" establishments along the way. Maybe he'd have better luck in Hollywood. There were a couple of places, the Limelight and the Crescent Moon, that sounded sort of romantic and glamorous.

Sheldon parked the car on a side street and walked into the Limelight. While the name might conjure up an image of Old Hollywood, this establishment apparently catered to an older, hard-drinking, decidedly unromantic crowd. These guys didn't look like they'd just come from the office. They looked like they'd been inside a tavern for a week or two. The Crescent Moon was no improvement. A dank, decidedly unwashed scent pervaded that establishment.

Never mind. He found himself heading home automatically. It was only 8:15. No doubt Jacques would cross-examine him upon his return. Did you talk to anyone? Where did you go? Sheldon willed himself to drive past his apartment complex and head toward Silverlake. Most of the bars in the area catered to a gay clientele. How about the Back Room? Tasteful, understated sign. Parking lot almost full. This looks promising.

STRANGERS IN THE NIGHT

Right away the place seemed inviting. A dark alcove opened almost immediately into a large room dominated by an impressive wooden bar, richly carved and polished to a satin finish. The back-bar was beautiful. Intricately fashioned dark oak arches framed mirrored panels that rose to the ceiling. It looked like every possible type of booze was available here. Standing at the ready on the mirrored shelves were all the recognizable brands as well as some obscure labels unknown to Sheldon. On either side of the bar were a series of cozy booths, upholstered in deep oxblood leather.

As soon as Sheldon walked in, the bartender glanced up and smiled. A waiter appeared and inquired whether Sheldon would like a booth.

"The kitchen's open until ten, and I can recommend the specials tonight," the waiter stated enthusiastically.

An inviting aroma of grilled meats emanated from the kitchen. Sheldon suddenly realized he was hungry. He opted for a booth and over the top edge of his menu he surveyed the room. Subdued lighting revealed that the other booths were occupied and several men stood at the bar. Sheldon was pleased to note that, in addition to the groups and couples in the booths, some of the patrons were definitely there by themselves.

He scanned the room again and was startled to find himself locking eyes with a very pleasant-looking young man: light eyes, fair hair—cut longer than what was considered stylish for a gay man in the late 1970s, but appealing nonetheless—a slender but muscular build. . . . The man smiled warmly, revealing beautiful teeth that seemed to sparkle in the muted light. Before he realized it, Sheldon was smiling back. Quickly he refocused his eyes on the menu. His heart was hammering.

Get a grip, Shelley, he instructed himself. Let's see, perhaps the grilled chicken breast or maybe splurge and have the petit filet mignon?

Someone had approached his table. Sheldon looked up from his menu to find, not the waiter, but the fair-haired young man standing there grinning at him.

"If you're not waiting for someone, do you mind if I join you?"

"No, not at all. I mean, of course, please sit down."

"You know, I noticed you the moment you walked in. I don't think I've seen you here before."

"First time here. I guess I don't get out much." Sheldon tossed the line off like a joke. He hoped this guy couldn't tell what a neophyte he really was.

"The food's great here," the man advised as he motioned for the waiter. "I'll have one of your burgers with everything on it and a Michelob."

"The same for me," Sheldon heard himself saying. "By the way, my name is Sheldon but people usually call me Shelley."

"I like that—Shelley, Shelley," his new friend repeated. "Oh, my name's Randolph but fortunately my friends call me Randy." They both laughed.

Sheldon thought this must be the best hamburger he had ever eaten in the nicest little restaurant with the most engaging young man. Randy was so relaxed, Sheldon felt like he had known him for much longer than however long they had been nestled together in this cozy leather booth. How long had it been? Sheldon glanced at his wristwatch while Randy continued to nibble on the remaining french fries from both their plates. It was almost eleven. Impossible.

Then, as if on cue, the waiter appeared. More beers? Dessert? Not the check just yet? Sheldon noticed that the place was really filling up.

The bar was packed two deep and the decibel level had risen significantly.

"I should be heading home," Sheldon commented as he paid the check.

"I'm sorry," Randy said. "What did you say?"

"I guess I lost track of the time—I should be heading home," Sheldon repeated in a louder voice.

"Do you live alone?"

"No, actually I have a roommate."

"Listen, thanks for getting the check. How about I buy you an after-dinner drink at my place? I don't have a roommate."

"I should be heading home. It's been a long day."

What was the matter with him? Wasn't this exactly what Sheldon had been waiting for? So why all the hesitation?

"Well, at least give me a ride home, Shelley. My car's in the shop and I'd rather not take the bus more than I have to."

BIG MAC

Home for Randy turned out to be a loft apartment above an Army/Navy surplus store in the heart of Hollywood. It was completely out of Sheldon's way, but he could hardly let his new friend take the bus. And what a good way to get to know Randy better.

A bit spartan, was Sheldon's first impression. A few small floor lights provided the only illumination. There was a long sofa, a coffee table, and an overstuffed chair defining the area just inside the door as the living room. A portable television set occupied a place of prominence against the far wall. A large, utilitarian armoire was stationed behind the sofa and blocked the view to the rest of the apartment. What was really remarkable, Sheldon realized, was the complete lack of any art on the walls. Not even a poster. Now, that's what I call minimalist, Sheldon thought. I guess this is one gay guy who didn't get the decorator gene, he mused.

"Make yourself at home," Randy said as he opened a bottle of white wine. "If I'd known you were coming over, I would have had some champagne."

"Please don't go to any trouble for me."

"Shelley, Shelley, Shelley. I want you to have a night you'll remember."

Randy poured the wine for both of them and then disappeared for a minute. When he returned he was carrying an old cigar box.

"I've got a few treats for you, my sweet new friend. Tell me if this is not the best bud you have ever had."

Sheldon was no expert, but the combination of Chablis, marijuana, and something Randy called Pig Poppers was having an effect. When Randy suggested they adjourn to the bedroom, there was no hesitation. Randy immediately began disrobing and Sheldon, fortified by weed, wine, and amyl nitrite, did the same.

"Shelley, sweet boy," Randy murmured, "lie down here on the bed. Let me rub your back. You were telling me about your rough day at the office."

As Sheldon rolled over, he glanced at his new friend's body. It was smooth, pale, and quite muscular—very pleasing. But Sheldon couldn't help noting that Randy showed no signs of sexual stimulation.

"What the fuck you looking at?"

"Nothing. Listen, Randy, I —"

"Shut the fuck up and turn over!"

What was happening? What had he done to piss this guy off? All of a sudden, Randy was acting like a different person.

Sheldon tried to move off the bed and suddenly felt a massive pain between his shoulder blades. What kind of a back rub is this? Oh God, this guy is too strong. Sheldon was pinned down. Randy grabbed Sheldon's arms and twisted them behind his back. He had his knee in Sheldon's spine. Sheldon's face was pressed into the mattress. He felt Randy's mouth near his ear.

"I've got a big surprise for you, Shelley," Randy whispered, and then Sheldon felt pain unlike anything he had ever experienced. Randy was jamming something immense up Sheldon's rectum. Oh God, he was being raped! He strained to lift his head.

"Stop!"

"Aw, Nellie Shelley. You just need to relax."

"You're hurting me," Shelley gasped.

"We haven't even started yet. That was just the appetizer. We need to get you ready for the main course."

Sheldon felt a moment of relief as Randy removed the instrument of torture.

"What was that thing?"

"Just an itty bitty black dildo. I call this guy Old Black Joe because it looks just like a nigger's dick. See."

To Sheldon's disgust, Randy started rubbing the dark rubber phallus across Sheldon's lips.

"Open wide!"

"No. Stop." Sheldon groaned and struggled to free himself. How could somebody as small as Randy be this strong? He had to get out of there.

"You talk too much, Nellie Shelley. Now, open wide for Old Black Joe."

Sheldon resisted and Randy punched him several times in the temple. Oh God, he was going to pass out. This guy was crazy—he might be planning to kill him. Sheldon had to stay conscious. Maybe it would be better to cooperate. He opened his mouth.

"Much better, darling. Now it's time to meet Joe's big friend, the star of the party."

Out of the corner of his eye Sheldon could see Randy pull something from beneath the bed. It had to be at least two feet in length and close to six inches across.

"Meet Big Mac!"

The pain radiated from Sheldon's anus up through his abdomen. He could feel his insides tearing apart—he could hear them giving way. He couldn't breathe. He realized that he had vomited with that first dildo still in his mouth. He was choking.

"Oh, yeah. That's good. Suck on this for a while."

The dildo was removed from his mouth and in its place Randy inserted his own, still somewhat flaccid organ. Sheldon was paralyzed with pain—the monstrous dildo was still inside him. A stench was pervading the room, a nauseating combination of vomit and feces and warm blood.

"Suck harder, Jew boy," Randy urged. Sheldon attempted to comply.

After a while he heard Randy announce: "It's time for Big Mac to move over." His face was again pushed into the mattress and the huge dildo was removed and replaced by Randy's own much smaller member. To Sheldon's surprise, the pain in no way diminished. Just stay calm, he told himself. It'll be over soon. And it was. With several self-satisfied grunts Randy concluded the sex act and rolled off the bed.

At first Sheldon did not think he had the ability to move. The pain was so intense—a hot, stabbing, unrelenting pain. But he had to get out of there.

He could hear Randy in the adjacent bathroom—water was running in the shower. He could hear his host singing. The next thing he remembered was seeing Randy standing near the bed, wrapped in a towel, holding a wineglass. Sheldon must have passed out for a second.

"Would you like some more wine?"

Sheldon couldn't believe it. This guy was acting like nothing had happened.

"Or how about another joint? Big Mac and I like to make sure all our customers are satisfied. Anything more we can do for you, Nellie Shelley?"

Sheldon did not attempt to answer. His mind held one thought: he had to get out of there before he lost consciousness again. He forced himself to stand up. The room swayed and he went down hard on his knees. His clothes. His car keys. Come on! Come on! He needed to use the restroom but it could wait.

He put his clothes on, found his shoes. His keys and wallet were right where he'd left them in his pants pocket. Okay. Okay. Now just walk out.

He half expected that Randy might try to prevent him from leaving or try to hurt him some more. But as Sheldon made his way to the front door, this tormentor, this torturer, barely acknowledged his departure. Randy had turned on the television and was carefully rolling another joint.

"See you around," he said as Sheldon opened the door and made a slow and painful exit down the flight of narrow stairs.

A Cup of Tea

"*Sacré bleu!*" Jacques exclaimed when Sheldon arrived home. "It's after 2 A.M.! You never stay out late. I was worried sick. You could have telephoned, you know. I made a *tarte Tatin* for your birthday. I could still heat it up if you like. You know, Sheldon, you look terrible. What is the matter with you? Are you drunk? Were you in an accident?"

Sheldon was sobbing. It was a combination of the relief at being home and the pain, which had not stopped at all—which actually seemed to be getting worse by the minute—and something else. The humiliation.

"What, what?" Jacques demanded, like an irate parent whose ordinarily dutiful child has disappointed him. "Where have you been? What happened to you?"

"I was raped," Sheldon replied, and then he lost consciousness.

When he opened his eyes, Jacques looked very worried.

"Oh, thank God, you're awake. You were out for at least ten minutes. I did not know what to do. I removed your clothes. There was much blood. I made some herbal tea. I drew a bath for you. That should help. Shelley, please talk to me."

"Yes. Tea. A warm tub. That should help calm down the pain."

But the tea and the bath did nothing to relieve the pain. If anything, it was worse. Sheldon had again lost consciousness briefly while in the bathtub. Jacques asked again, "What happened to you?"

"I told you, I was raped," Sheldon replied. He was lying in bed, clutching a pillow to his midsection. The pain had not abated.

"I think I'm going to be sick again," he gasped. Jacques quickly placed a large pot in front of his friend and applied a cold washcloth to his forehead.

"The blood in your underwear," Jacques persisted. "You must talk to me."

"He seemed like a nice guy. I went home with him. He used these rubber dildos on me. I think I'm hurt really bad, Jacques," Sheldon finally said between labored breaths.

"I'm taking you to the closest hospital. Right now. Let's get you dressed. You know, forget that, put on a robe. Let's go now. You look like shit." Jacques always pronounced it "sheet," which, until this moment, had always elicited a giggle from Sheldon. No one was laughing.

THE DAMAGE DONE

"You did the right thing by getting him to a hospital immediately," the surgeon informed Jacques. "Your friend would not have made it. He was in shock and suffering from advanced septicemia. The damage to the colon and surrounding tissue was profound. In fact, I've never seen anything like it. We did the best we could. And who knows? At some point in the future, it may be possible to reverse the colostomy. But for now, Mr. Silverman should be thankful he is alive."

Jacques was too stunned to reply. The doctor continued, in a businesslike tone, apparently oblivious of the effect his words were having.

"Now, I'd say we're looking at two to three weeks in the hospital, minimum, followed by a month of bed rest at home. The nutritionist will be working with Mr. Silverman regarding an appropriate diet. Eventually he'll be able to tolerate a regular diet, but not for some time."

Again Jacques found himself unable to reply. The doctor went on:

"Mr. Silverman was able to offer very little information regarding how he came to sustain these very serious injuries. However, I was able to ascertain that he was attacked and 'raped,' as he put it. Under such circumstances, I have a legal as well as an ethical obligation to contact the authorities."

"The police?" Jacques inquired.

"Yes. In this case, I've contacted LAPD Hollywood Division, based on where this crime occurred," the doctor explained.

"You know," he continued, "this is not the first homosexual rape case I've seen. It's certainly the most serious in terms of the physical damage sustained by the patient. I hope your friend has the courage to see this through. The others didn't."

Jacques nodded mutely by way of reply.

"The police will no doubt be contacting you as well," the surgeon continued. "I trust you will cooperate with them."

"Of course," Jacques responded, not really knowing what that meant.

YOU CAN'T KNOW TOO MUCH

Detective Oliver Swain was generally described by those who didn't know him very well as hard-bitten and streetwise, and I guess those terms apply, but they don't begin to give a complete picture of the man. Born and raised in South-Central Los Angeles, Ollie had joined the force at an early age, both as a way to extricate himself from the poverty in which he grew up and as a way to stake a claim to the power and principles he thought the LAPD embodied.

As a black man, Ollie was sensitive to the needs of his community and felt he could best do his part to meet those needs by working within the system. He identified with the victims of crime, who were so often those already socially and economically disenfranchised. But his concern for humanity was in no way limited to those in the inner city, as it is euphemistically called. To Ollie, a victim was a victim, and he was there to "protect and serve."

I first met Ollie when I was a freshly minted prosecutor, eager but unfocused. Ollie, although only a few years older, was already a detective. He impressed upon me the need for thorough investigation and attention to detail. "You can't know too much" was one of his favorite expressions. And Ollie applied that precept to whatever happened to be the subject at hand: a suspect's prior record, both federal and state, both as an adult and as a juvenile; the pattern of powder burns (referred to as stippling or sooting) at the site of a gunshot wound; the lighting, weather conditions, configuration of parked cars, and foliage at the time an eyewitness made his observations. You get the idea: you can't know too much.

For someone interested in the detail and minutiae of others' lives, Ollie played it very close to the vest regarding his own background. Folks generally can't wait to tell me everything about themselves. Total strangers will confide in me about their alcoholism, infidelities, or psychiatric treatment. I'm not sure why this is—perhaps because they sense a genuine interest on my part—but it certainly comes in handy in my line of work. My friend Ollie was reticent, even with me. It wasn't until we had known each other for a couple of years and had worked several cases together that he opened up to me.

"Most of my family thinks I'm nothing but a lousy Uncle Tom," he announced under his breath. We were having lunch at the Police Academy. I love that place. It was built by the WPA during the Roosevelt administration, and the stone and masonry work is remarkable. There is a beautiful Olympic-size outdoor pool nestled along one side of a lovely, shaded path. The sounds of gunshots from the nearby firing range hardly disturb the peaceful ambiance. There are two restaurants, one open in the evenings for dinner and special events and one open every day for breakfast and lunch. The latter offers reasonably priced, reasonably greasy food that we law enforcement types seem to favor.

I said nothing to Ollie, partly because I had a mouthful of tuna melt and partly because I didn't know how to respond.

"My sister's a schoolteacher. No one finds fault with that occupation."

"As well they shouldn't," I ventured.

"But there are days when I think my family has more love for my brother Anthony than they have for me, and that little shit is in the joint! Sometimes they act like I'm the one put him there just because I'm a cop."

"What's he in for?" I inquired.

"Armed 211. And he did time at CYA as a juvenile, so the sentence was fair. They gave him the low term."

"Sounds about right."

Ollie looked so disheartened, I didn't know what more to say. He was not the kind of man to be soothed by platitudes.

"Look," he said after a long sip of iced tea, "I didn't suggest lunch just so I could moan about my personal problems."

"I didn't think so. I imagine you want to moan about your professional problems."

That induced a modest chuckle and a brief synopsis of the crime.

"I took the crime report primarily from the roommate, a Jacques Lavin." Ollie had pulled out a sheaf of police reports from a blue binder and was consulting his notes as he spoke. "I also spoke directly with the victim, Sheldon Silverman, but only for a brief moment. He was obviously in no condition to be interviewed at length."

"When was this?"

"Last week. In the interim, I've talked to the surgeon and gotten copies of all the medical records to date, and I've interviewed the bartender who was on duty that night and the waiter who served them. They both remembered Silverman and his companion, Randolph Werner, but they seemed kind of hinky to me."

"Think they're hiding something?"

"I can't imagine what. Anyway, this case is just about the worst one-on-one I've ever seen. The fact that we're dealing with two homosexuals makes it that much worse."

"Actually, Ollie, the fact that we have two gay men instead of a man and woman is the whole problem. If Sheldon Silverman were Sheila Silverman lying in that hospital with those injuries, I bet you would have already hooked up this—what's his name, Randolph Warner?"

"Werner," Ollie replied soberly. "And you're right, Marissa, if the victim were female, the suspect would already be under arrest and the case would be filed by now. What's the matter with me? You think *I'm* bigoted?"

Ollie's question was genuine. He was wondering out loud about his own possible prejudices.

"No, I don't. But these facts make for a much harder sell in front of a jury. Getting twelve random people to overcome their individual and collective prejudices is always a challenge. But it can be done. Homophobia seems to be a particularly mindless kind of intolerance. In that way it's not so different from the cross-racial issues we deal with all the time."

"Right," Ollie replied, but he sounded unconvinced. "I can't think of a single D.A. who'd file this case."

"I can think of one." I smiled. "But only after you've attempted to interview Werner and I've interviewed Silverman. Then we'll see what we've got."

"I owe you big-time for this." Ollie grinned as he grabbed for the check. "What are you doing this afternoon?"

"I was going to attend a sex crimes investigators' meeting downtown, but I think I could skip it. Which hospital did you say our victim was in?"

THE FIRST STEP

On our way over to Queen of Angels, Ollie and I were both uncharacteristically silent. Generally you can't shut us up. If we're not talking about one of our cases, we're talking about someone else's case. If we're not talking about work, then we're talking about music, basketball, or, our favorite topic, food. If we hadn't gone into law enforcement, Ollie and I both would have been chefs.

I was mulling over what I would say to our victim, to Sheldon. I'm an advocate. My advocacy is not limited to the courtroom. In those days I spent a lot of time lecturing to community groups, medical personnel, and other lawyers regarding sex crimes and their prosecution. No matter what the stated topic of my speech, "Emergency Room Protocols for Suspected Victims of Sex Crimes" or "Interview Techniques for Patrol Officers" or "Community Watch Q&A," my personal message was also delivered loud and clear: we must report crime and prosecute the perpetrators.

Who is this "we"? All of us. Nobody signs up to be a victim or a witness to a crime. But it is our civic obligation to cooperate with law enforcement to see that justice is done. Many people don't want to get involved. Not until they themselves are victimized. And even then, some victims are so fearful of retaliation that they choose to remain mute. Was this the kind of speech I would give to Sheldon? It would depend on his attitude. If he was recalcitrant, I would be encouraging. And, sadly, if he was eager to prosecute, I would feel compelled to be forthright about our meager chances for conviction.

It had taken a matter of minutes to drive to the hospital. Being a passenger in Detective Swain's vehicle was not for the fainthearted. The man moved just as swiftly on foot, and I found myself nearly running to keep up as we rushed for an elevator and made our way to the third floor. The elevator doors opened to a warm greeting.

"Ollie! Nice to see you," a crisply uniformed Filipina nurse greeted us.

Ollie was on a first-name basis with a number of nurses and doctors at most of the hospitals in the metropolitan area. "Worked robbery-homicide before I transferred over to the sex table," he explained dismissively.

"This is Marissa Batt from the D.A.'s office. We're here to see Mr. Silverman. This is Maria Buyagawan." Introductions having been made, we proceeded to Sheldon's room, which, to my relief, turned out to be one of the few private rooms on the floor. An inquisitive patient in the next bed never enhances an interview with a sexual assault victim.

"You came at an excellent time," Maria said. "Sheldon's having a good day."

"We'll try not to spoil it," Ollie assured her.

At first glance, I didn't see our patient. The room was filled with so many contraptions—tubes, monitors, screens, bags of fluids—that he was almost obscured. And the sibilant sounds emitting from the equipment almost drowned out his voice.

"Hi, Maria. Hi, Detective."

"Hey, Sheldon, I'm surprised you remember me. You were not in such great shape when we first met." Ollie's talent for understatement was legendary.

Ollie introduced me and I spent a few moments explaining the purpose of our visit. Sheldon nodded solemnly when I commented on how important it is to have a commitment from the victim to see the case through. I liked him immediately. It wasn't just that he was so nice-looking—even in the hospital gown and with the tubes and bags—it was his tone. Straightforward, well mannered, and so very sad. Why is it that so many crime victims are such fine people? That certainly has been my experience.

There was nothing in Sheldon's responses to dissuade me from filing the case. In addition to his forthright manner, his memory for detail was excellent. I sensed no discordant notes in his narrative. I found him to be truthful and I found his story to be compelling. Of course, what I thought was secondary. What really mattered was how a jury would react, and it was my job to help them to see the case from my point of view.

"What happens now?" Sheldon wanted to know.

I explained that our investigation of the case would continue and that we would seek to interview the perpetrator. However, barring some unforeseen problem, it was my intention to file a complaint against Mr. Werner for the crimes he perpetrated: forcible sodomy, forcible oral copulation, and rape by instrumentality. I explained that, in addition to these crimes, we would also file what is called a "special allegation" alleging that, in the commission of the rape, the defendant intentionally inflicted great bodily injury. That allegation, if found true by the trier of fact (the judge or jury), could then be used to increase the sentence once the defendant was convicted on the underlying crimes.

"Just to be on the safe side," I continued, "I'll add a fourth count for assault by means of force likely to produce great bodily injury. Just in case we get a weird, homophobic jury that thinks you consented to all the sex acts. You see, Sheldon, consent is not a defense to assault."

"I think I'm following you." Sheldon spoke slowly and a look of pain disturbed his features. Was it something I said or did he need the nurse?

"All except what you said about a jury," he continued. "I don't want a jury trial. I don't want to have to talk about these things to twelve people. Twenty-four beady eyes staring at me . . ." Sheldon muffled a sob and turned his head into the pillow.

"Do you need the nurse?"

"No nurse," and, after a pause, "no jury."

"I understand your concern," I ventured, "but I cannot guarantee that we will be able to resolve the case without a jury trial. Of course, I'll do everything I can to encourage a plea bargain and avoid a trial, but you must understand that it's the defendant's right to have a trial by jury if he so chooses."

There was no audible response from Sheldon, so I continued, "Even if the defendant won't plead guilty, there's always a chance we could get him to waive jury and try the case before a judge."

"Yes," Sheldon replied. "I think I could tell this to a judge. I mean, I'm talking to you and Detective Swain right now. I could talk to a judge. But a jury—all those people staring at me—I'd be too embarrassed. Too ashamed."

"You have absolutely nothing to be ashamed about," Ollie said soothingly. "How were you supposed to know that this guy was going to turn into a sadistic monster as soon as he got you alone?"

Sheldon's apparent confusion over who could waive the right to a jury trial concerned me. I decided that it might be prudent to take the time now to explain some of the key events in the course of a criminal case. This was not the first college-educated victim who had only a tenuous grasp of criminal procedure. Sometimes we lawyers assume too much. We tend to forget that most people derive their notions about the justice system from fictionalized television shows and the usually distorted reportage of high-profile cases.

"The first step," I explained, "will be the preliminary hearing. It will involve a judge, not a jury. The judge will listen to your testimony and then decide whether or not there should be a trial. I can almost guarantee that the judge will find that there is sufficient evidence to bind the defendant over for trial."

Given the fact that the prosecution's burden of proof at a prelim is merely to demonstrate by "slight evidence" that the crimes alleged have been committed by the accused, this was a safe guarantee to make.

Poor Sheldon. He was looking relieved. But I had to tell him the unpleasant part:

"The hearing will have to be held here, in the hospital, due to your condition and the strict time frame under which we operate. Once the suspect is arrested, the clock starts running. If we waited to arrest Werner until you were out of the hospital, there would be problems. One, he might disappear. Two, his lawyer would argue that there was a preindictment delay that prejudiced his case."

Sheldon was nodding, a somber look on his face.

"So," I continued, "we will work with the hospital staff in order to handle the hearing in the best way possible so that your health and security will not be jeopardized. There will be a number of deputy sheriffs present, so you should have no fear of the defendant. But you understand, he has a constitutional right to be present."

"No way!" There was a look of horror and disbelief on our poor patient's face.

"Sorry," Ollie responded in his matter-of-fact fashion. "Sheldon, don't freak yourself out. You'll be a great witness, and Marissa and I will be with you every step of the way. But we need your commitment to see this thing through before we go ahead and arrest this joker. He almost killed you. He's got to be stopped. Think about it, he's probably done this kind of thing to other men."

"You're right, of course. I'll cooperate with you."

"You're going to be fine," Ollie announced as he managed to thread his big arms through the maze of tubes and give Sheldon a hug. "We're gonna nail this muthafucka, if you'll pardon my French."

Sheldon was giggling. I had never seen Ollie have this kind of an effect on a witness.

"Don't ever say 'pardon my French' to Jacques," Sheldon explained. "He hates that expression."

STRATEGY

"Tell me this," I asked as we sped back to the Civic Center. "Based on what Silverman told us, is it your intention to arrest Werner no matter what explanation he offers?"

"I never close my mind to new information, but I can't imagine what that perv could say to make me change my opinion on this one. What happened to Silverman is just pitiful."

"Mr. Pitiful," I intoned, knowing it would provoke Ollie's best Otis Redding imitation. I nodded approval as I heard the familiar lyrics:

> Call me Mr. Pitiful
> Baby, that's my name now
> Call me Mr. Pitiful
> That's how I got my fame
>
> But people just don't want to understand
> What make a man feel so blue
> They call me Mr. Pitiful
> Cause I lost someone just like you.

"I still think I should keep the day job," Ollie said.

I forced myself back to the subject at hand. "So, should I file this for an arrest warrant? If so, you're obligated to Mirandize him before asking him any questions. On the other hand, if your purpose in being there is merely to conduct an investigation to determine if any crimes have been committed, *Miranda* wouldn't apply until you decide you have probable cause to arrest. In either event, you should probably be armed with a search warrant. I hate to rely on getting consent, and without it you'd be in the position of arresting Werner first and then searching 'incident to the arrest.' Of course, then the ambit of the search would be more narrowly circumscribed."

Ollie had more legal knowledge than many lawyers I'd encountered.

I didn't need to cite the landmark case of *Chimel v. California* decided in 1969. Justice Potter Stewart, writing for the Supremes, had held that, without a search warrant, a search pursuant to a lawful arrest is limited to the area within the immediate control, or "arm's length," of the arrestee. The lawful arrest conveys the right to search the person, not the place.

"This is one of the two reasons I love working cases with you." Ollie beamed."You actually think like a lawyer."

"Well, thanks, Ollie. Dare I ask what the other reason is?"

"Your gumbo is better than my own momma's."

"Dude, you flatter me. You were probably just real hungry that day."

We resisted the impulse to segue into a discussion of the culinary arts and focused instead on the best way to approach Mr. Werner. Adhering to Oliver's adage "You can't know too much," we decided that no charges should be filed until we had heard his side of the story, assuming he wished to discuss things with the LAPD. We also decided that, although the matter was still in the investigative stage, Werner was our sole focus of attention as a suspect and thus should be Mirandized. This is a more cautious approach than many would take.

The basic rule is that a "custodial interrogation" is what mandates the advisement that a person has the right to remain silent and to have legal counsel present before any questioning takes place. Werner would not be in custody. Ollie intended to catch up with him either at home or at work (it had been determined that Werner worked as a part-time clerk at the surplus store on the first floor of his building). Although not in custody, would Werner be free to leave? The answer was no. If he declined to talk, he'd be arrested on the basis of our victim's statements. And if he talked, there was a real good chance he'd be arrested no matter what explanation he gave.

We also agreed that Ollie would not make contact with the suspect until we could get a search warrant prepared and signed. We didn't want to give him time to destroy any evidence. I glanced at my watch. It was almost five o'clock.

"We'll have to get a telephonic warrant," I commented. By the time we had prepared the warrant and the affidavit, the courthouse would be closed and all the bench officers would have left for the day. Fortunately, that never presented an impediment, because the appellate courts had ruled that warrants issued by a magistrate via telephone were to be given the same force and effect as those reviewed and signed in person.

"Or I could just swing by Judge Brown's house in Hancock Park on my way over to Hollywood. It's hardly out of the way," Ollie offered. Ollie preferred the more traditional approach, where the magistrate is presented with the warrant, affidavit, and all pertinent police reports for review, rather than having the generally voluminous materials read over the phone. And Judge Nancy Brown was one of a small handful of bench officers whose door was always open to police officers. She was the best—gracious, dedicated, knowledgeable, and focused—even in the middle of the night. She was the go-to judge when any experienced officer needed a warrant signed at an odd hour.

"Good idea," I agreed. "Wouldn't it be great if this case ends up in her court? Poor Sheldon deserves a sensitive, caring judge."

"Too bad there are so few." Ollie gave voice to my very thought. Not only had the collective legal scholarship of the bench officers been diminishing over the years, their personalities weren't improving either.

Aside from Nancy, it seemed that most female Superior Court judges were particularly venomous and ill-tempered. Lawyers openly speculated as to why this was so. One suggestion involved the black dye used in the robes.

"It's toxic and, over time, the wearer is poisoned. It seeps in through the pores in the skin and ultimately attacks the brain," one defense attorney explained in a professorial tone.

"That does not explain why most of these women are such castrating bitches from their first moment on the bench," another attorney pointed out.

"It has to do with the rarefied atmosphere on the bench," a prosecutor suggested. "There simply is not enough oxygen up there. The brain atrophies."

Question: How many female Superior Court judges does it take to change a lightbulb?

Answer: Just one—but she has to wait for the entire world to revolve around her.

You get the picture. We made jokes about it but it wasn't really very funny. I wrenched my mind back from Bitches on the Bench to the task before us.

"Uh, Ollie, is your partner Scottie still IOD?" This is cop shorthand for "injured on duty" and therefore not working.

"Yes, he is. But don't worry, little girl, I'll have backup."

I hated it when Ollie read my mind. But I didn't object to his calling me "little girl." Of course, if anyone else on the planet had dared to refer to me that way, I would have corrected him in the most vehement fashion. But when Ollie said it, it was a term of endearment. Not an ounce of condescension. Only love.

Ollie dropped me back at the Criminal Courts Building, a/k/a the CCB, while he went on to the Public Administration Building, a/k/a the PAB, or Parker Center, or, to you *Dragnet* aficionados, the Glass House.

I got to work on preparing the search warrant and the accompanying affidavit. Most of the language is boilerplate, and it took me less than half an hour to have the finished documents ready for Ollie to pick up on his way out to Hollywood. With that done, I generated the complaint against Werner, relying on the reasonable assumption that an arrest would be made. If the defendant could not be found, I intended to file the case for an arrest warrant.

I also had a lot of other work to catch up on. The People versus Randolph Werner was hardly the only case requiring my attention. There was a file cabinet full of other equally serious cases pending trial. Some were still set for preliminary hearing, while others were at the pretrial phase. In a separate drawer were cases where the defendant had been convicted but not yet sentenced. Plus I had mail to read and about a hundred phone calls to return. Just like all the other deputies assigned to the Sex Crimes Unit in those days.

THE ARREST

I insisted that Ollie tell me every detail of his contact with Werner, not just the distillation that would be memorialized in the arrest report. Ollie complied.

After visiting the ever-gracious Judge Brown, Detective Swain, now armed with a signed search warrant, met two uniformed officers in a marked patrol unit at the suspect's location on Vine Street in Hollywood. Ollie acquainted the officers with the facts of the case and that the suspect had a rap sheet. Before entering the building, he showed them the most recent mug shots of Werner.

Randolph Werner was thirty-two years old, five foot eleven, 160 pounds, blond over blue, with no observable physical oddities or tattoos. His mug photos failed to reveal more, and his prior criminal history likewise provided nothing that distinguished Werner from all the other garden-variety crooks we see every day.

Werner had a recent DUI that had resulted in a suspended license and two days in county jail. The rest of his California record began five years earlier when he moved to L.A. from Jackson, Mississippi. It included three prostitution convictions and one arrest for assault that had amounted to nothing more than a "D.A. reject," meaning the case had been presented to our office but not filed. There were no other entries.

Werner's Mississippi record was not automated, and phone calls to the Jackson authorities by the ever-diligent Ollie had netted little additional information. The suspect had a sealed juvenile record, had spent two years in a reformatory for "troubled" boys, and had suffered one arrest and conviction for marijuana sales as an adult on which he had done state time. Neither sexual assault convictions nor arrests. No weapons charges. Nothing else.

"There's our boy," Ollie exclaimed suddenly. The other officers looked up from the mug shots to see Randolph Werner in the flesh behind the counter of the surplus store.

As the policemen entered the business, Werner glanced in their direction and, after a split-second hesitation noticed only by Ollie, greeted his visitors warmly.

"Good evening, gentlemen, are you looking for anything in particular?"

"Actually," Ollie responded, "we're looking for Randolph Werner. Would that be you?"

The blond man readily acknowledged his identity and Ollie got right to the point. There had been a complaint registered with the police. A young man by the name of Silverman had accused him of a sexual assault involving dildos.

"It was weird," Ollie told me later. "He treated us almost like we were customers in the store looking for specific merchandise, rather than cops serving a warrant in his home."

There was no need to "toss" the apartment. After inviting them upstairs, Werner seemed happy to show the officers where everything was. In addition to the dildos described by Silverman, the warrant sought any items that could be used in sexual scenarios involving bondage and discipline or sadomasochism.

The officers ended up hauling out a truckload of leather and rubber goods—everything from the ubiquitous handcuffs to something called a sling, a contraption involving a leather harness with metal chains, that they found hanging from a closet ceiling.

The initial interview went almost too well. While the other officers were tagging evidence, Ollie turned on a portable tape recorder and gave the *Miranda* advisement. Werner immediately waived his rights. He would be happy to speak with the detective. He had no idea what the detective was talking about. He didn't know anybody named Silverman. He never assaulted anyone.

Detective Swain had decided not to wait until he got the suspect downtown. Although it is generally agreed that suspect interviews should be conducted at the police station or on neutral ground rather than in the perpetrator's own home where he might feel more comfortable, it is also generally agreed that the initial interview should be conducted as soon as possible, before the suspect has time to make up a story.

In response to Werner's complete memory lapse regarding any evening spent with one Sheldon Silverman, Ollie sketched in a few more details: the meeting at the Back Room, where the waiter remembered them both; the ride in Silverman's car, where Randy left a couple of fingerprints. . . . Suddenly Werner's recollection was refreshed. Oh yes, he did have a date with a guy named Sheldon who liked to be called Shelley. But nothing out of the ordinary happened. He couldn't imagine why Shelley had called the cops.

"He didn't," Detective Swain explained. "The doctor in the emergency room at the hospital did." When it became clear that Werner was more interested in finding out what the police knew than in providing any information himself, the interview was concluded. Detective Swain then proceeded to formally place Werner under arrest.

After the suspect was transported downtown by another police unit for booking, Ollie remained at the scene in order to make sure nothing had been overlooked in the execution of the search warrant. His tenacity did not go unrewarded. In a large metal trash can that Werner was apparently using as a laundry hamper, Detective Swain found a cache of physical evidence supporting Sheldon's allegations. Underneath a mountain of dirty clothes he found a set of soiled sheets and two bloodstained dildos.

"Can't we just snap a few pictures and leave this shit here?" one of the uniforms wanted to know.

"These queers make me sick," the other patrolman commented. "As far as I'm concerned, that Silverman guy probably got exactly what he deserved."

But Ollie insisted that the crime scene be preserved until he could take all the photographs he deemed necessary. Then all the potentially relevant physical evidence was tagged, bagged, and taken back to headquarters for booking into property. This was to be handled like any other crime scene. Ollie insisted that the officers be careful and thorough, but even as the patrolmen were unhappily complying with his directives, Ollie was filled with a sense of futility. Those two cops weren't alone in their feelings of disgust and revulsion. How could you find a fair jury to hear this case?

MEET SAM PARKS

A defendant's initial arraignment on a felony offense is generally a pro forma proceeding where the defendant is officially advised of the charges against him and of his constitutional rights. If he has not retained his own attorney and cannot afford to do so, the public defender is appointed to represent him. The deputy public defender selected to protect the interests of Randy Werner turned out to be Sam Parks.

Sam Parks was a well-known fixture around the courthouse in those days. The craggy face, the rumpled clothes, the shuffling gait, the pervasive scent of tobacco and alcohol that hung about him were familiar to all but the most recently hired lawyers. So was his sense of scorn and distrust for his clientele. Good, I thought, this is a definite bonus. With Parks in the mix, the likelihood of a plea bargain increased tenfold.

Sam was not known to be a vigorous litigator. If you couldn't find him in the afternoon, it wouldn't pay to look in the law library. A better bet would be the back booth at Hill's Code Seven, a popular hangout for both cops and criminal lawyers who liked to drink their lunch.

"So, Sam," I exclaimed a few days after the arraignment when I happened to see him in the hall, "the D.A. in the arraignment court tells me you're my worthy opponent on the Werner case."

"Yeah," Sam responded with no enthusiasm and apparently no recognition.

"You know," I continued, "the rape case with the dildos."

"Oh, right. The homo case," Sam responded. "Just my luck to get stuck with a case like that. Why does your office waste time filing these cases?"

I took a deep breath and decided to be as polite as possible. After all, antagonizing opposing counsel is never a good idea. I explained that the case involved great bodily injury and could not be ignored. I then informed Sam that he could expect a bedside hearing at the hospital unless his client was willing to waive time for the preliminary hearing until the victim had recovered sufficiently to be discharged.

Sam rubbed his prominent purple nose with a nicotine-stained forefinger and appeared to ponder this purely procedural issue. After a long moment and no audible response from Parks, I suggested that we should resolve these issues in court. Sam seemed relieved that no immediate action on his part was required and shuffled off down the hall.

Although I held out a shred of hope that the defense might agree to a continuance, I prepared Sheldon for the probability of a bedside hearing. Ollie, Nurse Buyagawan, and I decided that the patient would be more comfortable in one of the staff conference rooms. The idea of a dozen or so people crammed into a small hospital room was unacceptable. Sheldon's hospital bed would be wheeled into the much larger room where the attorneys and court personnel could take their places around the conference table. A minimum of three or four sheriff's deputies would be present to assure security, and the prisoner would remain handcuffed throughout the proceedings. The hospital administration was advised of and approved the plan.

BACK TO THE HOSPITAL

As expected, the defendant would not agree to a continuance. Therefore, on the date of the hearing, court proceedings were recessed in the CCB and reconvened at the hospital.

Jacques had bought Sheldon a new robe for the occasion, and although the IV line and the gastric tubes precluded his actually wearing it, Sheldon allowed Jacques to drape it over his shoulders.

"You look great," I lied when I saw our victim. He looked terrible. If possible, he looked even worse than when we'd first met. Shelley had lost weight and his face had a sallow cast. His beautiful dark eyes were sunken and red-rimmed, his cheeks hollow, his lips parched. The boldly colored satin robe seemed to accentuate Sheldon's pathetic appearance.

"Nice robe," I offered.

Sheldon shrugged and I could see his eyes filling with tears.

"Stop that right now," I found myself saying in a rather dictatorial tone. It seemed to work. Shelley struggled to collect himself.

"I'm O.K.," he said.

"You bet you are," Detective Swain's reassuring voice preceded him as he rounded the corner and entered the conference room. Ollie, ever the gentleman, had let me off at the front door and then gone to park the police vehicle.

"The rest of them will be here any minute now. I saw them piling out of the van. They've got Werner in leg chains as well as handcuffs, so don't worry, Shelley, that sorry soul is going nowhere."

A wan smile flickered across Sheldon's face.

I spent the remaining moments we had before "court reconvened" reminding Shelley of my Twenty-five Rules. After I had been in the office only a few months, it became clear to me that most witnesses, even the highly educated and otherwise articulate ones, are close to clueless when it comes to giving good testimony in court. I would routinely be obliged to lecture my witnesses on the rudiments of how to testify.

After a while I formulated my Twenty-five Rules, which, I am gratified to note, have been widely copied and circulated throughout the office. My rules contain such sage advice as "Don't answer a question you don't understand" and "If you need a break to use the restroom, ask the judge; don't sit there and suffer."

Obviously, in this case, nurses would be nearby to attend to Shelley's physical needs. I was much more concerned about the emotional demands this hearing would place on our victim.

Then, just like in the movies, the sound of jangling chains announced the imminent arrival of the defendant, in the company of four very large sheriff's deputies, followed by the judge, a tight-lipped, middle-aged white woman whose distaste for both the subject matter and the setting were almost palpable. The court clerk and the stenographic reporter joined the group. Where on earth was Sam Parks?

That schmuck, I thought. You'd think he could be on time for a bed-side hearing, for God's sake. I looked over to see if Werner was reacting to his lack of representation. He seemed unconcerned. I was relieved to note that he was not eyeballing our victim as so many defendants relish doing. Sheldon had already been instructed to look only at the individual who was propounding a question (Rule Seven) and look at the defendant only when asked to identify him (Rule Eight). He was following the rules.

Several minutes passed while the judge tapped on her watch crystal impatiently and the court reporter reinked her machine. Just when the exasperation level was about to rise another notch, Mr. Parks shuffled in.

"Another minute and I would have seriously considered a contempt citation," Her Honor informed him in an icy tone.

"Oh, sorry," was Sam's response. "I couldn't find a parking place."

"He couldn't find his ass with both hands, even if it was on fire," one of the deputies whispered in my ear.

As soon as Sam settled himself at the conference table next to his client, the judge called the case on the record. Sheldon was sworn as our first and sole witness. With Maria Buyagawan hovering nearby, his testimony was taken. First my direct examination and then Parks's cross-examination. I had prepared my witness for cross-examination and had given Shelley some examples of possible questions:

"Isn't it true that you agreed to go home with Mr. Werner?"

"Isn't it true that no one forced you to drink his wine, smoke his marijuana, and snort his amyl nitrite?"

"Isn't it true that you willingly went into Mr. Werner's bedroom?"

"Isn't it true that you voluntarily removed your own clothes?"

"Isn't it true that you went over to Mr. Werner's apartment with the hope that he would want to have sexual relations with you?"

"In fact, isn't it true that you spent several hours before meeting up with Mr. Werner at the Back Room, driving from gay bar to gay bar, looking for a potential sexual partner?"

Fortunately for Sheldon, Sam's cross was much less biting than my examples. Perhaps Sam was deterred by the hospital setting and the patient's obvious state of extremis. Or perhaps he was at a loss as to what questions to propound. My direct examination had been thorough but not unduly detailed. I always attempt to stave off difficult questions on cross by covering the issue on direct.

"So, you had been to a number of bars that night, Mr. Silverman. Were you drunk?" Sam wanted to know. Figures he would focus on the issue of alcohol consumption, I thought.

"No," Sheldon answered simply, following Rule One: If you can answer a question with a yes or no, do so.

"You found my client to be physically attractive, is that right?"

"Yes."

"Using those dildos was your idea, right?"

"No."

"You never contacted the police, did you?"

"I didn't."

"Why not?"

Generally speaking, it is considered a tactical mistake to ask The Why Question in court. Unless you are sure what the answer will be and it is an answer you wish to elicit, this question only serves to afford the witness an opportunity to explain his position. I was sorry we didn't have a jury impaneled to hear Sheldon's response:

"At first, all I could think about was getting out of the defendant's apartment and getting home. I was in so much pain. And I kept passing out. I needed medical attention. I needed a doctor, not a police officer."

"But you never called the police."

I could have objected on the grounds that the question—if it was a question—was argumentative, but Shelley was on a roll.

"By the time I regained consciousness after the emergency surgery, the police had already been notified."

"If they had not been notified, you would not have called them, would you?"

Again, I could have objected on the grounds that the question called for speculation, but I would have been quibbling and prolonging the proceedings. I could see that Sheldon was looking very tired, but his answer was strong.

"I certainly hope that I would have had the courage to do the right thing and make a police report. I believe I would have."

Before Sam could ask another question, Nurse Buyagawan interrupted the proceedings.

"I'm sorry, Your Honor, but I have to change this IV right now." I looked over to see crimson fluid filling Sheldon's IV line. The intravenous fluid was gone and the resulting vacuum was drawing Sheldon's own blood into the line. And poor Shelley looked like he couldn't spare a drop.

"We'll go off the record," Her Honor advised with a look of complete irritation, as though our witness were doing this just to annoy her.

Everyone in the room busied himself with something while Maria attended to Sheldon. Sam shuffled some papers, the reporter changed her paper, and the bailiff and his backup deputies averted their eyes. I glanced at Werner. He was looking at Shelley but quickly looked away when he became aware of my scrutiny. Our eyes locked for a moment. Was that a hint of a smile on his face?

"Back on the record," Her Honor announced as Maria finished her ministrations.

"No further questions," Sam said. Perhaps the interruption had derailed his train of thought.

"No redirect, thank you," I said without waiting to be asked. "People rest."

"It appearing to me that there is sufficient evidence to believe that the crimes alleged in the complaint have been committed and that the defendant, Randolph Werner, has committed the alleged crimes, I hereby order that the defendant be held to answer for the same in the Superior Court," the judge intoned and then went on to select the exact date and courtroom.

"I'd like to be heard on the issue of bail," Sam asked without attempting to dissuade the court on the fundamental issue of whether or not his client should be held to answer. Sam made a feeble and ineffectual plea to have his client's bail reduced. The judge was unmoved and so stated.

"The bail set is in conformance with the bail schedule and I have heard nothing at this hearing to suggest that a reduction would be appropriate. We are adjourned at this time."

The sheriff's deputies immediately hustled Werner from the room, and we could hear the diminishing sounds of his leg chains as he was escorted down the hall. The judge and her staff also departed swiftly. Ollie and I remained for a few moments.

"I'm exhausted," Sheldon said. "How'd I do?"

"I'd say magnificent would be an understatement," Ollie responded.

"I'm pretty picky," I added, "but I can't think of anything to criticize."

Shelley's eyes were beginning to close but a smug smile appeared briefly before sleep overtook him.

"I just gave him a mild sedative," Maria explained. "His blood pressure and pulse were elevated throughout the hearing."

"This sort of thing isn't healthy for anyone," Ollie replied in a voice filled with weariness. This was certainly an atypical comment for Detective Swain. I glanced at Ollie and was shocked to see how poorly he looked. His skin, normally a lovely shade of dark mocha, was gray and ashen. There were creases around his eyes I had never noticed before.

"Don't worry about me, little girl," Ollie responded to my unspoken concern. "I just need a good night's sleep. And if all the crooks in our city would just stop capering for a hot minute, maybe I could get some shut-eye."

DEPARTMENT 126

Cases are rarely tried in the court to which they are originally assigned. This is because we operate under what is known as a master calendar system as opposed to a direct calendar system. A case is assigned to a courtroom for pretrial purposes. When both sides announce they are ready for trial, the case is sent to the master calendar court for reassignment to a trial court. On occasion, the home court will be available to take the trial and the case will be sent back to the original court, but this is the exception rather than the rule.

I was thrilled with our original court assignment and hoped that, somehow, we would be able to keep the case there. The defendant was held to answer in Department 126, Judge Gordon Ringer. Judge Ringer was known throughout the county as the most learned and fairest bench officer. Many a defendant would waive his right to a jury trial and allow Judge Ringer to decide the case. Other defendants would plead guilty with the understanding that they would be permitted to have Judge Ringer sentence them.

You would think that such a renowned jurist would be tall and silver-haired, with an imposing presence. Not the case. Judge Ringer was a wizened man, with stooped shoulders, a balding domed pate, a beaklike nose, and beady eyes made beadier by thick lenses in his unfashionable horn-rimmed spectacles. His voice was raspy, the result of many decades devoted to the prodigious consumption of alcohol and tobacco. In the days before smoking was outlawed in public buildings, Judge Ringer would smoke on the bench while court was in session. No one thought to protest such behavior. When you were in the presence of Judge Ringer, you were in the presence of a judicial icon, a legal god.

The preliminary hearing had gone well, and now I found myself in the best possible courtroom. I had a smart, fair judge and a lazy defense attorney. So far so good. I had learned long ago not to count on a conviction until the verdict had been returned but I couldn't help feeling optimistic about the People versus Randolph Werner. Now all I had to do was convince Parks to convince Werner that waiving to Ringer was in his best interest.

"You're not getting any argument from me," Parks responded when I broached the topic a couple of weeks after the arraignment. "It's the client—he thinks he has a better chance in front of a jury. The guy's pretty streetwise. Hard to argue with."

"Well, it doesn't have to be Ringer. Maybe there's some other judge in the building we could agree upon. It would be nice to avoid all the extra work involved in a jury trial." I hoped my appeal to Parks's lazy nature was not too pointed.

"Any chance of working out a plea bargain?" Apparently Parks was warming to the idea of avoiding work. If a court trial was better than a jury trial, then a plea bargain was better still.

"There's always a chance for a dispo," I replied in my most conciliatory tone. "What are you looking for?" Sometimes it's better to let the defense pitch the first ball.

"Well—" Parks hesitated as his yellowed forefinger explored the stubble on his chin. "How about count four . . . as a misdemeanor?"

It was a ridiculous suggestion but I responded in an even tone.

"This case involves great bodily injury. The victim would have died if he had not received medical attention when he did. It would have to be a plea to one of the sex counts plus the GBI allegation."

"What about probation with a bullet?" Sam evidently found my plea offer palatable and was moving on to sentence negotiation. A bullet is courtroom vernacular for a year in the county jail.

"I think this is a state prison case," I replied, "but if your client wanted to plead open in 126, we could have a sentencing hearing and let Ringer decide."

Sam made no response while his finger scraped slowly and audibly back and forth across his chin. I waited. No sense appearing too eager.

"My client's pretty set on the idea of a jury trial." Parks sighed. "But I'll see what I can do. I think this would be a reasonable way to get rid of this case. He might go for it if he thinks he has a chance for probation." We shook hands—something I generally avoid where Parks is concerned—and agreed to discuss it further at the next court date.

The next court date was three weeks hence. I made no effort to speed the case along and was, for once, grateful that I had a slow-moving defense attorney. Sheldon needed the time to heal—physically and emotionally. He had been released to a convalescent hospital and was making good progress toward moving back home with Jacques. Jacques was eagerly awaiting the homecoming and experimenting with new recipes for tasty but medically approved menus. "Bland but not boring" was the way Jacques put it.

DEPARTMENT 134

Time passed. I focused my attention on other cases. And there were plenty of them. Defendants were held to answer. Defendants pled guilty. Defendants went to state prison. Some got probationary terms. The wheels of justice kept turning. My periodic calls to Sheldon were invariably encouraging: he was back at home, he had gained some weight, his spirits were improving, he was looking forward to getting the trial over. That was all I needed to hear. *People v. Werner* was coming off the back burner. I called Parks to check his schedule and pin him down on a trial date.

"Horace P. Neville," Sam said when I got him on the phone.

"Pardon me?"

"Horace P. Neville," Sam repeated. "Remember, you said it didn't have to be Ringer. We're willing to waive jury to Judge Neville."

Sheldon would be relieved. His trepidation about enduring a jury trial had not abated. I told Sam I'd get back to him within a day or two. I needed some time to check out Neville. Never having tried a case in his court, I wanted to consult with at least a couple of lawyers who had.

Neville was not a complete unknown to me. From reading his bio in the *Daily Journal*, I knew he was fifty-three years old, African-American, Princeton undergrad, Yale Law School, and had done criminal defense work as a private practitioner before being appointed to the bench by a Republican governor. Nothing to raise a red flag. So why was Sam willing to waive to Neville and not Ringer?

I had no appearances that afternoon, so I made what I hoped was an unobtrusive visit to Department 134 and took a seat in the back of Neville's courtroom. Nothing I observed affronted my sensibilities. The court was in the midst of a robbery trial, the jury was in the box, and the defense attorney was in the process of cross-examining the alleged victim, a timid-looking Korean woman testifying through an interpreter.

My olfactory sense, however, was affronted. The heavy and unmistakable scent of kimchee pervaded the courtroom. Amazingly, it appeared that no one was aware of the source. I noticed a burly male juror surreptitiously sniffing his armpit. The judge himself wore a puzzled expression. Then, without interrupting the proceedings, he motioned for a Spanish interpreter who had been seated in the audience to approach the sidebar. A brief colloquy ensued, and I could see the interpreter vehemently shaking her head. Instead of returning to her seat, she hurriedly left the courtroom, wearing a look of barely stifled laughter. I took the opportunity to follow her out the door.

"Carmen," I called after her. "What was that about?"

"He wanted to know if I had brought in tamales today." She laughed.

"Smelled like some rank kimchee to me."

"No doubt about it," Carmen responded. "See if I'll ever bring him my homemade tamales again!"

"Other than being an ignoramus when it comes to cuisine, what's Neville like?"

"Oh, he's okay. Most prosecutors seem to like him."

My discussions with several colleagues over the next few days netted similar assessments. "He's no Learned Hand," I was told. Well, I wasn't looking for legal scholarship, just a fair judge who would listen to all the evidence, render a just verdict, and then impose an appropriate sentence. "Then he's your man," the deputy D.A. assigned to Neville's court declared.

I wondered out loud if the judge had any issues regarding homosexuality and might have a problem with what amounted to a gay date-rape case.

"I don't think so," this same deputy told me. "After all, as a black man who's made it all the way to the Superior Court, he's got to be sensitive to bigotry and prejudice."

It was time to call Parks. Better lock in the jury waiver before his client changed his mind.

SATURDAY

The telephone call came too early on Saturday morning for it to be anything but bad news. My half-awake "hello" sounded like an inarticulate grunt.

"D.D.A. Batt? Marissa?"

"Yes?"

"This is Jeff Daly at the command post. Sorry to call at this hour."

I glanced at my bedside alarm clock. The numerals slowly came into focus. It was 5:30 A.M. or, as we ruefully put it, oh-dark-thirty.

"I've got some bad news for you," Jeff continued.

I was suddenly fully awake. I realized my heart was pounding. Was it Sheldon? One of my other victims?

"What?"

"Detective Swain, your investigating officer on your Werner case. He's in the CCU at UCLA Medical Center."

"A shooting?"

"No. They told us it was a massive heart attack. He's asking for you."

"I'm on my way."

I have no memory of dressing or driving to Westwood. The next thing I remember is standing in a small hospital waiting room. Muted lighting revealed the ubiquitous pastel institutional art on the walls. A small number of chrome-legged chairs, upholstered in matching pastel fabric, were all occupied.

It took me a moment to realize that I recognized most of the people in the room. Over the years, Ollie had shared many things with me, including photographs of his family members. His sister Norma and his favorite cousin Cynthia were there along with two men and another woman who looked familiar.

"You must be the D.A. that Oliver always talks about," one of the men said.

Before I could reply, an older woman on the arm of a minister entered the room. Her face was ashy gray and deeply furrowed like a dry riverbed. Everything about her, from her steel-gray hair to her gnarled hands, looked parched, except for her eyes, which were brimming with tears.

"Mrs. Swain?"

"Yes, chil'. Don' you worry. My boy is strong. He's a fighter and the Lord knows he's got a mess o' work left to do here on earth."

I was directed down a hallway, through a set of mechanized double doors, around a corner, and down another corridor to Ollie's bedside in the CCU. A nurse was adjusting an IV line. She looked remarkably familiar.

"Maria?"

"I trained here at UCLA and I still know most of the staff in the ICU and CCU, so"—she hesitated—"so here I am."

It would have been reassuring to see Maria except for the look of immense sadness on her face. Her tone, however, bespoke confidence.

"This is a great hospital and they are doing everything that can be done. Now, he can only have one visitor at a time and only for a couple of minutes, so sit down here"— she directed me to the one chair in the room— "and let him know you're here. He drifts in and out."

I hardly recognized Ollie. He seemed smaller and his face had a washed-out, slack-jawed look.

"Hey, Mr. Pitiful," I said, and was surprised to hear the quaver in my voice. There was no response, so I continued.

"Ollie, it's Marissa. I'm here. And Maria's here, so I know you are in good hands. Talk to me, baby."

Ollie's eyes flickered. I took his hand and bent closer to his face so I could hear his response over the beep and hiss of the monitors.

"Sorry." Ollie's voice was a hoarse whisper.

"As well you should be," I retorted in what I hoped was an upbeat tone. "I guess I'm stuck trying the Werner case all by myself."

"Tough case. One-on-one." Ollie's words came slowly.

"You just figured that out?" Maintaining my jocular manner was a challenge. I felt a tear roll down my left cheek.

Ollie was struggling to say more.

"Ollie, you should be resting. We don't need to talk about this."

"No. Want to."

I glanced at Maria, who nodded her approval.

"He's been wanting to tell you something about the case. I think it may give him some peace of mind."

I squeezed Ollie's hand and leaned down even closer so my right ear was next to his mouth.

"The clue's in the rap sheet" was what I heard him say. "Go back to the bar."

"Okay," I replied, although I had no idea what he meant. Ollie seemed to have fallen asleep, so I attempted to disengage my hand from his. His grip tightened for a second and he whispered: "Thanks for coming, little girl. We were a great team."

.   "I'll see you tomorrow. Be a good patient. Do whatever Maria says, okay?"

Ollie did not respond, but Maria gave me a hug and we agreed that we'd see each other the next day at Ollie's bedside. I made my way back to the waiting room and said goodbye to the remaining family members. On the way home, Ollie's cryptic words were playing in my head: *The clue's in the rap sheet. Go back to the bar.*

I got on the 10 heading east and must have been so preoccupied that, by the time I realized it, I had passed my off-ramp at Crenshaw and was heading downtown instead of home. Just as well. The file was in my office, and if I didn't look at the rap sheet right away, it would drive me crazy.

As I remembered it, there was nothing special that jumped out of the defendant's criminal record. When I got to the office, I pulled the file and found that my memory was correct.

Werner's Mississippi record was of no significance to the current prosecution. His drunk driving case was similarly insignificant. According to the probation report, the three prostitution convictions all involved undercover police officers in public restrooms. Nothing there.

The only other entry was the arrest for assault that had resulted in a D.A. reject. That hardly sounded promising, but I had nothing to lose in researching it further. Of course, it was Saturday morning and the office was empty except for a couple of other lawyers feverishly working on their own matters. I took my set of county keys and went down one flight to the seventeenth floor and the records department.

It took me a couple of minutes to find what I was looking for. In the days before computer technology became the accepted way of record keeping, navigating through the D.A.'s records unit could be a daunting experience. From floor to ceiling, row after row of metal shelves held manila file folders, each numbered and color-coded for ostensible ease in locating the one needed. The whole inventory was constantly moving, with new files coming in and older files being archived—that is, put in boxes and stored in a great subterranean warehouse in the very bowels of the earth under the Civic Center.

A corner of the room was devoted to rejected cases, and it was there that I found R047120. No case is ever rejected without a written explanation by the deputy making the decision. Over the years the color of the reject forms has changed from blue to pink to green. Back then, I was looking for a blue sheet, ideally, stapled to the crime report. And I was praying that what I was hunting for hadn't already been archived. Once that happens, it's like looking for the proverbial needle in a haystack. But I was lucky. There was R047120, right where it was supposed to be.

The blue sheet read: "The victim, male, white, 29 years old, homosexual, adamantly refuses to cooperate with law enforcement. Assault took place at suspect's residence. Assault involved rubber sexual apparatus. Victim refused M.T. [our shorthand for medical treatment] and stated he would see his private physician. Police had been contacted by neighbors who heard screams. Without victim's cooperation, case cannot be filed."

I realized I wasn't breathing and took a long gasp of air. If I could locate this young victim and persuade him to cooperate with me on the current case, I would have some of the most compelling 1101(b) evidence that could ever be put before a jury. The California Evidence Code provides in section 1101(b) that prior acts, whether or not they result in convictions, can be used to prove motive, opportunity, intent, preparation, plan, knowledge, identity, absence of mistake or accident, or whether a defendant in a prosecution for an unlawful sexual act could reasonably believe that the victim consented to the act. I was holding a blue sheet, but I felt like I was holding a piece of solid gold. Ollie was a genius.

I had to let him know. It wasn't even noon yet. I called UCLA and asked to be connected with the CCU. I asked for Ollie directly or his nurse, and the woman who answered put me on hold. It was a long hold, too, and I was about to hang up and call again when a familiar voice came on the line.

"Marissa, it's Maria."

"Maria!"

"Marissa, we've been trying to reach you at home. I've got some very bad news. Ollie passed away about an hour ago."

"No!" I didn't recognize my own voice.

"His mother was with him," Maria continued in an uncharacteristic monotone. "I don't believe he suffered at all. He never regained consciousness after you saw him. I've got to go." Maria was crying now. "Please take care of yourself."

I put the phone down and found myself staring at the device as though I had never seen it before. Nothing seemed real. All the familiar objects in my office seemed foreign and somehow alien. The very light in the room had an unnatural cast. At some point I looked out the window and was shocked to see that the sky had darkened. It was night already. My watch confirmed that several hours had passed. I needed to control myself. I packed up my notes on the Werner case and went home.

Ollie was gone. Messages on my answering machine reiterated that jarring fact. The command post had called. There was Maria's message.

And then there was a message from Ollie's sister Norma. There would be no funeral or memorial service. No uplifting sermon, no commendations to the Lord, no gospel music, no caravan of patrol cars, no honor guard. These were Oliver's wishes. There was a message from Ollie's partner Scottie, telling me about an impromptu wake at one of the LAPD's favorite watering holes, the Short Stop, near Dodger Stadium. The owner was opening the establishment on Sunday in Ollie's honor.

SUNDAY

Sunday morning arrived. There was a split second before I was fully awake when I felt fine, and then I remembered my new reality. My good buddy and the best cop I'd ever worked with was dead, and I was set for trial in less than two weeks on a one-on-one homosexual rape case with no more evidence to offer than what had been presented at the prelim.

After waiting until a reasonable hour, I picked up the phone and dialed the home number for one Ray Ricci, the recalcitrant victim identified on the blue sheet.

"Hello?" Despite my restraint in not calling earlier, the man's voice sounded drowsy.

"My apologies for telephoning on a Sunday morning," I offered, and then explained who I was and why I was calling. I was informed that Ricci had resided at that location but had moved, leaving no forwarding address.

"Wait a minute. Isn't this his phone number?"

"It was. When I moved in, the line was working so I just called the phone company and had them transfer the billing to my name. This is the first call for him I've had in about three years."

There was no reason to disbelieve the man on the phone. I apologized again and hung up. It wasn't like I had expected to locate another witness with just one phone call. Ollie had told me what to do next. . . .

Rather than going to the Short Stop, I made the Back Room my destination. Ollie would have wanted it that way. My concern that the place might be closed was allayed as I drove up. A banner proclaiming "Sunday Brunch, 11-3" was carefully draped across the front awning. I parked in the lot and went in. If the bartender was at all surprised to see a diminutive female with a bulging briefcase enter his establishment, his manner belied it. I was warmly welcomed and invited to a table. I chose instead to sit at the bar.

"What'll it be?"

"I'd love a cup of coffee."

"Could I interest you in a screwdriver or a Ramos gin fizz?"

"Ordinarily you could," I replied, "but today I'm here more for business than pleasure." I produced my badge (the bartender's expression changed from friendly to quizzical) and started to explain why I had come (his expression changed again, to wary). I quickly tucked my badge back in my purse and put my yellow pad on the floor next to my briefcase. I appealed to the bartender—whose name turned out to be Nick— as one human being to another. I had a big problem. Maybe he could help me.

I outlined the nature of the case and told Nick about the extent of the victim's injuries. I could see his features softening. By the time I got around to explaining why I was doing my own detective work, Nick was holding my hand.

"I think you could use a drink," Nick declared, and excused himself for a moment. I took the opportunity to look around. Sheldon's description had been accurate. The restaurant was beautifully appointed, and the brunch crowd all seemed to be in their twenties and thirties, well groomed and well behaved. Nick returned in a few moments with a tall, frothy, creamy-yellow concoction.

"Best Ramos gin fizz I've ever had, including those imbibed in New Orleans," I reported after the first sip.

"My specialty," Nick said modestly.

The ice had definitely been broken. I put my yellow tablet back on the bar and pulled a mug folder from my briefcase.

"In my business," I said, "this is what we call a six-pack."

I gave Nick the standard admonition. It is as important to exonerate the innocent as it is to identify the guilty. There is no obligation to pick anyone out. Take your time. Nick didn't need any time to point to Werner's mug shot.

"That's Randy," he said immediately. "I don't recognize any of the others." It turned out that my defendant had been something of a regular at the Back Room prior to his arrest, a fact that was known to most of the Back Room habitués. He was also known as "rough trade" and was studiously avoided by all but the "fresh meat."

"If you'll pardon the expression," Nick added delicately.

I asked Nick if he knew a Ray Ricci and had any idea where I might find him.

"That's a name from the past," Nick mused. "I had heard something about Randy setting him up for a night of B and D that got a little hairy. I don't think it was anything as awful as your case, but Ray moved out of town right after that. I think to San Francisco. No, it was New York, I think. Nobody's heard from him since then. When was that? A couple of years ago?"

"More like four years ago," I said sadly. Finding the Ricci blue sheet was a small miracle. Finding Ricci himself would be close to impossible. I took another tack and asked Nick if he was aware of any other unsuspecting young men who had fallen victim to Werner. Nick looked very uncomfortable and finally nodded affirmatively.

"There have been rumors about several men having problems with Randy, but everyone denies it—it's so embarrassing."

"Do you know of anyone who might talk to me? It would be a tremendous help. If I could get even one other man to testify to being similarly victimized by Werner, that would corroborate my victim when he testifies that it was not consensual."

Nick excused himself to fill a couple of drink orders and then returned to my end of the bar.

"I feel a little weird about this," he confessed, "but if you'd like to come back Wednesday evening, that's when we have a more leather-oriented crowd, if you know what I mean. Wednesday night we have what we call our Hump Night party, if you'll pardon the expression." Nick looked so sheepish that I actually laughed out loud.

"So, Nick," I said, "you don't think my presence at your Hump Night festivities will sound a discordant note?"

Now Nick was laughing. He encouraged me to come back and promised to introduce me to someone who had had some negative contact with my defendant.

"I don't know if he'll talk to you," Nick warned me, "but what do you have to lose?"

HUMP NIGHT

My first order of business on Monday morning had been to get a D.A. investigator assigned to the Werner case. It is simply not good policy for an attorney to conduct his (or, in my case, her) own investigations. It's a great way to become a witness in your own case, a situation that is, at best, awkward and, at worst, potentially unethical.

"Don't you remember when you told me . . . ?" is not a particularly artful cross-examination technique. And when your witness responds in the negative, you can't very well call yourself as a witness to testify to the contrary. By doing so, you would be putting your own credibility at issue. This presents the ethical dilemma.

So it came about that D.A. Investigator Ted Owens and I were sitting in his county car outside the Back Room at 10 P.M. Wednesday night. Ted was in a foul mood.

"Nothing personal. I always enjoy working with you," he grumbled, "but vice was my least favorite assignment when I was with the department and I'm not going in there."

"Ted, I need you as a witness, not as a chauffeur."

"I can't stomach these homos. 'Hump Night,' my ass."

"Poor choice of words, Ted."

Ted grunted. We had reached an impasse. In desperation, I suggested that I would go into the bar alone and, if I were fortunate enough to make contact with a potential witness, Ted would join us.

"Good luck," he mumbled as I emerged from his car.

The Back Room was a different place at night. The parking lot was filled with motorcycles, and inside it was clear that the preferred mode of attire was leather. And, although the place was crowded, my presence did not go unnoticed. I stifled my discomfiture and made straight for the bar. Two bartenders were working expeditiously, but I was dismayed to see that neither was my new friend Nick.

A big man wearing a leather vest over his bare chest graciously offered me his barstool. I sat down and got the attention of one of the bartenders. Nick had taken the night off but had left instructions: I was to be introduced to a man named Jeremy if he should come in. I ordered a tonic tall (no gin) and prepared to wait at least half an hour. To my surprise and relief, a young man who identified himself as Jeremy appeared at my side almost immediately.

"You weren't hard to spot," he remarked with a smile, and then suggested we sit in one of the booths where there might be modicum of privacy.

"I'll tell you anything you want to know," he said as we slid into the only available booth, next to the kitchen door. "Nick said you were good people."

"I'm glad I got the seal of approval."

My eyes had adjusted to the light, and I was astonished to observe a marked resemblance between Jeremy and Sheldon. Same slight build, same dark eyes, same coloring, same general features.

"What?" Jeremy asked. "Do I have something on my face?"

"No, no. I didn't mean to stare, but you look so much like the victim on my case, you could be brothers."

"I heard that Randy went for a certain type. Lucky me," Jeremy said ruefully. Without much prompting, he went on to tell a horrifying story.

He had met Randy Werner at this very establishment about a year ago. Randy had seemed like a nice enough guy, and Jeremy had invited him home. For some reason, Werner had insisted that they go back to his apartment instead, and Jeremy had agreed. Once there, Jeremy had been offered wine, marijuana, and amyl.

"I politely declined," Jeremy told me. "I'm asthmatic and I'm not much of a drinker. That seemed to piss him off. Anyway, he invited me into his bedroom. To be honest, I was in the mood until I saw the sling. S and M and B and D are not my thing."

"What happened next?" I prompted.

"He got real physical with me. Tried to pin me down like in some sort of wrestling move. I'd taken karate in college and I was able hit him in the solar plexus. Knocked the wind out of him. But not before he managed to break a couple of my ribs and knock a couple of my teeth loose." He showed me a slight scar on his upper lip.

"You were lucky."

"So I hear."

Jeremy would be a fabulous witness. I took out a blank subpoena form and started to fill it out. Jeremy immediately put his hand on mine.

"No subpoena."

"It's a formality."

"You don't understand. I'm not testifying about this."

"Your testimony is crucial. It may make the difference between a conviction and an acquittal."

"I don't care. If I'd wanted to be a witness, I'd have called the cops when this thing happened to me."

"But," I stammered, "if you didn't want to be a witness, why did you agree to talk to me?"

"Why not? I don't mind talking to you about it, but that is as far as it goes. I don't put very much faith in your criminal justice system. No offense."

"It's *our* criminal justice system, and it's only as good as we make it."

"No sermons. I told Nick I'd talk to you but that's it. Don't try to haul me into a courtroom—I won't remember anything."

I sat there in stunned silence as Jeremy walked out of the bar. It was time for me to go as well. I waved to the bartender on my way out.

"How'd it go?" Owens inquired as I slipped into the passenger seat.

"I struck out."

MONDAY MORNING

On Monday morning I checked my calendar to make sure I still had no conflicts with the court trial date Sam and I had set. With new cases being filed every day, a trial deputy's calendar is always subject to change. There were no impediments. I had no court appearances that morning, so I spent some time catching up on mail and phone messages. By midmorning I could procrastinate no further. I called Sheldon. His reaction to the news of Ollie's passing was predictable. He was close to inconsolable.

"I can't go through this without Detective Swain."

"And how do you think Ollie would react if he heard you say that?"

The pep talk I gave Sheldon was as much for myself as for him. The best way to honor Detective Swain's memory was to do an outstanding job on this, his last case. By the time we hung up, Sheldon's determination to see the case through had been restored. My own confidence was wavering. I had done exactly as Ollie had directed in our final conversation. I had studied the rap sheet. I had gone back to the bar. And I had struck out. It was still a one-on-one gay date-rape case. Where on earth could I find something to corroborate Sheldon's version of what happened? What would Ollie do?

In order to be a good prosecutor, you must be able to think like a defense attorney. There are only so many defenses available in any case, and it behooves a defendant to pick just one. Those who pick more than one reveal their guilt. I call it the Bart Simpson Defense: "I didn't do it. You didn't see me do it. You can't prove I did it." Not very effective.

So what would Werner's defense be? Obviously, consent. Some people have a taste for bondage and discipline. Sheldon was eager to engage in a sadomasochistic orgy and Werner was happy to comply. The injuries? An unfortunate accident. It happens. It's a known risk when you play these kinds of sex games. Or is it?

I suddenly realized that I was profoundly ignorant when it came to sadomasochism and bondage and discipline, or "S and M" and "B and D" as the practitioners called it. Did the participants want to hurt each

other or be hurt? Were injuries always accidental or sometimes intentional? How did participants convey their desires to each other? Were serious injuries or death common in S and M scenarios? I needed an
expert.

I picked up the phone and called the Gay and Lesbian Community
Services Center. After identifying myself as a prosecutor and giving a
brief outline of my case, I asked for their help. To my astonishment, I was
unable to connect with anyone at the facility who felt comfortable as-
sisting me. It wasn't until I hung up that I realized what the problem
was. I was asking an agency dedicated to the support and assistance of
the gay community to marshal its forces against a member of that community. No wonder I met with resistance.

There must be someone I could call upon. Someone familiar with
the milieu. A subculture within a subculture. A dangerous one at that.
There must be situations where the participants get hurt. Even killed.
Who would know about these things and be willing to talk to a prosecu-
tor? I picked up the phone and dialed a long-distance number in San
Francisco. When the receptionist answered, I asked for the coroner.

"Dr. Boyd Stephens speaking." The voice was professional, yet warm
and immediately reassuring. I explained my predicament and then
asked for help.

"Be glad to be of assistance. Sadly, this is an area in which I have
quite a bit of experience."

I had found my expert. Dr. Stephens answered a few of my questions
over the phone. Participants in true S and M activities are neither sadists
nor masochists. They are extreme game players who have no desire to
hurt or be hurt, at least not seriously. The danger implicit in their actions
is what intensifies the thrill of their encounter. Precautions are taken by
the wary and more experienced participants to avoid connecting with
those who do not share their proclivities or, worse, those with a true
sadistic or even homicidal bent. Further precautions are routinely taken
to avoid matters getting out of control during the sex acts themselves.

Time was short and Dr. Stephens was a busy man, but not too busy
to participate in the trial. It also happened that he was a certified pilot

with his own airplane and would be willing to fly down to L.A. when I needed him. I was awestruck. I expressed my appreciation, promised to send a subpoena for protocol purposes, and hung up. Ollie would have been so proud of me.

My next call was to Sam Parks. I wanted him to know immediately about my intention to call an expert witness. Failure to provide prompt and thorough discovery to the defense is unethical and can result in a variety of sanctions by the court.

Sam was surprised by the news. After a pause he said, "I may have to find an expert of my own."

THE CASE IN CHIEF

The trial day was finally upon us. Sheldon appeared a full hour early in my office looking pale and anxious. It was a chilly December day, and it was probably a combination of the weather and his mood that gave him such a wan look. We spoke about the weather, about Ollie, about food and what a great cook Jacques was. I asked Sheldon if he needed to review the police reports or the transcript of the preliminary hearing. He shook his head. He would never forget a second of that night. He didn't need to have his recollection refreshed.

I asked how he felt, knowing that it would all be over soon. Sheldon didn't know whether he was more relieved or terrified. I started packing up my materials for court. When I suggested that Sheldon remain in my office until it was time for him to testify, a look of momentary relief registered on his tender features.

The court in 134 was just finishing up the final case on its morning calendar when I arrived. I was happy that the habitually tardy Mr. Parks walked in a few minutes later. I took the opportunity to discuss a few last-minute pretrial matters. I provided Sam with a copy of my list of potential witnesses. I also had copies for the judge, court clerk, and court reporter.

In addition to Sheldon, I expected to call Jacques, the emergency room doctor, the surgeon who treated Sheldon, the arresting officers who had been present during Ollie's interview of the defendant in order to lay the foundation for the admission of the audio tape and to describe the collection of the physical evidence, and, last but not least, our expert, Dr. Stephens.

What witnesses did Parks intend to call? Sam wasn't saying. He didn't know if Werner would take the stand or not. He didn't know if he'd call an expert or not. Sam was not a great trial lawyer, but he was far from a nincompoop. He was under no legal obligation to reveal his defense strategy and wisely chose not to.

Judge Neville said "off the record" and then addressed Sam and me informally.

"I see you're here on a jury waiver. I trust this isn't a 'slow plea'?"

Sam and I assured the judge that this was a real trial where the issue of guilt would be fully litigated and, if the defendant were convicted of any charge or charges, the sentencing would also be a contested matter.

A "slow plea" is courtroom vernacular for a situation where the accused's guilt is understood by everyone except the defendant, who insists, against his own lawyer's advice, on going to trial. Typically the prosecutor and the defense attorney negotiate the sentence and the judge taking the case concurs that, once the defendant is convicted, the agreed-upon sentence will be imposed. The defendant is then advised that in all probability he will be convicted but, when he is, the sentence will be guaranteed. This way a recalcitrant or very stupid defendant can be protected from himself. A slow plea is, in effect, a very fast court trial.

But Sam and I were in 134 for a real trial. Judge Neville laid down the ground rules: there would be no bickering between counsel, no "standing" objections (giving a small speech rather than merely stating the grounds for an objection), and no lengthy opening statements and closing arguments. Pretty standard stuff.

The judge called the case and the bailiff produced Werner from the lockup. Randy emerged from the holding tank with a slight swagger and a look of supreme confidence on his face. That's okay, I thought; wait until I get you on cross-examination. I made a brief opening statement setting forth the prosecution's case, enumerating the witnesses and synopsizing their respective testimony. If this had been a jury trial, my approach would have been somewhat different and I would have spent more time introducing Sheldon as a person and providing the jury with more of his background.

Neville had made it clear that he didn't want to belabor matters, so I kept it short. Sam did me one better and waived his opening statement, reserving the right to make opening remarks prior to the defense case.

Jacques Lavin was called as the People's first witness. My hope was to establish, through a witness other than our victim, that it was not Sheldon's habit and custom to troll gay bars for sex partners. Sam sensed the judge's impatience with this line of questioning and began interposing objections.

"Irrelevant, Your Honor."

"Sustained."

"Calls for speculation."

"Sustained."

"Asked and answered."

"Sustained."

This was going nowhere fast. I concluded my direct examination of Jacques. No use irritating the judge at the outset. Plus, Jacques's testimony was not crucial to the case. I decided to call Shelley next without any further preface. I kept my eye on Randy as Sheldon entered the courtroom, was sworn, and took the witness stand. There was not even a hint of a reaction.

Sheldon's testimony at the trial was, if anything, stronger and more detailed than his prelim testimony. The defendant's demeanor remained bland and impassive, even during Sheldon's description of the rape and sodomy. Much to my relief, Sam interposed very few objections and his cross-examination was brief and, in my view, ineffectual.

"Wait just a minute," Judge Neville growled as Sheldon started to leave the stand. "I've got a few questions of my own." Never a particularly good sign, but I had warned Shelley about this possibility. Rule Twenty-five. The judge may propound questions. It doesn't mean he has a problem with your testimony, it just means he's awake.

"So, you make it habit to go to these homosexual bars?"

"No!" Sheldon responded a little too forcefully. I thought of objecting on the grounds that the question was argumentative, but it's rarely a good plan to object to the court's own questions. On the other hand, doing nothing isn't a brilliant tactic.

"Mr. Werner looked so good to you, you bought him dinner, isn't that a fact?" the judge barked.

"I thought he was nice-looking and I did pay for dinner," Shelley responded in a strained voice. His eyes flashed in my direction and the look on his face conveyed an unmistakable message: What is going on here?

What was going on was that I had made one of the worst tactical decisions of my career. In my eagerness to avoid subjecting Shelley to a jury, I had managed to steer the case into the courtroom of a vicious homophobe.

"You like it rough, don't you?" the judge continued accusingly, a look of loathing on his face.

"Objection!" I almost bellowed, rising to my feet. "Argumentative."

"I'm sure Mr. Silverman understands that I am not trying to argue with him. I am merely attempting to clearly understand the facts. That objection will be overruled. You may answer." Judge Neville's tone was icy and each word was enunciated with overt precision.

"No, I don't. Of course not," Sheldon answered. He was close to tears. "Do you think I wanted to end up like this?"

With that, Sheldon proceeded to unbutton his shirt and display a long red surgical scar that ran from his solar plexus to below his navel. The tubing connecting a colostomy bag was visible over the waistband of his trousers.

A hush fell over the courtroom. The only sound was Sheldon sobbing. The court reporter quickly handed him a tissue. Sam wore a look of complete astonishment on his face, while his client was grinning broadly and slowly rocking back and forth in his chair.

"We will have no exhibitionistic displays in my courtroom," Neville snapped. Sheldon attempted, unsuccessfully, to button his shirt with trembling hands.

"We're in recess," Judge Neville stated with a look that mingled contempt and disgust. He hurriedly left the bench without indicating when court might reconvene. The bailiff took Werner back into the lockup, and I approached Sheldon, who was still sitting in the witness box half undressed, tears staining his sallow face.

"I'm so sorry," I began. I didn't know what else to say. I put my arm around him and helped him down the two steps. Since there was no jury, the bailiff permitted us to use the jury room until court was back in session. Once we were alone, it took a few minutes for Sheldon to stop crying. When he finally did, a look of grim resignation settled on his features.

"We're going to lose," Sheldon stated flatly. "The judge hates me."

"I take responsibility for this," I replied. "I agreed to waive jury to him. Obviously, if I had checked him out more thoroughly, we wouldn't be in this situation. He looked okay to me."

"I know the feeling," Sheldon deadpanned. At that, we both started laughing hysterically.

"Listen," I continued when I had caught my breath, "it's not over with yet. I'm going to rest my case in chief soon, and then we'll see what Sam does. If he puts his client on the stand, I'm ready for him. If he doesn't, your testimony will go uncontradicted and the judge will be hard-pressed not to convict. Plus I have a rebuttal witness who may turn the tide on this case."

We reentered the courtroom with a sense of determination. Sam was still sitting at counsel table, the look of astonishment still in place. Sheldon resolutely resumed the witness stand and braced himself for whatever else Judge Neville had in store. The bailiff brought Werner out of the lockup, and a few minutes later Neville strode out of his chambers and ascended the bench.

"Call your next witness," he commanded. At least he was done tormenting Sheldon. The latter made a hasty exit from the witness box. My next witness was the emergency room physician who first attended to Sheldon. Perhaps a graphic description of Sheldon's physical injuries would help Neville to appreciate the gravity of this case. Sam's only questions on cross went to whether the doctor had noticed evidence of prior injury to the colorectal area. He had not. Further questioning by the defense elicited the acknowledgment that the victim's injuries were so severe that they might have masked prior trauma to the same area.

The testimony of the surgeon followed the same pattern. I established the severity of the injuries and that they were consistent with being inflicted by the dildos in evidence. Sam made his same point on cross: if there had been prior injury to the same area, it would have been obscured by the current injuries.

My final witness was one of the arresting officers. It should have been Detective Swain, but Officer Greene, perhaps aware of the role that had been thrust upon him, did an outstanding job on the stand. Whatever animus against homosexuals he may have felt, it did not taint his testimony. When I completed my direct examination, the defendant's incriminating and contradictory statements had been vividly recounted. Officer Greene also described in detail the execution of the search warrant and the collection of the physical evidence, including the numerous instruments of torture. Then, on what I hoped was a strong note, I rested the people's case in chief.

DEFENSE

My decision to save Dr. Stephens's testimony for rebuttal was a safe one. I knew Werner would be compelled to take the stand and assert a consent defense. That was exactly what happened. On cross-examination, my hours of preparation paid off.

Randy acknowledged that he had lied to the police. He admitted that all the sexual devices were his and that Sheldon had accurately described the sex acts in which they had engaged. Werner further conceded that he had not discussed his intentions with Sheldon beforehand but had assumed that he knew what Sheldon's desires were.

When I inquired as to what Sheldon had said or done that communicated his desire to be sodomized with an enormous dildo, Werner had no answer. The smirk that had been on his face throughout the trial faded and a hint of his angry, sadistic nature was finally revealed.

"I don't know, I just knew what he wanted, all right? It's what they all really want."

"'What they all want'?" I repeated with emphasis. "Would that include a young man who goes by the name of Jeremy who ended up with broken ribs and loose teeth thanks to you? Would that also include another man named Ray Ricci whom you raped with dildos?" I spoke fast to get it all out before Sam could register an objection.

"I don't remember," Werner responded vaguely.

"Objection," Sam interposed belatedly.

"Grounds?" asked Judge Neville.

"Compound?" Sam suggested tentatively.

"Overruled on that ground," Neville stated, "but sustained on the grounds that it is irrelevant, immaterial, and unduly wasteful of the court's time under Section 352."

Why wasn't I surprised? Neville wasn't interested in the truth; he just wanted the case to be over. Any chance of establishing 1101(b) evidence through the defendant's own testimony was now gone.

"No further questions, Your Honor."

"That's good," Neville retorted.

"Uh, no redirect," Sam added, picking up the theme. "The defense rests."

"Well," Neville said, "I'm ready to rule right now."

"Your Honor," I quickly interposed, "the People will be offering a witness in rebuttal."

"Just one?" the court wanted to know.

"Yes."

"All right then."

REBUTTAL

Dr. Stephens had flown in the night before and was patiently waiting in the hallway. I called him as my last witness and last hope. Dr. Boyd

Stephens was everything one could ever hope for in a witness: he was brilliant, articulate, responsive, engaging, and thoroughly knowledgeable.

I had met with him the night before in his hotel room and gone over the facts of the case in detail. My cross-examination of the defendant had been tailored to provide a platform for Dr. Stephens's rebuttal.

I started to lay the foundation for the doctor's expertise relative to sadomasochistic behavior. Sam immediately leapt to his feet and, rather than objecting, offered to stipulate. I happily accepted. I had been concerned that this might be a stretch even for a renowned forensic pathologist from San Francisco. Sam had really helped me out, even though it was clear that his sole intention had been to ingratiate himself with Neville by speeding up the proceedings.

"Doctor," I began, "in the context of homosexual sadomasochistic game playing, what are 'flags' and what is their significance?"

"The current fashion in this milieu is for both the dominant male or 'top' and the submissive partner or 'bottom' to advertise their desired roles by wearing 'flags.' These are colored handkerchiefs that are typically worn in either the right or left hip pocket. Left would denote dominance and right would indicate that the wearer is a 'bottom.' The color of the handkerchief indicates the particular interest of the wearer. For example, red identifies the man as someone involved in 'fisting,' yellow indicates an interest in 'water sports,' blue —"

"I think I get the picture," Neville interrupted. He looked like he'd just smelled something foul.

"In addition to flags," I pressed on, "are there other physical indicators of preference and proclivity worn by members of this milieu?"

"Yes. An earring worn in the left ear indicates dominance, the right ear submission. Also a prominently worn set of keys on the right or left side of one's jeans can serve the same purpose."

"In addition to flags, earrings, and keys, do the participants in S and M behaviors typically discuss their desires beforehand?"

"Absolutely. This is crucial so that the participants are clear on the parameters of what will be acceptable behavior. Also, the participants always establish a 'safe' word or phrase."

"What is that?"

"If matters become too intense for the submissive partner, he needs to have some means of bringing the action to an immediate halt. Under the circumstances, saying 'stop' or 'you're hurting me' would be interpreted as part of the game. A 'safe' word or phrase is always something incongruous to the activity. Some favorites I've heard over the years include 'Mickey Mouse' and 'Richard Nixon.'"

This met with a pronounced chortle from the rear of the courtroom. I glanced back and observed an older gentleman with a prominent florid nose, dressed in a threadbare suit and no tie. He smiled and winked at me. I nodded slightly and smiled back. It was Carl, one of my most devoted court watchers. Over the years, he and his cronies had followed my career closely. Many times I was flattered to find Carl and his group watching a case I was trying rather than a more high-profile prosecution down the hall.

My next line of inquiry concerned the use of the dildos. Dr. Stephens explained that only the most experienced practitioners would attempt to use an apparatus of the size involved in this case. I picked up "Big Mac," the item now known as People's number 22 for identification. I had to use both hands to carry the exhibit up to the witness stand.

In response to my questions, Dr. Stephens told the court that he had encountered the use of dildos of this size before, but only in the context of X-rated movies. In order for a bottom to accommodate such a device, years of training would be required. The capacity to use such an item was of such rarity that the film Loving Arms was a veritable classic among the S and M crowd. Dr. Stephens was personally acquainted with the participants in the film and had spoken to them about these very matters.

Neither Sam nor Judge Neville had interposed a single objection to Dr. Stephens's testimony. Perhaps this was attributable to my witness's unimpeachable credentials coupled with the nature of his testimony. I had accomplished my goals on rebuttal.

"No further questions of this witness, Your Honor."

There was a long pause and then:

"No questions," Sam mumbled.
"No further witnesses. People rest rebuttal."
"Anything further, Mr. Parks?"
"We have one witness on surrebuttal."

LAWRENCE PRESCOTT-HUGHES

The defense called Mr. Lawrence Prescott-Hughes, B.A., M.A., M.F.C.C., Ph.D.

"Dr. Prescott-Hughes," Sam began.

"Your Honor," I cut in immediately, "the People will stipulate that Dr. Hughes possesses bachelor's, master's, and doctorate degrees in sociology and has written the best-seller *Glory Hole: Indiscriminate and Anonymous Homosexual Encounters in Public Places.*"

"And that he also works as a marriage and family counselor?" Sam added.

"We so stipulate," I answered.

"Very well, the court accepts the stipulation," His Honor stated.

Of course, the stipulation meant close to nothing, and I wasn't about to agree that this pompous, self-absorbed twit had any expertise relative to S and M behaviors. Luckily, I had read Hughes's book, which had enjoyed an enthusiastic reception among psychologists and social workers when it was initially published some five years before. Calling it a best-seller was a stretch. It was a tactic designed to flatter the witness and, ideally, put him off his guard.

Mr. Hughes, or Dr. Hughes, as he preferred, was, by his own admission, a man who had suffered through a long, loveless marriage, sired five children, and then, in middle age, come to the startling realization that he was a homosexual. His own forays into the world of anonymous sex were chronicled in his book along with data he had purportedly gathered in a scientific fashion from other gay men leading a dual existence.

Sam's attempts to use Prescott-Hughes to contradict Boyd Stephens met with vigorous objection from my end of counsel table.

"But, Ms. Batt, you stipulated to his expertise," the judge chided.

"Not in this area, Your Honor."

"I'm going to let it in. I think this is a matter for cross-examination. It goes to the weight, not the admissibility, of the evidence." This was something I'd heard many judges say over the years when they were obviously hesitant about the Rules of Evidence. When in doubt, allow the testimony in and let the opposing party argue that it should be given little or no weight.

The tenor of Hughes's testimony was clear: when homosexuals engage in anonymous and indiscriminate sex they are, in effect, consenting to whatever happens to them. After all, he should know, he'd written the book on the subject!

On cross-examination, I established that Dr. Lawrence Prescott-Hughes had never engaged in a sadomasochistic encounter and knew of no one who had. He sported no flags, earrings, or keys and had never heard of their significance until today. He had no personal familiarity with dildos and did not know what a sling was. Likewise, he had just learned about safe words from my synopsis of Dr. Stephens's testimony on that subject. He could not comment on the distinctions between a sadomasochistic player and a true sadist. Nonetheless, he felt eminently qualified to rebut Dr. Stephens's expert opinions.

Dr. Prescott-Hughes left the witness box with a look of haughty indignation. Someone had had the temerity to question his credentials. The defense rested and the case was over except for the argument.

With All Due Respect

If Judge Neville had effectively masked his homophobia, I might have been lulled into a false sense of security and waived my opening argument. Because the prosecution bears the burden of proof, it is afforded two opportunities to argue to the court. In court trials it is not uncommon for the prosecutor to waive the opening argument and merely respond to the defense argument. The opening argument is crucial in jury trials, where it is used to review the evidence, explicate the applicable law, and demonstrate how the evidence supports the legal prerequisites to conviction. One likes to assume that judges do not require such instruction.

Judge Neville had not inspired my confidence. I launched into my opening remarks with the hope that my powers of persuasion would not fail me. Logic and dispassionate reason were the hallmarks of my presentation, but the court was not moved. Neville interrupted me incessantly with carping questions and biting comments.

"Your so-called victim didn't have to go over to the defendant's house, drink his wine, smoke his weed, and jump into bed with him, now did he?"

"Who are you to say that Mr. Silverman didn't sign up for everything he got? You weren't there, were you?"

"You play with the bull, sometimes you get the horns." This last comment was accompanied by a soft little chuckle from His Honor.

I drew a long breath and mentally lectured myself not to be drawn into an acrimonious confrontation with the judge. I decided to concentrate on Count 4, the assault charge. I pointed out to the court that the law is clear: a victim cannot consent to an assault.

"I know why you filed that count," Neville snapped. "I'm not impressed by that argument."

Time to change gears again. In desperation, I revisited the sex counts and argued that the court would not take the same position if the victim were female.

"Probably not," Neville acknowledged, "and your point would be?"

"My point," I responded slowly and deliberately, "is that the law is gender-neutral. The legislature has seen fit in recent years to rewrite the code sections at issue here. All references to the victim of sex charges as female and the perpetrator as male have been deleted.

"If the victim in this case were a young woman who had been brutally raped and tortured and left with serious and permanent injuries, I do not believe this court would be reluctant to convict. The court's apparent impediment is the gender of the victim.

"Under the law, this is inappropriate. The facts of this case are hardly in dispute. The defendant acknowledged that everything the victim said was true. His only defense is that he thought the victim had consented. That is inherently preposterous.

"The defendant's own actions show his consciousness of guilt. He lied to the police and claimed at first that he didn't even know the victim. The fact that the bloody sheets and dildos were found secreted beneath a pile of dirty clothes in a laundry receptacle also indicates consciousness of guilt.

"I would urge the court, with all due respect, to put aside whatever prejudice it may have toward homosexuals and apply the law as it is written to the facts of this case."

Had I said enough? Had I said too much? Would anything I could say make a difference? I glanced back toward the audience and caught Carl's eye. He looked grim and I saw him shake his head slowly from side to side. I sat down. Before Sam could begin his argument, the Honorable Horace P. Neville spoke:

"I do not need to hear further argument from either side. Both sides in this case agreed to waive their respective rights to a jury trial. Both sides agreed that I should be the sole trier of fact. I have listened with great attention to all the evidence presented by the People and by the defendant. The court even interposed its own questions on occasion. I am satisfied that I have a clear understanding of the facts of this case.

"I am also satisfied that I have a clear understanding of the applicable law"—at this juncture Neville fixed me with a derisive stare—"and I find, with all due respect, that the prosecution has failed to meet its burden of proof beyond a reasonable doubt on all counts. This case is dismissed."

With a flourish of robes, Neville swept off the bench and disappeared into his chambers. As I left the courtroom I could hear Werner laughing. For me, the worst was yet to come. Shelley would be waiting in my office. We had agreed that we would go out to lunch, no matter what the outcome of the case. Of course, we were hoping we would be celebrating, not commiserating.

"You don't have to tell me," Sheldon said as I walked in. "It's written all over your face."

"Yeah, I'm a lousy poker player," was all I could manage.

At lunch we raised our glasses of iced tea and toasted each other.

"To Sheldon, who will always be a winner and a survivor, no matter what."

"To Marissa, who is still my favorite prosecutor."

"And to the memory of Oliver Swain," I said softly.

Just then the waiter came with our Cobb salads and for a couple of minutes we busied ourselves with our food. Sheldon broke the silence.

"I prayed about this case. I prayed for justice. Do you believe all prayers are answered?"

"Yes, I do."

"Even now?"

"Yes, Sheldon. But sometimes the answer is 'no.'"

JUSTICE

Justice is like the sun. A society that lacks justice is as though shrouded in darkness. No one can stop the sun from rising. No cloud can hide the rays of the sun indefinitely. "Opening the eyes" means causing those whose hearts are steeped in darkness to recognize the existence of the rising sun of justice.

— Daisaku Ikeda, *Faith into Action*

BRAIN DEAD

Victoria Cathcart

The first time Victoria Cathcart met Robert Norton, she had a very bad feeling. Over the seventy-nine years of her stay on this earth, Miss Cathcart had come to trust her feelings.

It wasn't so much Robert's appearance that gave her qualms. He was six foot three inches tall with light brown hair—always neatly combed—light blue eyes, and a pink complexion that made him look like he'd just pinched his cheeks. He had a bulky frame that was more fat than muscle and was always encased in clean, sharply pressed clothes. Miss Cathcart could not remember ever seeing Robert in jeans, a point that set him apart from all the other twenty-five-year-olds she knew.

It wasn't really his manner, either, that bothered her. He was always soft-spoken and extremely polite. His speech was replete with "no, sirs" and "yes, ma'ams." Had Victoria been familiar with New Age vernacular, she might have said that there was something unwholesome about his aura. If she had been a psychologist, she might have described him as hypervigilant. But as it was, there was nothing Victoria could put her finger on and nothing she could put into words.

So when Robert Norton asked Victoria Cathcart if he could join the Hollywood Stalwarts, she hesitated but said yes. The Stalwarts were Victoria's pride and joy, her creation, her legacy.

Miss Cathcart had moved with her family to Hollywood from Kansas when she was still a baby and Hollywood was still a small town nestled amid orange groves and oil wells. Victoria grew up going to public schools. After graduation from Hollywood High School, she continued her education at UCLA. She became a middle school teacher and ended her career as principal at her own junior high school.

In retirement, Victoria had become more active than ever. Having never married and with few surviving relatives, Miss Cathcart devoted her life to her community. Nothing mattered more than Hollywood—its beautification, its education, its preservation. She was involved in the Conservancy, she was on the board at the Hollywood Y, she donated time to a literacy program at the local adult school, she was a frequent and vocal presence at City Hall.

But one night two years before, Victoria had come to the sad realization that she still was not doing enough. She had parked her '59 Buick Special in her drive and was walking up the path to her door when she noticed a shadowy figure in her front yard. It was too large to be one of the many lawn gnomes that spotted her garden.

As she moved closer, Miss Cathcart realized that it was a man, on his knees, throwing up all over her prize rosebushes. How revolting! She scurried inside and called the police. Of course, it took them forever to respond even though the station was about three blocks away. It wasn't a murder, a robbery, or a hot prowl burglary, she was told by the responding officers. A down drunk barfing in the bushes was a low priority.

That same night the seed that would become the Stalwarts began to germinate. Hollywood could never be restored to its original grandeur when the detritus of the world freely roamed its streets and plagued its residents. Victoria contacted her cronies at City Hall and her colleagues at the Chamber of Commerce. She made friends with the watch commanders at the LAPD and demanded guidance. Something more than another Neighborhood Watch meeting was in order.

Not just anyone merited membership in the Stalwarts. First of all, you had to be a friend of Victoria's. Of course, that included about half of Hollywood. Next, you had to be willing to be trained by the LAPD and give up at least one night per week to patrol the neighborhood. And you had to have a sense of compassion and be able to exercise restraint.

The creed of the Stalwarts was to be nonconfrontational. Undesirables were to be "walked out" of the neighborhood. This tactic was accomplished by a number of Stalwarts hovering near the miscreant in question—tagger, drug dealer, prostitute—and politely asking the offending individual to leave the vicinity.

You might not think this strategy would be particularly effective, but it was. Typically, the object of the Stalwarts' collective scrutiny was more than happy to walk a few blocks in order to rid himself of such a bizarre coterie of onlookers.

The Stalwarts were an eclectic group: old and young, gay and straight, professional and blue collar, and every ethnicity under the sun. Their shared concern for the neighborhood transcended any differences they may have had. And their diversity was a living testament to Victoria Cathcart's generous nature and tremendous heart. Anyone who was interested in the betterment of Hollywood and was willing to contribute his time was welcome.

And yet, when Robert Norton asked Victoria Cathcart if he could join the Hollywood Stalwarts, she hesitated. And then she said yes.

JOHN R. WINSTON

Life had been good to John R. Winston. He had been blessed with a clear and sonorous voice. Combined with his perfectly clipped British accent and precise diction, this gift had permitted John to earn a comfortable income working in the entertainment industry. Commercials and voice-overs were his bread and butter, but the legitimate theater was his passion. He had never done anything beyond off-off-Broadway during his time in New York City, his first stop as a recent arrival from London when he was still a young man. But his failure to see his name in lights on the Great White Way never dampened his enthusiasm for the work itself.

In middle age Mr. Winston had moved to Los Angeles, drawn by the lure of sunshine and television. He had not been disappointed. While in New York, he had been obliged to augment his income as an actor by waiting tables. In L.A. the commercial work alone supported a lifestyle that included a craftsman-style bungalow above Franklin Avenue, a new car every ten years, and an annual holiday abroad.

Mr. Winston led a life unencumbered by a wife or children. He had no close friends but many acquaintances with whom he enjoyed limited but cordial contact. He had owned a dog once, but its death had left John with a deep sense of loneliness and desolation that had taken months to dissipate. There would be no replacement canine.

Now in his late sixties, Mr. Winston had surprised himself with a previously unknown desire. It was the urge to help others. Perhaps meeting Victoria Cathcart at a Neighborhood Watch gathering had provided the impetus. Or perhaps it was a dawning recognition that he had led a comfortable but selfish existence and that, with each passing day, Mr. Winston was twenty-four hours closer to his death. What would be said about him at his memorial and, for that matter, would anyone be there to mourn his passing?

Through Miss Cathcart, Mr. Winston had been introduced to the literacy program at Hollywood High's night adult school, and there he had met Jesús Ramírez. Jesús was twenty-two years old but looked no older than seventeen. In this country less than a year, alone and "undocumented," he was already remarkably fluent in English. His voice was sweet and resonant, his manner polite and deferential. But what struck John Winston was his appearance. Jesús was simply beautiful— John would later say "flawless"—from his smooth olive skin and dark eyes to his full lips and strikingly white teeth. Jesús had what Mr. Winston called "star quality."

In no time, Jesús became Mr. Winston's star pupil. Although the other students were oblivious, Mr. Winston was concerned that he was neglecting them and focusing too much of his attention on his favorite. A man of strict moral rectitude, John resolved to cure the problem by inviting Jesús for private tutoring at his home. Jesús was happy to accept the invitation. This was the first time in his life anyone had paid any attention to him.

As the eldest of eleven children from a small town in Mexico called Los Cerritos, Municipio de Amatlán de Cañas, Provincia de Nayarit, Jesús was used to dirt floors and a diet limited to rice and beans and a bit of chicken every other week. His exodus to the north had been encouraged by his parents, who, like so many from his village, expected the older children to seek employment in the States and send money home.

Jesús was a quick study and soon after his arrival had determined where the most lucrative vocation could be found. Within a week he was associated with a Latino gang and selling marijuana on the street.

Mr. Winston was aware of Jesús's employment but chose not to make an issue of it. His greater concern was that Jesús refrain from smoking the stuff himself. On more than one occasion, his protégé had shown up for his lessons high as a kite. John had tried to lay down the law. What Jesús did outside his presence was not John's business; after all, he wasn't the young man's father. But Jesús was simply not welcome at John's house unless he was sober.

Jesús struggled to comply with John's edict regarding sobriety. It wasn't easy, because he really liked to smoke dope and pound down those tequila shooters, but it was certainly to his benefit to please the old guy. Where else could he get free food, a place to stay overnight if he chose, and periodic gifts? Once it was a couple of shirts and a pair of slacks. Really nice stuff, too. Another time it was a watch—a Seiko, not a Timex or a Casio.

Despite what his dirty-minded homies thought, there were no strings attached. Mr. Winston was not *un viejo degenerado*. John seemed to really like him as a person, not for what Jesús could do for him. As far as Jesús was concerned, that put John in a class all by himself. Even his parents expected him to send money home once a month. John never asked for anything . . . except that Jesús leave the weed and the booze alone.

JEAN-LUC ST. PIERRE

There were days when he missed the French Quarter, but most of the time Jean-Luc was happy that he'd made the move to Hollywood. After his lover of ten years had died, New Orleans seemed to lose some of its cachet. What had been exquisitely beautiful and historically significant now seemed old and tired. A lot of friends were gone now, too. AIDS had taken its toll.

Jean-Luc's predominant thought was how fortunate he was to be alive, to be able to make a fresh start in a new city. But there were still those dark moments when he felt like giving up. Bereft of friends and family, battling one opportunistic disorder after the next, seeing his round, cherubic face slowly morph into something gaunt and hollow, it was a challenge to remain hopeful about the future.

Two things kept Jean-Luc out of the doldrums: his Buddhist practice and his membership in the Stalwarts. He had been introduced to Buddhism while still in New Orleans by a man he'd met at his doctor's office. The man was visibly sick, but his manner was so upbeat and positive that Jean-Luc had asked him what his secret was. Medicinal marijuana? No, the man had responded, the secret was something he would happily share. It was the Law of the Universe, it was the One Essential Phrase, it was the Mystic Law of Cause and Effect, it was Nam-Myoho-Renge-Kyo.

Within a week Jean-Luc was chanting, attending Buddhist meetings, and feeling more like the man he had been before his diagnosis. His involvement with the Stalwarts had begun within a month or two of his move to Los Angeles. The owner of the dry cleaning establishment where he worked was a close friend of Victoria Cathcart's and hence a member of the group. When Jean-Luc heard about the Stalwarts, he knew it was something he wanted to do.

When one is battling a devastating disease, it's easy to become self-absorbed. Buddhism teaches the importance of practicing for oneself and for others. In the parable of the Two Slender Reeds, the Buddha teaches that we are all inextricably connected with our environment and that, in fact, the person and the environment are one. To live in contravention of this truth is to be a solitary slender reed, buffeted by the winds of circumstance. However, when two slender reeds lean against one another, they will not be so easily uprooted by the storms of bad fortune. As a member of the Stalwarts, Jean-Luc was able to contribute something to others and make a difference in his new neighborhood. He was no longer a solitary, slender reed.

The Stalwarts became Jean-Luc's extended family. Victoria was a ready-made grandmother. A gay couple, George Clarke and Jorge Moreno—known to everyone as the Georges—became good friends. George worked as an architect and Jorge as a florist, so you can imagine how beautiful their house was. Soon Jean-Luc had moved from his dingy apartment to the Georges' bright and airy pool house.

The Mansouris also became close friends. Aram and his southern-belle wife Dixie ran a private primary school in the area and were active in the Stalwarts. Dixie was a fabulous cook, and at least once a week Jean-Luc was their guest for dinner. She was determined to fatten him up, and her fried chicken seemed to be working.

Lloyd Linden, a transplant from Pictou, Nova Scotia, and his wife, Shirley, also became Jean-Luc's instant friends. Lloyd was a retired lobsterman with a taciturn, gruff manner that belied his warm heart and munificent spirit. Shirley was generally reserved but possessed a wry sense of humor that she would reveal once she got to know you. The Lindens both spoke French and enjoyed conversing with Jean-Luc in his preferred language.

The camaraderie and friendship that the Stalwarts offered buoyed Jean-Luc's soul. They were a great bunch and their mission in Hollywood was commendable. There wasn't a single member of the group Jean-Luc didn't like. Well, to be completely honest, there was one. There was something about that Robert Norton that made Jean-Luc feel uneasy. Maybe it was the way Jean-Luc would catch Norton looking at him with those small steel-blue shark eyes. There was something creepy about that guy.

A Warm Summer Night

All told, there were about fifty members of the Stalwarts. Some were older residents who were unable to patrol the neighborhood. Everyone wanted to participate in some fashion, so the Stalwarts invested in walkie-talkies, and those whose infirmities precluded their joining in the nightly walks monitored the activities of the others via radio. This was not something merely designed to placate the less than ambulatory members of the group. Victoria felt it was an important safety precaution. Although there had been no violent incidents since the group was formed, you couldn't be too careful.

On the night of June 9, an unseasonably warm Friday night, two separate patrols were out on the streets and Victoria was covering home base. Her hip replacement six months before had left her dependent on a cane, and she was obliged to move much more slowly than she desired. Miss Cathcart was determined to be completely mobile by the end of the year, but meanwhile she was glad that the Stalwarts had invested in the walkie-talkies. She had just gotten comfortable on the settee with an ample dish of coffee ice cream and DuBois, her Persian, on her lap when the radio started to crackle:

"Miss Cathcart, I mean, home base, please come in. This is Patrol Number Two." It was Jorge, patrol leader of the second team that night.

"This is home base. Over."

"Can you hear me? I don't want Robert to overhear. He's here with my patrol and he's brought those two friends of his again. They're all dressed in fatigues. I think Robert has a can of Mace on his belt. What should I do?"

How irksome! The rules that the Stalwarts had set down for themselves were simple: no uniforms (not even berets), no weapons, and no untrained interlopers. It sounded like Norton was violating all three policies tonight.

"Jorge, this is home base. Please invite Robert and his friends to go home. We must follow our own regulations and he has been warned about this before."

"Roger, home base."

Victoria returned to her ice cream, which now resembled a small, pointy island in a beige sea. DuBois was in for a treat. Not only did she not favor melted ice cream, Miss Cathcart had lost her appetite. Nerves did it to her every time. If she were just out there on the street herself, she'd make sure things were running smoothly. Could Jorge be relied upon to insist that Norton and his cronies leave? Would that resolve the problem?

The answers were yes and no. Jorge promptly relayed Miss Cathcart's directive, but before Norton and his two friends could respond, something happened. Jorge's group had been moving slowly northward on Highland Avenue from Melrose toward Sunset and had just reached Fountain when the group's collective attention was drawn to a young Hispanic man running across Highland. He was wearing jeans and sneakers. His bare chest shone smooth and golden under the streetlight and his jet-black hair glistened.

What a cutie, thought Dixie Mansouri, who was part of Jorge's group. But something was wrong. The young man seemed oblivious to his surroundings. He crossed the northbound lanes without looking. Cars braked suddenly, tires squealed. The man then danced around one of the palm trees in the median before dashing across the southbound lanes. More cars braked rapidly, and the man ran up to where the Stalwarts had gathered on the west side of Highland. The look on his face revealed no recognition of the danger in which he had just placed himself.

"Marijuana?" the young man inquired vaguely. It was obvious that he was under the influence of something much more potent.

Jorge attempted to communicate with the man, first in English and then in Spanish, to no avail. The man began giggling uncontrollably and then lurched toward a parked car and perched on the hood.

"You can't talk to people on angel dust," Robert Norton advised Jorge authoritatively. "You have to subdue them."

Before any of the other Stalwarts knew what was happening, Robert had removed the Mace canister from his belt and was spraying the young man in the eyes. The man cried out and slid off the car, clutching his face. He landed in a heap on the pavement, clawing his eyes and moaning.

Norton began prodding the man with his shod feet. Then he kicked him hard. His military-style boots found their mark on the man's rib cage. Norton's two buddies were laughing.

"Stop!" Dixie screamed. "What is the matter with you?"

"It's what's the matter with the Stalwarts," Robert shot back. "You will never be effective without the use of appropriate force." But at the same time he had stopped kicking the young man.

To Dixie's relief, Robert's victim slowly staggered to his feet and began wobbling off down Highland. Jorge took the opportunity to repeat Miss Cathcart's orders. Surprisingly, Robert offered no argument. Instead he motioned for his friends to follow him. Dixie watched the three of them swaggering eastward on Fountain. At least they weren't following that poor inebriated young man.

Jorge checked his watch. It was just 10 P.M. He called home base on his radio to report that all was well. Robert Norton and his friends were going home.

In the Shadows

Meanwhile, the members of Patrol Number One were walking on Las Palmas Avenue, south of Santa Monica Boulevard. Nothing out of the ordinary had been encountered. Just your usual denizens of Hollyweird: the pierced, the tattooed, the transvested, the transgendered, the occasional voyager from a parallel universe. George was functioning as the patrol leader that night and had just checked in with Victoria to report on the uneventful evening.

Later that night, as the group rounded the corner across from the Circus Disco, Lloyd Linden thought he saw something. It looked as if Robert Norton and his two friends were chasing someone. Lloyd thought it looked like a young Hispanic man wearing only jeans, but it was just a quick glimpse. Lloyd called back to Jean-Luc to use his binoculars and tell him what he saw.

"Sorry," came the report, "I couldn't see anything. They must have headed up Seward."

Patrol Number One crossed Santa Monica and started toward Seward with Lloyd and George in the lead, Aram and Shirley and four other members following behind, and Jean-Luc bringing up the rear.

Jean-Luc's health had been pretty good for the last several months, but a bout with cryptosporidium had slowed him down a bit. He had started using the binoculars as a way of keeping up with the rest of the group. Maybe he couldn't walk quite as fast, but he was able to see things that the others missed. On this occasion, however, he wasn't sure what he had seen. He continued to walk, as quickly as he could, following the rest of the group east to Seward.

As he reached the northwest corner of Santa Monica and Seward, Jean-Luc observed his fellow Stalwarts crossing Seward on the diagonal and pausing just north of the corner. Further up on the east side of the street, his binoculars revealed another scene: three or four individuals clustered together near the wall of a warehouse. There were long shadows cast by a nearby streetlight. Jean-Luc walked as quickly as he could northward on the west side of Seward, pausing every few yards to look through his binoculars.

The shadowy scene across the street came into sharper focus. Robert Norton and his two companions were facing the warehouse wall. Norton was crouched down on one knee, while his friends were standing just behind him. It looked like there was someone or something on the ground adjacent to the wall. Norton was holding something over his head—was it a flashlight?

Then there were a series of cracking, crunching sounds as Norton repeatedly slammed down whatever he was holding. What was he doing? Norton's two friends were in Jean-Luc's line of sight. Jean-Luc quickly walked northward without crossing the street until he was parallel with Norton and his friends. Through his binoculars he saw that there was definitely someone down on the ground. There were what appeared to be dark shadows on the pavement near the person's head.

At the same time, Jean-Luc observed the members of Patrol Number One slowly approaching Norton.

"Wait there!" Norton screamed. The other Stalwarts docilely stopped several yards south of where Norton remained crouched. Apparently he was unaware of Jean-Luc, who continued to peer through his binoculars, refocusing in an attempt to get a clearer view. It looked like a man on the pavement, but it was hard to tell.

Suddenly Norton stood up and crossed the street, walking directly toward Jean-Luc. Norton motioned for the rest of the patrol to follow him.

"He's just stunned. It's okay. We don't need any trouble. Let's head toward La Brea," Norton advised everyone within earshot. George and the others crossed back to the west side of Seward while Norton's two buddies appeared to be bending over the man on the pavement.

"Let's go!" Norton yelled at them and they also crossed back to the west side of the street. Norton suddenly noticed Jean-Luc.

"What are you doing with those damn binoculars?"

"Nothing. What's going on over there?"

"Nothing. That asshole was trying to sell me some marijuana. I just taught him a little lesson, that's all." Jean-Luc noticed beads of sweat on Norton's forehead and dark semicircles of perspiration staining his camouflage-style shirt. Norton kept one hand on a long metal flashlight, which was holstered in a ring on his leather belt.

"Did you hit him?"

"No! I just scared him. He's playing 'possum. Let's get out of here. He's probably a gang member and his homeboys are probably nearby. We don't need any trouble."

The other Stalwarts had now gathered around, apparently waiting for some direction.

"All right," George responded. "I think Robert's right. Let's move on."

The group started walking rapidly south on Seward toward Santa Monica. Norton and his two friends took the lead, with the rest of the group following several yards behind. As usual, Jean-Luc lagged even further behind. Every few feet he would turn around and look back at the area where the man was on the pavement. Apparently he had yet to move. This was very odd, Jean-Luc thought. He couldn't still be stunned, could he? None of the other Stalwarts seemed at all interested. No one else gave a second glance at the man on the ground.

When Norton reached the corner at Santa Monica, he called back to the others that he was tired and was calling it a night. He headed west on Santa Monica. The others followed in the same direction at a much slower pace. By the time Jean-Luc reached Santa Monica Boulevard, Robert Norton was nowhere to be seen. Jean-Luc was feeling exhausted himself. He also decided to head home. The rest of Patrol Number One kept moving toward La Brea.

A Second Look

It took Jean-Luc less than ten minutes to get home. As he made his way through the exquisitely landscaped backyard toward the pool house, he noticed that the Georges had yet to return. He wished they were home. He needed to talk to someone about what he had seen, or, more precisely, what he *thought* he *might* have seen.

What if the person on the ground was injured rather than merely stunned? But what if the person was a dangerous gang member? What should Jean-Luc do? As soon as he was inside his home, he got down on his knees in front of his Buddhist shrine and began to chant: "*Nam-Myoho-Renge-Kyo! Nam-Myoho-Renge-Kyo! Nam-Myoho-Renge-Kyo!*" Immediately, Jean-Luc knew what must be done.

He literally sprinted to his car and began driving back to the Seward Street location. There was no time to walk. Jean-Luc needed to know the truth. Then he would know what to do. He prayed that the man would be gone. He prayed that his sense of panic was merely a product of an overactive imagination. Do not be such a drama queen, he instructed himself.

His car rounded the corner at Seward and he pulled to the curb just south of the warehouse. He hurriedly grabbed his flashlight and jumped from his vehicle, leaving the motor running. He intentionally hadn't brought his binoculars. Whatever there was to see, Jean-Luc was going to see with his naked eyes.

There were shadows on the pavement, but there was something else. And it wasn't moving. Jean-Luc took a deep breath and strengthened his resolve. It wasn't that he was a particularly timid or easily frightened man, but he was all alone on a dark, deserted street with a single streetlight casting unnerving shadows, and there was *something* on the pavement that had to be examined at closer range.

Holding his flashlight in front of him like a shield, Jean-Luc edged closer. It *was* a man lying on the pavement. The man was not moving a muscle. In the darkness, Jean-Luc forced himself to move even closer and allowed his flashlight to illuminate the shadowy area near the man's head. The flashlight shone on the pavement and on the man's brown, unclothed shoulders and on his glossy black hair and on the shadows around his head which were not shadows at all but rather large pools of blood and something else . . . clods of something gray . . . and bits of something white. . . .

In horror, with his heart pounding in his thin chest, Jean-Luc ran, faster than he thought he could, to the Circus Disco parking lot a block over between Cherokee and Las Palmas. In that moment he had forgotten that he had driven over to Seward. He ran to the guard station and screamed for help.

"What? What's going on? Is that you, Jean-Luc?" Chris Fox knew most of the Stalwarts by name and had participated in their training. The security personnel at the disco were grateful to the Stalwarts, whose work had dramatically cut down on the establishment's problems with drug trafficking and male prostitution.

"There's a man on the sidewalk—I think he's dead!"

"Get in my patrol car. We'll go see." Chris had one of those calm, reassuring voices with just a hint of a southern accent. Jean-Luc was in a state beyond reassurance, but he obediently got in the vehicle and allowed himself to be driven back to the scene of the crime.

When they reached the warehouse on Seward, Chris pulled the car to the curb and both men walked cautiously toward the dark shadowy lump near the wall. Each man was armed with a flashlight, and Chris had a baton and a canister of Mace on his belt. There was no need for weaponry. What was on the pavement presented no danger.

"Oh God!" Chris gasped when his flashlight illuminated the scene. Jean-Luc looked again, with the vain hope that his prior observations had been wrong. Not so. This time, perhaps emboldened by Chris's company, he bent down close to the man's head. The thick dark hair was matted with blood and the side and back of the man's skull were crushed. A portion of the skull was missing and what Jean-Luc knew must be brain tissue—although he had never seen it before—was exposed. There was more gray matter on the pavement, and bits of bone. A wave of nausea suddenly engulfed Jean-Luc. He lurched to the gutter and was immediately sick to his stomach.

Chris directed his flashlight beam into the man's eyes, which were wide open and unblinking. He bent down, careful not to disturb any of the physical evidence. There was a sound. It was almost imperceptible above the white noise of the traffic on Santa Monica. It was something between a gurgle and a wheeze. The man was still breathing. Chris pulled out his cell phone and punched 911.

THE DIGESTIVE SYSTEM

The life of a calendar deputy in the L.A. D.A.'s office is in a permanent state of flux. Cases are constantly flowing in and out of your courtroom. It is always a struggle to make sure that the output keeps pace with the input. If you fail to expeditiously move the cases through the system, then things back up and the caseload can burgeon to a frightening number. I have always prided myself on my ability to whittle a caseload down to a manageable size.

I view the criminal justice system as an organism. Those deputies assigned to the Complaints Division as filing deputies function as the mouth of the organism. They review police reports and determine what, if any, charges should be filed. They feed the organism. Then the peristalsis begins in the alimentary canal that is the court system. The judges and police and probation officers and defense attorneys all function like enzymes, breaking down the case into its component parts so that it may be processed or digested. And the calendar deputy stands guard at the sphincter.

The reward for any efficient calendar deputy is not necessarily a small caseload and a more mellow day-to-day courtroom experience. Sometimes the reward is a transfer to another courtroom where the previous calendar deputy has not been so efficient. That reward was bestowed on me in the summer of 1996. You've got to take these things like a man—even if you aren't one.

So there I was, at a little after 6 P.M. on a warm Thursday evening in late August, in a new office, acquainting myself with my new caseload of more than two hundred active filings. By active, I mean undigested, in the metaphorical sense. These were all cases where the defendant had yet to plead guilty or be convicted. I view anything pending sentencing as ready for excretion out of the system.

The files I was reviewing that night were all pending trial. It was a load. My late father, who had spent many years in the navy, would have called it "a blivy—ten pounds of shit in a nine-pound bag." Of course, metaphorically speaking, these matters hadn't reached the descending colon yet.

How to approach such an onerous task? Cull out the oldest cases and determine what must be done to resolve them. There was no time to worry about decorating my new office; these files demanded immediate attention.

The oldest case in my stack proved to be something called *People v. Robert Norton.* It was more than a year old, having been filed in July of the previous year. What had caused the delay in the prosecution of the case? I noted that a series of different defense attorneys had appeared for the defendant: first the public defender, then the alternate public defender, then a well-known panel attorney, followed by a privately retained defense attorney.

It appeared from the notations in the file that the trial had recently been continued, *yet again,* because the defendant had just retained *yet another* defense attorney. This time he was to be represented by someone known as J. T. Sloats, a name with which I was unfamiliar.

The outside of the file jacket indicated that it was a homicide case. It was labeled 187(a), but the charging document inside the file read 664/187(a), indicating an attempted murder. A second count in the information alleged the crime of violating Penal Code Section 245(a)(1), assault by means of force likely to produce great bodily injury and with a deadly weapon. The weapon was identified as a flashlight. So, was this a murder case or an attempt-murder case?

I began reading the police reports. There was an initial investigation report or crime report. Numerous individuals were listed as witnesses, but the body of the report failed to contain their individual statements. There was an arrest report and a rap sheet for Norton. It appeared that this was the defendant's sole contact with law enforcement. He had no prior arrests or convictions.

There was a property report listing numerous items removed from the defendant's home at the time of his arrest, including an eighteen-inch metal flashlight, a canister of Mace, military boots, and camouflage clothing. The report noted that the flashlight had been found in the kitchen sink. The Mace, boots, and clothing had been returned to the defendant, but the flashlight had been booked into evidence as a weapon used in the commission of a crime.

If this were a murder case, there should be an autopsy report. None was present in the file. If this were a murder case, there should be a murder book. This is a three-ring binder, typically blue in color, compiled by the detectives on a homicide case. It is always organized in the same fashion, with preprinted tabs identifying the contents. It is my practice to secure a copy of the murder book for myself at the earliest opportunity. That way, the prosecutor and the detective can be literally on the same page. I could find no murder book anywhere in the office.

Okay, if I was looking at an attempt-murder case, the file was still way too thin. Where were the supplemental or follow-up reports? Where were the photographs of the scene and of the victim's injuries? Where were the medical reports from the hospital? It looked like nothing had been done on this case since its filing. Apparently my predecessor's reputation as a worthless drone was warranted. I picked up the phone and dialed a number I knew by heart.

"Hollywood detectives," came the familiar greeting on the other end of the line.

"Hi. It's Marissa Batt calling from the D.A.'s office for Detective J. Wilson."

"Hi, Marissa. Great to hear from you. This is Tom Pritchard. I just got reassigned here last week. And I thought working Southwest was a pain in the ass."

"Better than working Rampart, Tom."

"No shit. Let's see, you wanted to reach a 'J. Wilson.' Seems like we have two of those on the roster."

"Serial number 05778926."

"He was just transferred to Metro. His caseload was divided between a couple different dicks here. You know how important those Metro cases are. God forbid Wilson should have to keep working any of his old Hollywood capers."

"Well, it looks like he didn't exert himself too much on a case I have pending trial right now in Department 118. Either that, or the deputy D.A. who had the case managed to lose half the file."

"What's the case?"

I provided Tom with the defendant's name and DR number. I think DR stands for "departmental reference" but I could be wrong. It's one of those abbreviations that has taken on a life of its own, and no one remembers what it stands for.

"Took me a while to track that one down," Tom apologized after keeping me on hold for several minutes. "And I've got some bad news," he continued. "It seems like your Norton case was never reassigned to anyone."

"Hey Tom," I responded in my most cajoling tone, "how would you like to be my I.O. on this one?" I.O. stands for investigating officer, and

I couldn't think of a more dedicated detective than my old buddy Tom Pritchard.

"Wish I could," Tom said in a wistful tone. "It would be like old times. I'm stuck working the desk. IOD."

"What happened?"

"Oh, I forgot that I'm a fat, middle-aged, slow-moving fart. I went in foot pursuit of a young hoodlum. Actually, I almost caught him, but he bolted over a chainlink fence right as I was closing in and I went over after him. Managed to tear out a couple of ligaments in my right leg."

"What about the crook?"

"They set up a perimeter and Buddy got him. The suspect had shimmied under an old jalopy in a neighbor's yard. The canine chomped him pretty good."

"A little street justice, huh? Anyway, if you can't help me out on this Norton case, can you find someone good for me?"

"I'll talk to the lieutenant and have someone call you tomorrow."

"Thanks, Tom. And take care of yourself."

"You too. Great talking to you. It's been too long."

A COUPLE OF PHONE CALLS

I looked at my watch. Not even seven yet. Might as well call a few civilian witnesses on the case to introduce myself and see if they still remembered anything. I needed to wait for my new I.O. in order to conduct proper interviews. This is one of the cardinal rules. Never interview witnesses without your detective present.

From my reading of the file, a Victoria Cathcart was the logical person to call first. I dialed and was overjoyed to hear a crisp, friendly voice answer after the first ring. I quickly identified myself and apologized in advance if I was calling at an inconvenient time.

"No, no, my dear," Miss Cathcart hastened to reassure me, "I'm pleased to finally hear from someone in the D.A.'s office."

"No one has been in touch with you on this case?"

"Not a soul. I spoke very briefly with a police detective right after the incident but have heard nothing since then. When Robert comes to our Stalwarts meetings, he acts like nothing is happening. Has the case been dismissed?"

"Not at all. It is my intention to get this case to trial as soon as possible."

"I don't mean to be critical, my dear, but what has taken you so long?"

"That's something I've been trying to figure out myself. I've just been reassigned to this courtroom, and this case appears to have been continued numerous times by the defense. I intend to oppose any further continuances."

"I'm glad to hear that, and I know the other members of the Stalwarts will be pleased to know you're on the case. Let me make sure I know how to spell your name correctly and that I have your telephone number." Miss Cathcart's no-nonsense style appealed to me and I happily provided the information she requested.

"Miss Cathcart," I continued.

"Call me Victoria, my dear, everyone does." Victoria was fast becoming my new best friend.

"Victoria," I responded dutifully. "You said Norton continues to attend your meetings?"

"Much to our collective irritation, I might add. He's threatened to bring the media to our next meeting. He's demanding that we vote to endorse the dismissal of the charges against him. He's also been soliciting us to contribute to his defense fund. Pretty nervy, if you ask me."

"When is the next meeting of the Stalwarts?"

"Next week. We meet on the second Tuesday of each month."

"Would you mind if I attended? It would give me the opportunity to introduce myself to your membership, many of whom are listed as witnesses on this case."

"You'd be very welcome."

"My only concern is avoiding any contact with Norton. At best it would be awkward; at worst, unethical."

"I understand completely. Robert has been persona non grata at our meetings since that night. I know I will be speaking on behalf of the entire membership when I make it official."

"Thanks. One last thing occurs to me, Victoria. Would you happen to know how the victim is doing?"

"Poor Jesús. I saw him only once. It was about six months after the attack. John dropped by on his way from County-USC Medical Center to the rehabilitation facility. He had Jesús in the car, the poor thing. I had to look away—it was so bad. I understand that he was a very nice-looking young man before this happened."

"Do you know how he's doing now?"

"You'd better call John—that's John Winston. He's been taking care of Jesús since this happened."

I thanked Victoria for all her help and quickly put in a call to John Winston. Again I was rewarded by a swift answer (did everyone on this case sit by the phone waiting for it to ring?) and an exceptionally pleasant voice. I began to explain who I was and why I was calling. Before I could finish, Mr. Winston unleashed a torrent of verbiage. He had been waiting an eternity for someone from the D.A.'s office to call, he was at his wit's end trying to care for Jesús, the death penalty was too good for the monster who perpetrated this atrocity.

I started to respond but stopped when I realized that Mr. Winston was sobbing.

"Are you okay?"

"I'm so sorry. I'm generally much more self-restrained. Please forgive me."

"Where is Jesús now?"

"He's staying with me. He has been with me since he was released from the Rancho Los Amigos rehabilitation facility. He's an outpatient now, and I take him there six days a week for physical therapy. I'm worn out. But I'm the only one he's got. His entire family is in Mexico. I'm in touch with them, but they have no money and there are no medical facilities in the vicinity of their village. I can't just send him back."

"Sounds like I need to nominate you for sainthood."

I heard a sardonic snort on the other end of the line.

"I'd like to meet Jesús as soon as possible."

"Well —" Mr. Winston hesitated. "Would you like to come over for a visit?"

"Actually, I'd prefer to meet him here in the Criminal Courts Building. He'll need to be here for the trial, so we might as well get him acclimated to the setting. What do you think?"

"I'll bring him in to meet you, but I doubt he'll be able to testify to anything. Have you seen his medical records?"

"I need to study them," I answered. Just like a lawyer, I thought harshly. Technically truthful, but fundamentally misleading. Would it be preferable to tell the poor, suffering Mr. Winston that I hadn't even glanced at a medical record because no one had bothered to do diddley on this case, including subpoena any documents?

Mr. Winston and I agreed to meet within the week. We wished each other good night and I hung up. I was exhausted. Just thinking about what John Winston had been living with for over a year had sapped all my energy.

GETTING ORGANIZED

With morning came renewed strength and determination, provided perhaps in part by a triple grande latte. I bustled into my office a minute or two before 8 A.M. and was startled to see someone sitting in one of the side chairs facing my desk. It was a young woman with close-cropped dark brown hair, sensible shoes, and an unflattering polyester suit that failed to disguise the fact that she was wearing a 9-mm automatic on her belt.

"Detective Lee Benson at your service on the Norton case," she said, rising and extending a beefy hand, fingernails bitten to the quick.

"That *is* service," I exclaimed. "I was hoping for a phone call, maybe."

"Pritchard let me know what you're up against."

"We have at least half an hour before I have to be in court. Let's see what we can accomplish."

I scooted my chair around to Lee's side of my desk and we got to work. In short order we had a page-long list of action items with notations on which one of us would be responsible for each. For example, I would prepare subpoenas for all the medical records and schedule an interview with the brain surgeon; Lee would order aerial and night photographs of the crime scene and send the flashlight to the crime lab for serology testing; we would both attend the next meeting of the Stalwarts and participate in interviewing the numerous witnesses. I was feeling much better.

"It's been a joy meeting you and I look forward very much to working with you on this case," Lee announced as I left for court.

"Me too," I responded with a grin. I made a mental note that I owed Pritchard, big-time.

As the days clicked along I gained familiarity with my new caseload. There were other cases that also needed special attention, including a couple of paper cases. One was a nasty yearlong embezzlement that involved lots of bank records and stock transfers. The other involved two crime partners bilking an old woman out of her life savings. But between my work on all my other cases, I continued to get the Norton case ready for trial. It was still my top priority.

The day before John Winston was scheduled to bring Jesús downtown for an interview, he called.

"I'm unhappy to report that Jesús is back in hospital. He was having difficulty eating without choking. He was losing a lot of weight, so the doctor decided to hospitalize him so they could feed him through a gastric tube."

"That sounds serious."

"Actually, he's only been off the feeding tube for a couple of months. I hope this is just a minor setback. But we'll have to reschedule our meeting with you."

I reassured John. The case wasn't even on the trial calendar yet. As much as I wanted to move the case along, I had to be mindful of my witness's constraints. And there were a few things I needed to do to be completely ready for trial. I had prepared the subpoenas duces tecum, or SDTs, for the medical records, but I wasn't happy about the unavoidable delay in serving them and then waiting for the hospital to respond. I decided to contact the neurosurgeon directly.

It did not take long to find Dr. Gregory Miller. I started with Cedars-Sinai Medical Center. That was the hospital to which the paramedics had taken Jesús after they had peeled him off the pavement. A helpful woman in their records department explained that Dr. Miller had been the attending physician on the case.

"I remember hearing about this case when it came in last summer," she volunteered. "Everyone said that if Dr. Miller hadn't been working in the ER when they brought the case in, that young man would have died. There isn't another doctor on staff here who could have saved him. Not with an open depressed skull fracture in the parietal region. I heard that half his brain was left on the street. Everyone at Cedars knows about this case. You know, Dr. Miller is probably the finest brain surgeon in the country."

"I didn't know that."

"Oh yes. He's not actually on staff here. He had been called in to assist on another head injury case that night. Very lucky for your young man. If you fax me an SDT, I'll ship the records out to you today."

"That's great. I need them as soon as possible. I'd also like to be able to contact Dr. Miller directly. Can you help me?"

"No problem." She provided me with a Beverly Hills address and a telephone number. I hung up and dialed Dr. Miller. I got a recording that offered three options: if it could wait, leave a message; if it was urgent, enter a numeric page; or, if it was an emergency, hang up and dial 911. I selected option number two and hoped that the doctor would find my assessment of urgency to be legitimate.

Figuring it might take some time for a famous brain surgeon to return a page, I pulled a stack of files onto my desk and started preparing on upcoming pretrial matters. To my amazement, my page was answered within fifteen minutes.

"This is Dr. Miller."

"This is Deputy District Attorney Marissa Batt. This involves your patient Jesús Ramírez, the open depressed parietal —"

"I know the case," the doctor cut in. "I continue to follow this patient. He's currently undergoing rehabilitation at Rancho Los Amigos. Has something happened?" There was an edge to his voice, and I immediately felt guilty for paging him. I quickly explained that I was preparing the case for trial and needed to interview him as an essential witness. I hastened to add that, other than the gastric feeding, I had been told that his patient was doing okay.

"That's good to hear. So you need me as a witness? I've never testified in a criminal matter before. I've been a witness in a number of civil lawsuits. Should I have received a subpoena?"

"You will as soon as we get a trial date and a courtroom. I wanted to interview you as soon as possible and check your availability. I imagine you're a busy man." This comment was greeted by laughter on the other end of the line. I was starting to like this guy. As far as I'm concerned, a sense of humor is one of the more crucial attributes in a well-integrated personality.

"I'm taking a red-eye to Montreal tonight. I'm scheduled to speak at a symposium there through Saturday, then I'm off to London for a conference on neuromotor impairment as a result of brain-stem trauma, then —"

It was my turn to interrupt. "Doctor —"

"Perhaps I've told you too much?" More laughter. From both of us.

"How about tonight?" Dr. Miller continued. "If you could meet me at my office around seven, I'll be happy to discuss the case with you. I have all the films on file here."

He made sure I had clear directions to his office and we hung up.

In the Field

Beverly Hills was a dramatic contrast to downtown. I happen to like downtown L.A., but Beverly Hills does have its own appeal: tree-lined avenues, exquisite boutiques offering outrageously priced baubles, trendy restaurants, designer clothing shops, art galleries. . . . Good thing I've never been assigned to the Beverly Hills courthouse, I thought. My county salary wouldn't last very long in this high-tone neighborhood.

Dr. Miller's office was definitely on a par with its surroundings; housed in a gleaming chrome and glass postmodern edifice, it encompassed a third of the top floor. I entered a richly upholstered elevator, pushed the button labeled PH, and was soundlessly whisked upward. Just a little different from what we have at the CCB, I thought as the doors opened on a tastefully lit vestibule. An enormous frosted Lalique vase containing an array of fresh flowers stood on an impressive pink marble table.

Just as I was wondering in which direction to turn, the good doctor appeared. And he too was on a par with the surroundings. He was absolutely gorgeous (I should remember to pick a jury heavy on females) and looked much younger than his curriculum vitae indicated was possible. I bowed slightly and then offered my hand.

"Dr. Miller?" I ventured, wondering for a split second if I was in the right office.

"Ms. Batt?" he smiled, taking my hand. "Don't say it—I hear it all the time—I know I don't look old enough to have finished med school. I'd say we both have that problem. You look like a kid yourself."

"Actually, I find it can be quite disarming in the courtroom. Sometimes my opponents will underestimate me because I appear so completely nonthreatening."

"How handy. In my case, it's usually a disadvantage. Takes me a bit longer to establish confidence and trust. I had one patient, on the operating table, demand to see my driver's license."

"What did you do?"

"Well, I didn't have it on me. I signaled for the anesthesiologist to start and I showed the patient my license the next day, after a successful surgery. She had no memory of ever asking to see it."

"Are you sure the surgery was successful?" We both started laughing.

"Dr. Miller," I said after composing myself, "we should probably get to work on the Ramírez case. I know you have a plane to catch."

"There's plenty of time, don't worry. Come on back to the conference room and I'll show you the films. I had one of the secretaries burn you a copy of all the charts so you won't have to wait for the hospitals to send them. I know how long that can take."

He ushered me down a wide hallway hung with modern art. I recognized an Ed Ruscha and a particularly intriguing piece by David Hockney before we turned a corner and I found myself entering an immense conference room through etched glass doors. The far wall was one sweeping window, floor to ceiling, framing a southwest view of Century City. It was now dusk and a few lights were already twinkling.

"Thank you," I murmured, trying hard not to sound awestruck. The next thing he'll do is offer you a drink, I mused.

"How about a drink?" he said. I almost laughed out loud.

The conference room was a study in understated elegance, from the plush carpet and fabric-covered walls to the highly polished furniture.

"Make yourself comfortable," Dr. Miller said, gesturing toward a chair at one end of a massive black granite table. Normally I don't like doctors very much, but I could make a big exception where Dr. Greg Miller was concerned.

"We've got the soft and the hard stuff, wine, orange juice, you name it," he continued as he opened an expansive refrigerator housed beneath a polished black granite built-in buffet at one end of the spacious room.

"What are you having?" I asked.

"A Perrier," and then in a somber tone, "I'm told that alcohol kills brain cells." More laughter.

"You put it that way, I'll have the same."

We toasted each other with sparkling water and then Dr. Miller started putting x-ray films up on numerous light boxes that were affixed to the wall.

"I know they don't complement the decor. The interior designer tried to veto it but we use them all the time. Let me show you what kind of injuries we are dealing with."

The doctor proceeded to point out on the x-ray films the extensive damage to my victim's cranium.

"Here in this CT scan you see numerous fractures. Most notable is the large depressed fracture of the right parietal area. This injury required an immediate craniotomy, elevation of the fracture, evacuation of the subdural hematoma, and debridement of the parietal contusion, along with repair of the dura and placement of an intracranial pressure monitor."

"What am I looking at in this film?" I inquired, pointing to another x-ray that looked like it would make a nice courtroom exhibit.

"This provides a good view of the mandible fracture, the maxillary sinus fracture, the sphenoid sinus fracture, and the fracture of the zygomatic arch."

"All the damage was to the victim's right side?"

"Yes, for the most part. These injuries indicate to me that the initial blow probably incapacitated the patient and the subsequent blows were all delivered while Mr. Ramírez was immobilized on the pavement."

"Were there any injuries to the left side of the victim's face?"

"The damage to the mandible was extensive and bilateral. I believe there were numerous fractures to the jaw and multiple tooth loss. I'm less familiar with this aspect of the case. You'll need to contact Dr. David Kane, the oral surgeon, to get all the details. But for starters I've got a complete set of the medical records for you, from Cedars, County-USC, and the Adult Brain Injury Unit at Rancho Los Amigos Hospital."

"Thanks. I've got a lot of reading to do."

"You know how to read medical records?"

"Oh yes. I've had lots of practice over the years. So the patient was transferred from Cedars to County Hospital at some point and then to the rehabilitation facility?"

"That's right. We kept him at Cedars for over a month. The mandibular osteotomy and autologous bone grafting were performed by Dr. Kane at County Hospital. An initial stabilization of the mandible with titanium plates was performed by Dr. Martin Harper at Cedars. He was seen by ophthalmologists at all three facilities."

"In your opinion, are all these injuries consistent with the weapon being a metal flashlight weighing approximately five pounds, in excess of a foot in length, and roughly an inch and a half in diameter?"

"Yes. One of the paramedics reported that a flashlight of that general description was probably the weapon used. In this film you can clearly see the open depressed parietal fracture. From this angle, we can measure the depression and conclude that is consistent with being caused by such an instrument. See the curvature of the depression? Offhand, I can't think of an object other than the butt end of a flashlight that would cause this exact type of damage."

"These injuries are appalling. And these films graphically prove the viciousness of the attack. I'm going to show some of these x-rays to the jury and have you explain them. The jury will love you. After all, you brought this patient back from the grave!"

"Thanks for the kind words, but it was truly a team effort. The other doctors on the trauma team did a great job. And Jesús has had excellent follow-up care at USC and at Rancho Los Amigos. Rebuilding the mandible, for example. I've never seen finer work. Also, Dr. Daniel Sacks, the ophthalmologist at Cedars, could not have done more with what he had to work with. The fact that Mr. Ramírez has any vision left is a small miracle."

"Of course, if it hadn't been for your efforts, the patient would not have survived to have his eyes and jaw repaired."

The good doctor smiled at me indulgently. Don't argue with a prosecutor when she is determined to compliment you.

I checked my watch. I didn't want to take up too much of the doctor's time, but I had a few more questions.

"Is there a chance that the patient's condition might improve over time with proper therapy?"

"Highly doubtful. I think he's recovered as much as he ever will. His condition remains guarded and he will always require medical attention for as long as he lives."

"Could he die from these injuries?"

"That's always a concern in a situation like this. He simply cannot be left unattended. He could aspirate food. His gag reflex has been compromised. Pneumonia is a constant and chronic problem."

"And his mental condition?"

"The injuries left him gravely impaired," Dr. Miller said sadly. "I had no choice but to excise the necrotic tissues. He lost a significant amount of brain tissue as a result of the blunt force trauma and then more as a consequence of the surgery. Jesús is profoundly mentally disabled. I wish you good luck on this case."

"Thanks. I really should be going now."

"Here's a copy of my fee schedule for work on a case as an expert witness," the doctor announced blandly, handing me a piece of paper containing some astronomical figures. I was in a state of shock. There was no way the County of L.A. could pick up a tab like this. Furthermore, Dr. Miller was not technically an expert witness, someone appointed by the court to educate the jury on a subject outside what is considered to be common knowledge. Dr. Gregory Miller was an essential eyewitness to the injuries. I was speechless, but I'm sure the expression on my face betrayed my thoughts.

"You know," the world's finest brain surgeon said, "I'm overdue for some pro bono work. Let me make a gift to the cause of justice." With that he extracted his fee schedule from my hand, wadded it into a tidy ball, and sent it sailing gracefully into the most beautiful alabaster waste basket I had ever seen.

"Like I said," he went on, "this is my first criminal case, so you will have to forgive my ignorance and my presumption."

"Nothing to forgive. We just don't have adequate funds available to finance our prosecutions. We make our own charts and diagrams, take our own photographs—it's a do-it-yourself kind of operation."

"What if a doctor didn't agree to donate his time?"

"Oh, then we'd pay him our standard witness fees—eighteen dollars per day!"

"That's all?"

"Plus parking." We both laughed.

A LITTLE LEGAL ANALYSIS

The next night and part of the weekend were devoted to studying the voluminous medical records on Jesús Ramírez. All told, there were at least forty-five different doctors who had attended him on various occasions at the three medical facilities. In addition to the oral surgeons, the ophthalmologists, the gastroenterologists, the team of neurologists and neurosurgeons, and a small army of radiologists, there were ear doctors and audiologists. It turned out that, in addition to all the other injuries, Jesús had suffered significant hearing loss as a result of the head trauma.

I had no intention of calling each doctor involved in the case as a witness. That would be a dandy way to wear out a jury and infuriate a judge. However, it would be important for the jurors to have a clear understanding of the injuries. My preliminary plan was to see if the defense attorney would agree to stipulate to most of the medical testimony.

A stipulation is an agreement between the attorneys as to certain facts in a case. If the stipulation is entered into by the attorneys and accepted by the court, then it must be accepted by the jury as conclusively proven.

Why would an attorney agree to stipulate to part of the opposing counsel's case? There are many reasons. If the facts are uncontested—that is, if no evidence to the contrary will be offered—why not? It saves time. Sometimes agreeing to stipulate is a tactical maneuver. If the witness providing the testimony is particularly powerful or charismatic, it might be wise to offer a stipulation in lieu of testimony. Naturally, I intended to call some live witnesses regarding the victim's injuries: one of the paramedics, the victim's primary doctor at Rancho Los Amigos, and of course the unparalleled Dr. Gregory Miller.

It's always smart for a prosecutor to think like a defense attorney. Obviously, this case was going to trial. If the defense had been interested in a plea bargain, I was sure my lazy predecessor would have cut a deal. This had the flavor of a case that had to be tried but nobody was eager to do it. So, if this case was going to trial, what would the defense be? There are two basic defenses in an assault case: self-defense and alibi. Since there were quite a few witnesses, I figured we were talking about self-defense, but the magnitude and multiplicity of the injuries would make this a hard sell.

There was a great bodily injury allegation appended to both the attempt-murder and the assault charges. Norton was charged with intentionally and personally inflicting great bodily injury on the victim in the course of committing the crimes. Not difficult to prove in this case, and worth an additional three years in the state prison. The attempt-murder charge is punishable by five, seven, or nine years in the state prison, while a felony assault carries a low term of two years, a mid-term of three years, and a high term of four years.

A maximum sentence of either twelve or seven years for bludgeoning another human being into a literal pulp. With conduct credits (good time and work time), Norton could cut his actual time in custody almost in half. And the likelihood of a high-term sentence on a first-time offender was remote. And the probability of getting a conviction on attempted murder was even less likely.

Attempted murder is one of the most difficult crimes to prove—much more difficult to prove than murder itself. In both murder and attempt-murder cases, the prosecution must prove malice aforethought. Express malice aforethought is the specific intent to kill another human being. Implied malice aforethought involves proving that the act was intentional, that the natural consequences of the act are dangerous to human life, and that the act was done deliberately, with knowledge of the danger to and with a conscious disregard for human life.

Here's the catch: In a murder case, malice may be either express or implied. In an attempt-murder case, only express malice will do. Obviously, it is a much simpler task to prove the elements of implied malice. How does one prove express malice? Well, if you are lucky, the perpetrator will announce his intention to kill at the time he does the deed: "I'm now bashing this fellow's head in with the specific intent to kill him." Right. How many times does that happen?

But what about arguing that the nature of the injuries demonstrates the perpetrator's intent? In this case, it was a fluke that Jesús survived. The defendant struck numerous blows to the victim's cranium, fracturing the skull to the point that brain tissue was found on the pavement. No, that's *implied* malice.

Well, what about the fact that Norton hurried away from the crime scene, leaving his victim unconscious on the sidewalk? He told the witnesses that the man was merely stunned, thus attempting to ensure that no one else would render aid. Doesn't that tell you that he wanted the victim to die? Nice try, but that's still *implied* malice.

I figured the attempt-murder charge was a loser in this case—unless I could find someone to whom Norton confided his murderous intent. And perhaps that individual would be one of the Stalwarts. . . .

LIGHTS, CAMERA, ACTION

The date of the Stalwarts' monthly meeting had arrived, and Lee and I were in attendance in a large classroom at the Mansouris' Hollywoodland Schoolhouse. Victoria conducted the meeting with assistance from Aram Mansouri, who was apparently second-in-command. His wife Dixie read the minutes from the previous meeting in a lovely southern drawl. They were immediately approved as written and she sat down with a look of satisfaction.

Next on the agenda was the introduction of guests. Detective Benson and I rose and nodded amiably at the assemblage. I inquired if I could briefly address the members at some point in the evening. "Right now would be fine. You are the next item on our agenda," Miss Cathcart informed me.

I began by thanking the Stalwarts for allowing us to attend and explaining the purpose of our visit. The Norton case was finally going to trial and we needed to interview all the witnesses. Perhaps not everyone who was on patrol that night would be called to the stand, but we wouldn't know until we had talked to everyone. I sensed unrest in the room. Not atypical at all—show me someone who wants to be a witness and I'll show you someone who has an ulterior motive.

Preparation is the key to good trial work, and experience had taught me well. I pulled a pack of subpoenas from my briefcase and started calling names as though I were taking roll. As each member responded, I handed out a subpoena. Nothing beats personal service!

The D.A.'s office doesn't have the manpower to personally serve all the witnesses on all the cases we handle. We typically mail our subpoenas, requesting personal service only when we think a witness is going to be uncooperative. Personal service is a prerequisite to the issuance of a body attachment, or arrest warrant, for a missing witness.

A subpoena sent through the United States Post Office is not legally binding, but most folks don't know that and will respond to a mailed request to appear. If that were not the case, our office would be in deep ca-ca, so keep this to yourself.

Since we didn't have a specific trial date, I had to be inventive. The case was set in another week on the pretrial calendar as "zero of thirty," as we say, written on the file as "0/30." This means that, absent another waiver of the defendant's right to a speedy trial, jury selection would begin on the thirtieth day after the pretrial date. I made an educated guess as to what a realistic date would be when witnesses might be called and filled out the subpoenas accordingly. I also didn't know in which courtroom the case would be tried, so I put down the number of my calendar court with an explanation on each subpoena.

"Please be available from the date on the subpoena until otherwise notified," I explained, "and since you all reside within a half hour's drive of the courthouse, you can all be on-call to me so you won't have to spend days waiting in the hallway until it's your turn to testify." That statement engendered a few smiles from the audience.

Next, I passed out copies of my Twenty-five Rules for Giving Effective Testimony and encouraged my prospective witnesses to read them at their convenience. Finally, I cautioned everyone not to discuss the facts of the case with each other. They would be contacted within the next few days so we could schedule individual interviews prior to trial. I thanked everyone again and sat down.

Before Victoria could announce the next item on the agenda, there was a commotion at the door. A well-fed young man dressed in a dark suit strode into the room along with a heavyset middle-aged woman with bleach blond hair. She was wearing a bright floral print dress and carrying a pile of papers. They, in turn, were accompanied by an entire television crew including a reporter, cameraman, soundman, and lighting technician. I turned to Victoria with a quizzical expression.

"It's Robert Norton," she whispered. "Believe me, I told him he was no longer welcome here. But he has threatened to do this. He's already given several interviews to the local newspapers and now this."

Everyone grew quiet as Norton marched to the far end of the room to afford the minicam operator with an establishing shot of the room and its occupants. The big woman in the bold dress started distributing her handouts. I shot Victoria another quizzical look. "His mother," she whispered in response.

I took one of the handouts. It had a fuzzy photograph of Norton, wearing the same dark suit, under the heading VICTIM OF LAW EN-FORCEMENT!!! Beneath the picture was:

MODEL CITIZEN ARRESTED AND CHARGED AFTER DEFENDING SELF AGAINST ARMED ATTACKER! HOLLYWOOD STALWART NEEDS YOUR SUPPORT TO DEFEND HIMSELF AGAINST UNJUST CRIMINAL CHARGES!!

The rest of the flyer contained blank spaces for a supporter's name, address, telephone number, and amount of contribution.

"I think you all know why I am here tonight," Norton began in a loud, nasal voice. The camera was rolling. "It is to get your support for me as I defend myself against this unjust prosecution. Persecution would be a better word for what is happening to me."

"You should leave, Robert," Aram interrupted. "You are not on the agenda tonight."

"I am not on the agenda!" Norton repeated in a shrill voice. "Well, I should be! There is nothing more important to discuss. What is happening to me is a crime and I demand that the Stalwarts give me support. You owe it to me. I was out there on the streets doing your work for you. Doing what most of you are afraid to do for yourselves. I was risking my life for you!"

"That's right!" the mother chimed in.

"Robert," Victoria said calmly, as she planted her cane on the floor and pushed herself up to a standing position. "This is not the time nor the place for such a debate."

"There is nothing to debate!" Norton shot back. "I'm the victim. The police and the D.A. are out to get me. All I did was defend myself against a drug-crazed dope addict with a knife!"

"That's right!" the mother repeated.

"All I am asking for is a vote of support and a contribution to my defense fund. That is the least you can do under the circumstances. I put my life on the line for you!"

The mother was nodding vigorously. The camera was still rolling. Lee and I exchanged looks. What a blustering fool. I wondered if his lawyer knew what Robert Norton was up to. Lee was busily taking notes for a supplemental or follow-up report.

"I demand a vote on this right now. Everyone voting to support me raise your hands."

There was an uncomfortable silence. No hands were raised.

Then Lloyd Linden cleared his throat and said in a gravelly voice: "The problem is this, Robert. A number of us weren't even out on patrol that night. Some of us were in the other patrol group and didn't see what happened. You can't expect us to support you when we don't know what happened."

"I'm telling you what happened!" Norton bellowed, and then, apparently realizing that he was still on camera, stated in a softer tone, "You all know me. You know what a good citizen I am and that I have done nothing wrong. They have accused me of committing crimes! Felony crimes! I am being persecuted. I need your vote of support. And I need your financial help."

George Clarke took out his checkbook and wrote Norton a check for fifty dollars. "Here," he said, handing it to Robert. "Please do not misunderstand what this signifies. I believe everyone deserves a fair trial, even the guilty. This is my contribution to your fair trial—nothing more." Norton responded as though he had not heard George's disclaimer, waving the check in front of the cameraman and announcing to the television reporter that he had the support of the Stalwarts.

I noticed Aram and Victoria conferring in lowered voices. Then Aram stood up and made an announcement: "This meeting is hereby adjourned. We ask that you all leave the premises promptly. We will notify you of the date and location of our next meeting. Please have a safe trip home, whether you are walking or driving." He started turning off some of the lights and everyone got the message, even Norton and his TV crew.

Detective Benson asked if anyone needed a ride, and Miss Cathcart immediately accepted. Walking was still out of the question, and she drove as little as possible because it seemed to aggravate her hip.

"Aram had picked me up, so you'll be saving him a needless trip over and back. Thank you for the offer."

"Tell me something, Victoria," I said as we were getting into Lee's patrol car. "How would you suggest I go about getting copies of the stories about this case that appeared in the local Hollywood papers?"

Victoria grinned. "Well, all you'd have to do is ask me. I've kept a scrapbook on this case, and every article ever printed about it is in there."

She agreed to let me borrow her compilation of materials so I could make copies. What good fortune. I had envisioned hours spent culling through back issues of throwaway papers, hunting for articles relating to the case.

Just as Lee was about to pull away from the curb, a thin young man approached on the passenger side.

"The meeting ended so abruptly, I didn't get a chance to properly introduce myself. I'm Jean-Luc St. Pierre. I'm the one who went back and found the body—I mean, the man. I expect you'll want to interview me."

"Yes. I wanted to say something to you when I was handing out subpoenas, but I didn't want to mention anything about the facts of the case in front of other potential witnesses. You are, without a doubt, the most important witness in this case. And I'm sure you realize that if you had not had the wisdom and fortitude to return to the scene, the victim would have died."

"I've heard he's in real bad shape. Maybe I didn't do him such a favor?"

"He's alive. 'The foremost treasure of sentient beings is nothing other than life itself.'"

"That sounds familiar. Is that a quotation?"

"It is. Those are the words of the Buddha."

"A prosecutor who quotes the Buddha. You have no idea how happy I am that you are on this case."

DISCOVERY

As soon as I got home, I fixed myself a cup of ginger tea and cuddled up on the couch with Victoria's scrapbook. There were approximately ten articles about the case, and the defendant was quoted extensively in each of them. His statements were rife with inconsistencies.

In an early article, Norton was quoted as saying that he saw something shiny in the victim's hand and was not sure whether it was a gun or a knife. A subsequent article had the defendant describing the knife in rich detail. In one article, Norton described the victim as "spinning around" with the knife held sideways as though to "slash" him in the abdomen. In another piece, Norton recounted that the victim "sprang" on him from the shadows and attempted to "stab" him in the neck.

Of course, Norton would claim that he had been misunderstood and misquoted. I added to my list of action items the preparation of subpoenas for these reporters. When Robert Norton took the stand, I would cross-examine him on the conflicting statements he had made to the media. If he denied it, the reporters could be called as rebuttal witnesses.

When I got back from court for the noon recess the next day, there was a voice-mail message from Detective Benson.

"Hey, Marissa. You will not believe what I unearthed over here at the bottom of the file cabinet where we were keeping our case packet on Norton. A roll of film! I've shipped it out to the lab to be developed. Really hope and pray that it's in good enough condition to make prints. It's got to be shots of the crime scene. We'll know soon. Meanwhile, I got the aerials and the night pictures back. We're still working on putting a map together for you. Would it be okay if we just blew up the relevant page from the Thomas guide? Let me know."

I called back and left a message for Lee telling her to start with a blowup of the Thomas guide page. I had other ideas involving clear overlays: one would show the routes each patrol took on the night in question, while another would indicate where the crime occurred, where the Circus Disco is located, Norton's route home, and Jean-Luc's route home and back.

If the mystery roll of film proved to be crime scene photos, we'd be in good shape. Without them, it would be more difficult to get the recent aerials and night shots before the jury—how would I prove that they accurately depicted the scene as it appeared over a year ago? I'd have to rely on the memory of the residents, and that could be problematic, especially if there had been any changes in the interim involving trees, buildings, lighting, and so forth.

Lee was in my office when I got back from my afternoon calendar call. Photos were spread out on my desk and a large map page glued to a piece of cardboard was resting against the wall. The photos were of the crime scene.

"I love you, Lee!"

"I thought you'd be pleased."

"No pictures of the victim?"

"None. I went ahead and contacted the paramedics. One had been transferred and didn't seem to remember much. I think the other one—Ramón Estrada—will be a pretty good witness.

"Estrada tells me that their RA Unit arrived on the scene first. They assessed the situation and determined that the victim was in danger of expiring at any moment and needed to be taken to the closest ER as quickly as possible. They were just leaving with the victim as the police were rolling to the scene. So you have no pictures of our victim on the ground.

"We do have a couple of photographs showing the pool of blood on the sidewalk where Jesús had been lying. What do you think of the aerial and nighttime photographs? I hope we got what you wanted. Oh, and here are copies of all my follow-up reports to date and another set of photos for the defense attorney."

"Thanks." It is such a pleasure to work with an experienced detective who knows that every item of evidence must be duplicated and supplied to the defense.

"Your timing is exquisite," I continued. "This case is on calendar tomorrow, and it will be nice to be able to provide the discovery to the defense attorney in a timely fashion."

I studied the photographs and started picking out which ones I would use in court. I'd have them enlarged and mounted on cardboard with appropriate captions. I think it's tacky to introduce a stack of small snapshots in a jury trial. The jurors are obliged to take turns looking at them. It's distracting and wasteful of court time. Such a lack of preparation demonstrates a basic disregard for the jury and a disinterest in the case. In my view, the importance of the variety, number, order, and quality of exhibits cannot be overestimated.

If at all possible, an exhibit should be large enough so that all the jurors can view it from where they are seated in the jury box. With the advent of overhead projectors, even small exhibits can be magnified and projected on a screen for the jury's convenience. This is done routinely in the D.A.'s office today, but back when I was trying Robert Norton, we did not have the technology at our disposal, so we did it the old-fashioned way.

"How are we doing on scheduling interviews with the Stalwarts? I'd like to get Jean-Luc to walk us through everything he saw. I'd like to see those binoculars. We should meet with him at night so we can, as much as possible, approximate the same conditions. I need to get a clear picture in my mind of what he saw. The distances. The lighting. I need to understand the time frames. Maybe it would be something for a jury view?"

I was thinking out loud. Lee was happy to join in.

"I like it," she said, "assuming good lighting and powerful binoculars. We could have each juror stand where the witness said he was and then look through his actual binoculars at the place on the pavement where the crime occurred. How about a reenactment of the crime?"

"Now you're getting carried away. I'll be lucky if the trial judge permits a jury view. You know how much they hate those things. At least in this case the defendant isn't in custody. Makes it a little less involved."

"I've been meaning to ask you about that," Lee said. "Why isn't he in custody?"

"The deputy D.A. at the arraignment must have been asleep, that's all I can figure. The defense apparently made a motion to lower bail. I'm sure they must have argued lack of prior record and self-defense and the judge must have bought it. The bail set is about half what is called for in the bail schedule. Maybe the prosecutor in the arraignment court didn't know the extent of the injuries. Anyway, the defendant bailed out."

"That's too bad. If he'd stayed in custody, the case would have been tried already."

Lee was right. Once a defendant bails out, the impetus to exercise the right to a speedy trial seems to dissipate.

J. T. SLOATS

Getting the Norton case to trial was the foremost thought in my mind when I entered my courtroom the next morning. John Winston had called with the good news that Jesús was off the feeding tube and doing much better. So much better that John had agreed to bring him down to meet me at the CCB that afternoon. After more than a year of delay, I wanted to be able to provide John with a specific trial date.

As soon as I walked into court I noticed Norton and his mother sitting in the back of the courtroom—same dark suit, same bold floral frock. Did these people have a closet full of identical suits and dresses, or did they simply eschew rudimentary hygiene? I banished these unkind thoughts and concentrated on working through the morning calendar call.

About half of my caseload belonged to the deputy public defender assigned to the courtroom, Frank Nakashima. We typically agreed on the value of a case and rarely set a matter for trial. Why have twelve people with limited information decide something that two people with all the data can decide? A trial is always a crapshoot, and Frank and I were not gamblers.

The rest of the calendar involved privately retained attorneys, panel attorneys appointed by the court, and alternate public defenders. They generally wandered in between nine and ten. Frank and I were both punctual and always tried to resolve as many of our cases as we could before the other defense attorneys showed up.

Attorneys came and went, pretrial motions were heard and ruled upon, defendants were arraigned and their bail amounts were set, cases were resolved or continued. The morning wore away and no J. T. Sloats appeared. The Norton case was the last matter remaining on our calendar, and the judge was becoming impatient. Finally he asked the defendant where his attorney might be. "We have not heard from attorney Sloats, Mr. Norton. Have you had any contact?"

Before the defendant could reply, the double doors at the back of the courtroom crashed open and a corpulent woman in a beige business suit barreled into the room. Her hair was short and slicked back behind her ears with the aid of some sort of oleaginous pomade. Her complexion was mottled and shiny. It seemed to me that even the fabric of her suit had a greasy sheen. She was pulling one of those large, cumbersome briefcases on wheels and managed to slam it resoundingly against the little swinging door that separates the audience from the attorneys. J. T. Sloats was a woman who knew how to make an entrance.

"May I have a moment to speak with defense counsel off the record?"

I asked. The judge nodded, so I immediately introduced myself and provided the new discovery materials I had recently acquired.

"What the hell is this?" Ms. Sloats growled as she snatched the reports and photographs from me and started hastily shuffling through them. I was taken aback, but I always resist being drawn into an argument. I explained that I had just been transferred to this courtroom, had discovered that this case needed attention, and had been working diligently to get the case ready for trial.

"Why didn't I get this stuff before now?"

"Because none of it existed until yesterday. The first time I myself saw these reports and photographs was at about 3 P.M. yesterday."

"Right," my opponent barked in a tone bristling with disbelief.

"Your Honor," I said, redirecting my attention toward the bench, "if we could go back on the record?"

I've found it preferable to converse with difficult attorneys on the record for two reasons: it usually serves to tone down the rhetoric, and having one's representations memorialized is a good thing when your opponent is the type who might be capable of inventive or selective recollection. Something told me that Ms. Sloats and I would be talking exclusively on the record for the duration.

There was another reason that militated against needless personal contact with this defense attorney. She reeked! This was not just a mild case of B.O. — this was felony B.O. with an enhancement for the added stench of heavy, sweet perfume and stale, sour coffee breath. Ugh. Being in close proximity to Ms. Sloats made me feel like puking.

Could I, literally, stomach an entire jury trial with this woman? I positioned myself at the farthest end of my side of counsel table, and the rest of our colloquy was conducted on the record and at a distance. Unfortunately, this did nothing to improve the content.

"Your Honor," Ms. Sloats began angrily, "the prosecution has just handed me some last-minute discovery materials. I need time to review them. I must demand a further continuance of the trial date."

"You have thirty days from today, Ms. Sloats," His Honor replied mildly. "I can't imagine that Ms. Batt has given you anything so complex that it would require more than a month to 'review,' as you put it. The trial date will remain."

"This is a discovery violation!" Ms. Sloats roared. "I demand sanctions against the D.A.!"

"Ms. Sloats," the judge replied in a tone one might use to lecture a dull-witted child, "there is no violation of any sort. I couldn't help overhearing your conversation with Ms. Batt. You could not have received this discovery in a more timely fashion. Many lawyers wait until the case has been sent to a trial court before they provide copies of photographs and other potential exhibits. This case is sent to 100 on the date previously set. Bail up to stand."

"One hundred?" Ms. Sloats asked, looking completely blank.

"Perhaps your practice doesn't bring you to the CCB often?" His Honor responded with the hint of a smile. "Department 100 is our master calendar court. If this case does not settle in 100, it will be assigned to a courtroom for jury trial. And you can save your paper, it is unlikely this matter will be back before me."

I doubted Ms. Sloats knew what the judge meant by "paper." He was referring to an Affidavit of Prejudice, declaring an attorney's belief that a particular judge is unfit to hear a particular case. Paper can be used as a noun or a verb, as in "I laid some paper on that idiot in Department 134" or "I papered the bozo in 134."

"Incidentally," His Honor continued, "what does J. T. stand for?"

"If you don't mind, I prefer to be addressed as J. T. Sloats. This is the name I use. The initials will have to suffice." With that, J. T. Sloats turned on her heel and stamped out of the courtroom, her briefcase once again colliding with the swinging door. Norton and his mother followed her, like loyal retainers, into the hallway.

"Oh brother!" the court reporter said, blinking his eyes and fanning the air in front of his face as if that might dissipate the odor. "Oh brother!"

AN EXHIBIT

I had talked to John Winston. I had talked to Victoria Cathcart. I had talked to Dr. Miller. I had read the entire medical file and looked at all the films. And I was still completely unprepared for what I saw that afternoon.

John Winston and Jesús Ramírez had been ushered into the conference room on the eighteenth floor. The receptionist, Eva Cortez, buzzed me in my office. Her voice was a strained whisper.

"Marissa, there are two gentlemen here to see you. A man with a British accent and a . . ." Her voice trailed off.

"Thanks, Eva. Do you want to send them down to my office?"

"Uh, I think it might be better if you came over here," Eva said, still whispering.

I took her advice, gathered up my file and a yellow tablet, and walked over to the conference room. I stopped at Eva's desk on my way in. Before I could say a word, she spoke.

"Marissa, I've worked here almost thirty years. I've been the receptionist for four district attorneys. And I've never seen anything so awful. The death penalty is too good for whoever did this!"

I nodded sadly and walked into the conference room. A tall, distinguished gentleman with beautifully coifed silver hair immediately rose from his seat and extended his hand.

"It is a pleasure to finally meet with you in person. I'd like to introduce you to Jesús. Jesús, this is Ms. Batt. Can you shake her hand? Can you say 'hello'?"

I extended my hand and hoped that my features were composed. The individual who now rose laboriously to his feet bore only a fleeting resemblance to a human being. The head was hideously distorted, permanently tilted like a planet on its axis with a deep indentation in the right side of the cranium and the rest of the skull a collection of acute angles. The cheekbones, eyes, and mouth presented a horror of asymmetry. The right eye hung distended from its socket, a milky film covering the iris, while the left orb darted incessantly from side to side in a nervous nystagmus. The mouth was contorted into a lurid grin, investing the face with a perpetually grotesque expression. I could see an expanse of naked gums with only two teeth visible, like a couple of old tombstones tilting out of the ground.

Jesús Ramírez politely extended a hand, which I clasped in both of mine. I felt my throat constricting and tears forming. Jesús was making strange noises that sounded like high-pitched giggles interrupted by an occasional choking sound. I managed to offer a greeting and was astounded to hear Jesús respond with "*hola*" in a muffled tone. Then the giggling and choking resumed.

"The giggling is a result of the brain damage, I'm told," John explained. "It can be a trifle off-putting at first, but you get used to it. The choking, on the other hand, is a serious problem. It's an impairment of the gag reflex, as it's called. Jesús has to think about swallowing very carefully, don't you, dear boy?"

"*Sí, mucho cuidado,*" came the muffled rejoinder.

"Oh, that's another matter," John told me. "Jesús has reverted back to Spanish since the injury. I believe he no longer has any English at his disposal. What little he says, he says in Spanish. If you'd like to put any questions to him, I'd be happy to translate. I'm fluent in several languages—French, Italian, and Spanish."

I took John up on his offer and confirmed my suspicions: Jesús was much more an exhibit than a witness. He had no memory of the attack whatsoever and was unable to comprehend most of my questions. I chose not to prolong the interview. It was an obvious strain on both Jesús and Mr. Winston. And it wasn't doing me any good, either.

I rose from the table and thanked both men for making the trip to visit me at the courthouse. I explained to John that I did intend to call Jesús to the stand but that my questioning would be very brief.

"The jury needs to see what that fiend did to another human being," John stated flatly.

"Exactly."

"Oh, one last matter before we go," John said. "Jesús has been asking if he might visit his mother in Mexico. Perhaps just for a few days. His uncle will come up and get him and then bring him back. I personally think it would do Jesús a world of good. And we'd have him back before the trial starts. The doctor at Rancho Los Amigos has given his approval, but I thought it prudent to check with you as well."

"*Extraño a mi madre. Tengo que volver a mi casa,*" came the muffled entreaty.

"He says —" John began, but I interrupted. No translation was necessary. How could I refuse such a request?

"Just make sure Jesús is back in L.A. before the trial starts" was all I could say.

RASHOMON REVISITED

Lee had spent quite a bit of time scheduling interviews with the various members of the Stalwarts. A few retirees were willing to come down to the CCB for interviews. The members with jobs were not eager to take time off from work to be interviewed, so we scheduled them in the evenings at their homes. This made for some long days for Lee and me, but it was worth it not to alienate any of our witnesses.

Because there were so many people to interview, Lee and I decided to concentrate our attention on the members of Patrol Number One, those who had been present during the attack: George Clarke, Lloyd and Shirley Linden, Aram Mansouri, Larry and Susan Goldfarb, Donna Ritter and Rachel Stern, and, of course, Jean-Luc St. Pierre.

We visited George Clarke at home. Jorge greeted us at the door and invited us to sit out on the patio. It was a balmy evening. The pool lights were on, and the rippling water cast an undulating light on the pool house at the far end of the property. A dozen or more amber glass lanterns hung from the wooden beams overhead, and the sound of crickets and wind chimes added to the ambiance.

Jorge immediately offered lemonade, which we accepted. Before I could take my first sip, I knew something was going on. Both men seemed nervous. Jorge kept running back to the kitchen—for napkins, for candles, for coasters. George was pacing back and forth. I looked at Lee. She shrugged her shoulders.

"Is something wrong?" I asked. Obviously something was.

"You haven't heard?" Jorge responded. I shook my head.

"Well," George said, "that fellow John Winston has sued the Stalwarts! Apparently, Robert sued Jesús Ramírez for attacking him first, and Winston countersued, or whatever you lawyers call it, on behalf of Jesús against Norton and all of the Stalwarts."

Great, I thought, just great. It always complicates a criminal prosecution to have a civil litigation waiting in the wings. The witnesses are more concerned about sidestepping liability than telling the truth. And the most scrupulously honest witness will have his credibility questioned whenever money is involved. Invariably the jury will learn of the pending civil case. It's hard to argue that it isn't relevant.

"I'll talk to Mr. Winston and find out what's going on," I began. "But meanwhile we have to prepare for the criminal case, which will go to trial next month. It could take years for the civil matter to be resolved. And, quite frankly, from what I know of the facts, it seems that Norton was acting alone and his tortious acts couldn't possibly be imputed to anyone else. Now, I'm not a civil lawyer and I cannot give you legal advice, but I can tell you this: don't let this civil case get in the way of justice. Just tell the truth and don't worry."

"It's easy for you to say," Jorge said. "You're not one of the defendants."

"This whole situation is unnerving." I forced myself to speak calmly. "But we have got to keep ourselves focused. First things first. Let's prepare for the criminal trial. I would guess that once Norton is convicted, the civil matter will no longer have any viability. That's not any fancy legal reasoning—that's plain common sense."

That seemed to have a beneficial effect on the Georges. They both sat down at the patio table and I interviewed George.

Before beginning I suggested, perhaps too delicately, that it would be better if Jorge were not present during the interview. By being present, Jorge made himself a witness to everything that George said and thus could conceivably be called by the defense to impeach George. Jorge was, both literally and figuratively, unmoved by my entreaty. He stayed put and, perhaps for emphasis, put his hand on George's forearm.

After all of that, I learned very little from George. He stated that he had heard what he believed was Norton's flashlight striking the pavement approximately four to six times. He did not actually see what happened because it was dark and he was too far away. He never got close enough to the victim to see whether or not he was injured. He had relied on what Norton said and had gone home without checking for himself. He recalled that, in addition to Robert, the only other people close enough to see whether or not the victim had been injured were Robert's two friends. He had met them only a couple of times and thought one was named Jim something and could not remember the other man's name.

During the next few days, Lee and I interviewed the rest of Patrol Number One. Lloyd and Shirley were happy to come downtown and meet us at the courthouse. They seemed less concerned than the others about the pending civil lawsuit. "Bunch of foolishness" was what Shirley said. "Pack of ruddy lies" was Lloyd's assessment.

We interviewed the Lindens separately and didn't learn much from either of them regarding the night in question. Neither had actually seen the attack. They both had heard sounds like metal striking pavement. Neither had checked on the condition of the victim. Shirley thought George might have gotten close enough to see something, but Lee and I knew otherwise. Lloyd was pretty sure Norton's two friends were named Jim Weaver and Cameron Hill. "Couple of losers, if you ask me," Lloyd added.

Aram Mansouri met us over the lunch hour at the Hollywoodland Schoolhouse. He offered us tuna sandwiches, apples, and Fig Newton cookies, the menu for the day. He could not have been more gracious. Nor could he have been more garbled in his rendition of the facts. He was foggy on everything from what day of the week it was to what time it was when the patrol arrived at Seward and Santa Monica. He could not recall who was in Patrol Number One nor remember what, if anything, Norton had said that dissuaded the others from approaching the victim.

The only thing Aram remembered clearly was the sound of the flashlight striking "that poor man's head." Of course, he didn't know at the time what had caused the sound. He had learned most of what he now "knew" from reading all the articles about the case that had appeared in the local papers. Aram Mansouri would be useless as a witness.

It was a marathon effort, but Lee and I continued the interview process at an average pace of at least one witness a day. Of course, this was on top of all our other work and had to be accomplished when I wasn't obliged to be in court.

We met with Larry and Susan Goldfarb late one afternoon in my office. They had recently retired (he from the garment industry and she as a librarian) and moved to Los Angeles from Manhattan to be with their son who lived in the Hollywood area. They suddenly had time on their hands and had decided to do volunteer work. Thus their involvement with the Stalwarts.

We interviewed Larry first. He also was worried about the ramifications of the civil lawsuit and was reticent to say anything. Once Lee and I reassured him, he proved to be a cooperative witness and remembered quite a few details regarding the evening in question. He remembered that Robert had told everyone to go home and that Jean-Luc had lagged behind after the rest of the patrol left Seward. He himself never looked at the man on the pavement.

Susan Goldfarb also had a good memory. She remembered the times involved, the route the patrol took, who was present, and what Norton had said. She recalled that only Norton and his two friends got close enough to see the man on the pavement. She remembered that Jean-Luc had used binoculars and thought maybe he had seen something that could be helpful.

We met Rachel Stern at her home in Hollywood after work. She and her partner, Donna Ritter, were both landscape designers. They had met Victoria Cathcart through the Conservancy and had met the

Georges by virtue of their business. With those connections, their involvement with the Stalwarts was assured.

"We didn't have a choice" was the way Rachel put it.

Donna was out of town, but Rachel made it clear that they both would cooperate with us even though they weren't thrilled to be witnesses. Rachel's memory was good on many points and she was particularly helpful regarding the changes that had occurred on Seward Avenue in the months since the attack. She pointed out that the trees had grown markedly and that one of the warehouses had been repainted.

Like the other witnesses, Rachel never got close enough to see the man on the pavement. She thought Lloyd might have seen something, but, again, we knew otherwise. Lee and I thanked Rachel for her help and made a note when Donna would be back in town.

We had saved our interview with Jean-Luc for last. As he was our most critical witness, we wanted to know what everyone else's testimony would be before we spoke with him. He was standing in front of the Georges' home, binoculars around his neck, when we came by to pick him up. We had decided to wait until dark and have Jean-Luc walk us through the entire evening, including the attack and his return to the scene and discovery of the victim.

The time Lee and I spent with Jean-Luc was invaluable. He was calm, coherent, and detailed in his recollections. After taking the guided tour with Jean-Luc, we knew firsthand the route taken by Patrol Number One, the lighting conditions, the distances, and the time frames involved. We even knew how objects appeared through the very same binoculars our witness had used on the evening of the assault.

We had done it. In less than two weeks, Lee and I had interviewed all of the members of Patrol Number One including Donna Ritter. We ended up interviewing her telephonically because we felt it was important to provide Ms. Sloats with a complete set of follow-up reports as quickly as possible. I didn't need more static from her.

Lee and I were exhausted and we should have had a sense of accomplishment, but we didn't. The problem was that no one—not a single person—had seen what actually happened. Not even Jean-Luc.

A DELICATE MANEUVER

Wait a minute. There were two people who had probably witnessed the entire attack, Jim Weaver and Cameron Hill. I called Victoria and confirmed that Lloyd had gotten their names right. Lee's face wore a resigned smile. I didn't have to tell her what to do. Find those two losers and interview them.

It was Friday. Another two weeks and we'd be in trial—finally. I needed the weekend. I wanted some uninterrupted time to concentrate on *People v. Norton*. I know what you're thinking. Why not take a couple of days off and just relax? There was simply too much work to do and most of it was the kind I had to do myself, by myself.

I needed to collect my thoughts. Many trial lawyers write their closing arguments before they even pick a jury. I'm one of those. It's an attempt to envision the entire trial, not just your own case in chief, but also the defense case and possible rebuttal. I also pull all the potential jury instructions well ahead of time. Without a legal framework, you cannot build a strong factual case. If you don't know what you need to prove to convict someone of a particular crime, you won't know which witnesses to call and what questions to ask.

The order of witnesses is important, as is knowing which witness will be used to lay the foundation for which piece of physical evidence. If you want your jury to see Exhibit One early in the trial and Witness A is the only one who can lay a foundation for that piece of evidence, then you'd better call Witness A to the stand early in the game.

One of my favorite parts of a trial is cross-examination of the defendant. It doesn't always happen. Sometimes the defense strategy will involve keeping the client off the stand and harping on all the weaknesses in the prosecution's case. This strategy is usually employed when the client is so obnoxious that it is a guarantee the jury will hate him. Whether or not the prosecution's case has weaknesses is generally a secondary consideration.

In this case Norton would have to take the stand in order to explain to the jury how he was forced to defend himself against a raging, knife-wielding lunatic. I knew that the defendant would be obliged to lie, and it was on that premise that I began composing my cross-examination. No knife had been found at the scene, none of the witnesses had observed one, and I was convinced that Jesús was unarmed at the time of the attack. I intended to ask detailed questions regarding the appearance of the knife and the manner in which Jesús allegedly used it.

Would the defendant say that he struck the pavement with his flashlight or would he acknowledge that he bashed in the victim's cranium? This was the key area for cross-examination. By the time Norton took the stand, he would have heard all the witnesses say that it "sounded" like a metal flashlight striking the pavement but that they never actually saw what happened. Would he say that he merely struck the pavement? If so, I would nail him. Is that the way a rational person defends himself against someone coming at him with a knife? If Norton didn't strike Jesús, how did Jesús get those devastating injuries? And why wasn't Norton injured?

On the other hand, if Norton admitted striking the victim with the flashlight, he'd be in trouble. How many blows did it take before the victim was incapacitated? And, if the victim was injured, why did Norton tell the rest of the Stalwarts that he was merely "stunned" or "playing 'possum"? What kind of monster shatters a man's skull and leaves him to die on the street with brains and blood oozing out onto the pavement?

I was so deep in thought that I failed to realize that the phone was ringing. When the sound penetrated my consciousness, I ran down the hall and snatched up the receiver.

"This is Marissa," I said and then realized it was Saturday morning and I was at home. I quickly revised my greeting: "I mean, hello."

"Are you all right?" It was Lee Benson.

"Yeah. I forgot where I was for a second. I've been working on our case since early morning and I guess I thought I must be at work. What's up?"

"Located both of the 'losers' for you."

"I'm writing a letter of commendation to your captain. Or maybe I should just send it straight to the chief."

Lee explained that it hadn't been hard to find Weaver and Hill. Running them through DMV was all it took. Neither had a criminal record. Both resided in Hollywood. Lee had "door-knocked" their respective apartments and left business cards the night before with no results.

"What do you think?" I asked.

"What do *you* think?" Lee responded with a laugh.

"I say let's give it a shot right now."

"Why am I not surprised? I'll pick you up in fifteen."

"This is going to be a delicate maneuver, Lee."

"I know. If they're not prosecution witnesses, then they're accessories after the fact."

"You're reading my mind again. I'm not big on formal grants of immunity—tends to undermine the value of a witness's testimony. On the other hand, I'll need to assure them that they are not potential defendants."

Saturday morning proved to be an excellent time to find both Weaver and Hill at home. We hit Weaver first at his studio apartment on Las Palmas near Lexington. It was around 10 A.M. when he answered the door wearing a doofus expression, green plaid boxer shorts nestled beneath a prodigious belly, and little else.

"Oh man" was the only greeting he offered. We each identified ourselves by producing our badges and business cards and then apologized for intruding at such an unseemly hour and on the weekend. Jim seemed slightly flustered, asked us to excuse him for a moment, and shut the door. Minutes elapsed and just when Lee and I were wondering if he had slipped out the back, the door opened and Mr. Jim Weaver reappeared, now garbed in jeans and a Metallica T-shirt.

"Uh, I'd invite you in but the place is kind of a mess right now. Would it be okay if we just talked in the hallway?" It was fine with me. Over the years I had been to more than my share of filthy, foul-smelling, vermin-invested dumps. If Weaver said his place was a mess, I was willing to take his word for it.

Before I did anything else, I handed Jim a subpoena. If things got tense, I didn't want him running back into his apartment without being served. He looked at the document as though he had no idea what it was.

"It's a subpoena," I said helpfully. "You know, a court order that you appear as a witness in the case involving Mr. Norton. I know you'll want to help in any way you can. We want to make sure we understand the true facts of the case, and we believe you can help us." This was my standard opening gambit when dealing with a potential defense witness.

Lee had one foot propped up on an old ash can that was sitting in the hallway. Her notebook was open and resting on her knee. She began by asking Weaver the standard questions regarding his name, date of birth, driver's license number, and so forth. We then segued into his relationship with Norton ("good buddies"), how long they had known each other ("since we were kids"), what he was doing with the Stalwarts on the night of the attack ("just hanging out"), and then what he actually saw ("not much").

That would never do. Lee and I pounced on Weaver. We let him know that we had a whole legion of witnesses who would testify that he was inches away from the victim when Norton struck him. That information had the desired effect.

"Okay," Jim responded, his pale complexion becoming suddenly blotchy. "I'll tell you everything, but don't let Robert know I talked to you. He told me not to."

Lee and I exchanged glances. Such a promise was not possible; everything Weaver told us would be memorialized and given to J. T. Sloats in the form of a supplemental police report. Norton would know exactly what Weaver told us.

"Just tell us what you saw and you won't have anything to worry about," Lee said in her most reassuring tone.

"Well," Jim began, "I was standing right behind Robert when he caught up with the dope dealer. It was kinda dark. Robert took a swing at him with his flashlight and the little guy went down. Then Robert got down on one knee and kept swinging that big flashlight. Then we left." Jim's face was now completely flushed.

"When he was swinging the flashlight, did he hit anything?" I asked, being careful not to lead the witness. Weaver hesitated, so I continued, "Everyone told us that there was this loud cracking sound, so obviously the flashlight was connecting with something."

"Yeah," Jim agreed, a stricken look on his face.

"The witnesses also told us that you took a close look at the dope dealer before you left the scene," I said in a measured tone. No one had said anything of the sort, but I figured I had nothing to lose.

"Yeah," Weaver agreed, looking extremely unwell.

"What did it look like?" My choice of pronoun was intentional. Dehumanizing the victim would make it easier for Norton's good buddy to tell the truth.

"It was pretty gross," Jim confessed. When I looked at him expectantly, he continued, "There was a lot of blood around the guy's head and there was some stuff on the ground. I guess it was his brains or something. I didn't hang around. I just wanted to get home."

"I don't blame you," I said soothingly, and Lee echoed my expression of sympathy by vigorously nodding her head. Weaver's complexion was slowly returning to its original sallow hue.

Now that the ice had been broken, Jim Weaver seemed happy to tell us everything. He seemed relieved, as if, by telling us, he was absolving himself of any complicity in the crime. The information began to pour out of Weaver like someone had opened a spigot. There was no need to interpose a question. Lee was writing furiously. If Robert Norton was counting on Weaver as a defense witness, our defendant was in for a rude surprise.

As soon as we were outside Weaver's apartment building, Lee and I practically bolted for her patrol car.

"Think we can make it in time?" I asked.

"Not before he calls him," Lee answered. "I just don't want to have to go looking for him."

We arrived not a second too soon. Cameron Hill was heading down the steps of his apartment building just as we were walking up.

"Mr. Hill," Lee said, "this is for you." Lee wasted no time in serving Hill with his subpoena.

Cameron Hill was tall and rangy, with bad skin and eyes so pale I could not discern if they were blue or green. He was dressed in shredded blue jeans and an AC-DC tank top. Completing the ensemble was a small tuft of yellow lip hair, a tattoo of barbed wire encircling one meager bicep, and ears pierced to accommodate earrings that in every way resembled wine corks.

"Oh shit" was Cameron's initial comment. Although it was clear that he knew who we were and why we were there, Lee formally introduced us and we went through our badge and business card routine.

"Would you like to talk inside or out here on the street?" Lee wanted to know.

"I was just going for a burger," Hill informed us.

"We'll give you a lift," Lee responded cheerfully, wrapping one of her muscular arms around Cameron's thin shoulders and guiding him toward the patrol car. Before he could think of an excuse, we were rolling toward the nearest McDonald's. Cameron ordered two Quarter Pounders, and had his Coke and fries supersized. When presented with the bill, he hesitated and turned to us.

"Sorry to disappoint," I said, "but we have a policy against buying meals for our witnesses or providing them with anything that could be interpreted as consideration for their testimony. I'm sure you understand." Cameron scowled slightly as he dug a wad of bills out of his pocket.

We sat down at a table, Lee with a cup of coffee, I with an iced tea, and watched Hill inhale his meal.

"You must have a great metabolism," Lee commented, a tinge of envy in her voice.

"My mom says I must have a tapeworm." Cameron laughed. The food seemed to be improving our witness's disposition, so I started firing questions, and between mouthfuls Cameron provided answers. He knew Robert through Jim and had only known our defendant for about a year. Although he also referred to the victim as "the dope dealer," he hadn't actually seen any contraband. Nor had he seen a knife. Nor had he seen the victim attack Norton.

"He just sort of spun around when Robert came up behind him."

"What happened next?" I asked the prosecutor's favorite question.

"Robert hit the guy with his flashlight and the little dude went down." It seemed like everyone took note of Jesús's small stature. This, I knew, would not be lost on the jury. Cameron told us that, although he didn't actually see Norton hit the victim again, once he had him on the ground, it was obvious that he had struck him in the head.

"Why do you say that?"

"Because I heard his head was bashed in."

"Did you see it?"

"No. I didn't look. The sound was enough for me."

STATE OF MIND

"That went rather well," Lee commented on our way back. "You should be thrilled. You handled those two losers perfectly. Wait until I type up these follow-ups and you give them to the defense attorney. I bet Norton will want to plea bargain."

"Don't count on it. You know, I should tell Lloyd Linden that his judgment was too harsh. Jim and Cameron may not be winners, but I don't think of them as losers anymore."

I liked Lloyd. He was opinionated but backed up his opinions with fact. Even though he hadn't actually seen it, he knew that Norton had bashed in that young man's head. But was it attempted murder or merely an assault with a deadly weapon? Lloyd had been positive that Norton had intended to kill Jesús. On what facts was he basing this opinion?

Lee looked exhausted. I decided to handle reinterviewing Lloyd on my own. Lloyd was a thoroughly cooperative witness, so there was no need to have my detective there for impeachment purposes. I'd take my own notes and make a copy for J. T. Sloats.

It was early afternoon by the time I got home. I immediately picked up the phone and called Lloyd. I was prepared to get in my car and go back to Hollywood, but Lloyd suggested I spare myself the trip and interview him over the phone.

As clearly as I could, I explained the legal and factual problems associated with proving an attempt-murder charge. "Not only do I have to prove what Norton was thinking at the time of the attack, I have to prove his state of mind beyond a reasonable doubt."

"You've got your work cut out for you," Lloyd said. "How can I help?"

Robert Norton was on his own personal crusade to clean up Hollywood, to rid the city of pimps, prostitutes, drug dealers, and other undesirables. I asked Lloyd to tell me about any statements Robert might have made or anything he might have done that would demonstrate this fervor.

There was silence on the other end of the line. Then Lloyd spoke.

"I'm not sure this is what you have in mind, but there were a couple of episodes with Robert that I found very disturbing."

Lloyd proceeded to tell me about an attack on two transvestites. It had occurred about six or seven months prior to the assault on Jesús. Lloyd and Robert were assigned to the same Stalwarts patrol on this occasion, and when Robert came upon a couple of transvestites walking on Hollywood Boulevard, he left the patrol to follow them. Lloyd felt uneasy and decided to follow Robert. He observed Norton swinging his flashlight and screaming at the two individuals.

"Do you remember what Norton was saying?"

"I'll never forget it. He said, 'You degenerates make me sick. If I catch you out on the streets again, you're dead. I'll bash your ugly heads in.'"

I was writing this down word for word. Under Evidence Code Section 1101(b), this testimony would probably be admissible to prove Norton's intent to kill Jesús.

The other episode was more recent. About a week before our crime, Lloyd had seen Robert confronting a young Hispanic man outside Robert's house on McCadden. The young man was holding a spray paint can and Norton was screaming at the top of his lungs.

"Do you remember what he said?"

"Sure do. He tells the man not to move a muscle. Then Robert runs to his car, which was parked right in front of his house. He opens the trunk and pulls out a shotgun! Good thing I happened to be driving by. It was early in the morning and there wasn't a soul around. I stopped my car right in the middle of the street and jumped out. Norton racked the shotgun and the man started running. I asked Robert what he intended to do with that shotgun. Know what he said? 'If you hadn't shown up, I'd have blown his head off!'"

"Are you positive that's what he said?"

"Positive."

THE TRIP HOME

My telephone was ringing as I entered my office a little before 8 A.M. Monday morning. It was one week before the Norton matter was set to go to trial. I snatched the receiver off the hook before the voice mail could kick in.

"This is Marissa."

"This is John Winston."

"Oh, I'm glad it's you, John. I didn't recognize your voice for a second. You're on my short list of folks I need to talk to. I've been told that civil lawsuits have been filed. That Norton has sued Jesús and that, on behalf of Jesús, you cross-complained against Norton and all the Stalwarts. Is that correct?"

"Not anymore." I realized that John was crying.

"What's going on?"

"Jesús is gone." John's voice quavered.

"John, we all agreed that the trip to Mexico was a good idea. I know you're fond of him and you must miss him, but you needed a rest too."

"No, you don't understand. He's gone—gone. His uncle rang me up early this morning and told me. Jesús passed away last night."

"No!" It took me a moment to process what John was saying. "Tell me what happened."

John relayed what little information he had. There had been a party in honor of Jesús's homecoming. His mother had made tamales. All the neighbors had come over. Apparently Jesús had choked on a piece of food and no one knew what to do. By the time a doctor arrived from the nearest town, Jesús was dead. Because of the lack of mortuary facilities in Los Cerritos, Jesús had been buried immediately.

"John, I'm going to have to call you back. There are some things I need to check on immediately, and I'll be back in touch later on today. Please try to take care of yourself, okay?"

"Okay," John responded without conviction.

As soon as the connection with John was broken, I dialed another number.

"Department of the Coroner, Office of the Medical Examiner, may I help you?"

"Hi, Esther. This is Marissa calling for Dr. Lakshmanan."

"Hey, Marissa, how are you doing? I think he's in a meeting—as usual."

"Normally I wouldn't ask you to interrupt a meeting, but I need to talk to him immediately. I just got word that my victim on an upcoming trial died last night in Mexico and it's an attempt-murder case and I need to know if we ever send a coroner to a foreign country and how should I handle the exhumation and —"

"Wait, wait," Esther interrupted. "I'll get him on the line for you."

In a matter of moments, I was speaking to the coroner of Los Angeles County. Dr. Lakshmanan Sathyavagiswaran and I had known each other professionally for many years. We had first met a decade earlier when he was one of a dozen deputy medical examiners performing autopsies downtown.

I had been given a special assignment involving the prosecution of two Italian gentlemen for "fixing" drunk driving cases in one of the outlying courthouses. Law enforcement was sure that organized crime was involved and was convinced that a full investigation would reveal that the judges in that jurisdiction were on the take. My key witness was a twenty-three-year-old crook who had found God, found true love, and wanted to make amends before he married the girl of his dreams.

My youthful snitch had worked as the capper for the two defendants.

He had been the one who would make the initial contact with the arrestees and let them know that, for a fee, the deuce, or drunk driving charge, would—magically—be memorialized in the official court records as a moving violation, or what we call a mover. His testimony would provide the linchpin evidence connecting the defendants to the court personnel.

The night before the preliminary hearing, my informant turned up dead. In an attempt to secure some easy brownie points with my macho boss, I offered to attend the postmortem, confident that my supervisor would direct me not to—and equally confident that my willingness to subject myself to something so gruesome would be noted with approval. To my utter chagrin, my superior was delighted with my suggestion and ordered me to be present at the autopsy.

I had never attended a postmortem examination before, and the stress of the event was intensified exponentially by the fact that I had known the victim. And known him well. I had met his family and his fiancée. I had spent hours with him, day after day, as he explained the intricate methods used by the defendants to falsify official documents. And I had become privy to the man's motivations. This was someone who had decided to change his destiny, to rid himself of his criminal past like a snake shedding its skin, and to spend the rest of his life as a model citizen.

If it had not been for Lakshmanan's professionalism, sensitivity, and utter kindness, I do not believe I would have been able to muster the emotional strength to witness the autopsy. He helped me transcend the grisly scene before my eyes and focus my attention on the forensic issues. Had my young snitch taken his own life, died of natural causes, been the victim of an accident, or—as I suspected—been murdered?

That question will never be answered, although the autopsy did reveal the cause of death. My witness had died as the result of a drug overdose. The drug was codeine. Both the stomach contents and the serology report confirmed this conclusion.

I was able to add something to the equation. I knew that my witness had been a migraine sufferer and this was his prescribed medication. That information supported a finding of accidental death or suicide. Suicide was unlikely. There was no note, and the victim had not demonstrated depression or voiced any suicidal ideations. On the contrary, he was looking forward to his new life as one of the good guys.

Was there evidence that the victim had taken the medication against his will? Had someone screwed a gun to his head and forced him to swallow too many pills? A dissection of the esophagus disclosed no trauma. But a close examination of the heart showed massive occlusion of the coronary arteries. My twenty-three-year-old witness had been carrying around the heart of a sick old man.

Over the intervening years, Lakshmanan and I had become more than professional associates. Our shared appreciation for Indian music, dance, and cuisine laid the groundwork for an enduring friendship. I was thrilled when Lakshmanan was selected as *the* coroner. I always dropped the title "Dr." when we spoke, because I knew I was addressing him by his first name, employed as a last name only to facilitate pronunciation by the linguistically timid.

Mindful that Lakshmanan had been called out of a meeting to take my call, I spoke quickly and provided him with only the essential facts.

"I am sorry, Marissa," the doctor said, "but there is nothing we can do. Even assuming you could cut through red tape and get the body exhumed immediately and we could fly an autopsy surgeon down to Mexico with a portable laboratory, it would be too late. It is already too late. Given the climate of the region during the summer months, combined with an unembalmed subject, the degree of decomposition would make a meaningful autopsy impossible—particularly in this case where examination of the brain and cranium is essential. The brain would have liquefied by now. I am sorry."

I thanked my friend for his help and we both promised that, when time permitted, we would meet for dinner at our favorite restaurant, the Bombay Palace, and that we would discuss everything—everything except work.

A Hinky Feeling

What else could go wrong? I had pushed the case to trial, only to have my victim die before we could even pick a jury. If Jesús had expired in Los Angeles and there had been a prompt postmortem, I would probably be amending the charges against Norton to strike the word "attempt." As it was, there was no way I could establish the causal connection between the bludgeoning and the death. So there I was, obliged to try what I knew was a murder case as a mere assault.

And I was worried about John Winston. Losing Jesús had emotionally eviscerated him. He called several times a day, just to talk. About Jesús. About what I thought would happen to the case now that Jesús was dead. About how miserable he was. John was driving me crazy.

My strategy was to give John assignments to perform. It was a device designed to help me and to force John to do something productive rather than moping around the house all day and calling me incessantly. One assignment was to locate before-and-after photographs of our victim. The painful counterpoint would be graphically demonstrated for the benefit of the jury.

The Stalwarts' collective reaction to Jesús's death was what you might expect: genuine sorrow coupled with relief that the civil lawsuit had died with him. If anything, our victim's demise had served to galvanize the Stalwarts and strengthen their resolve to be good witnesses for the prosecution.

The day set for jury selection was upon us. I arrived at the courtroom of Judge R. Jay Ferry having done everything I could to prepare the case for trial. My opening statement and closing arguments were written, all jury instructions that could possibly pertain to the case had been pulled, every potential witness had been interviewed, and all my exhibits were in order.

Instead of being filled with a sense of abiding confidence, I had what we in law enforcement call a hinky feeling. It was a somewhat amorphous sensation, a vague but persisting cloud of unease.

I kept having the weird feeling that I was being followed. I'd be appearing on a matter in court, I'd be walking over to Olvera Street or Chinatown, I'd be eating lunch at one of my favorite hangouts on First Street, and out of the corner of my eye I'd see a large woman in a bright floral dress. At first I tried to dismiss these observations as a series of strange coincidences or figments of an overactive imagination. But it kept happening.

Lee had agreed to join me in court for jury selection—something many detectives rigorously avoid. My preference is to have the investigating officer in court, for a couple of reasons. First, it sends a strong signal to the jury that this is an important case. Second, a good I.O. can provide invaluable assistance during the voir dire process. I waited for Lee outside the courtroom and was gratified to see her round the corner with an armload of exhibits.

"You doing okay?" was her greeting.

"I'm fine. Why? Is something wrong?"

"No. Everything's fine. You just look like you feel a little —"

"Hinky?"

"Well, yes. You're not nervous about this case?"

"No, it's not that. Lee, you're going to think I've lost it, but I've been having this unnerving sensation that someone is stalking me."

"Someone in a floral dress?"

"Yes! How on earth did you know?"

"I didn't want to upset you, but I've been aware for some time that the defendant's mother had taken an unwholesome interest in my favorite prosecutor."

"You should have told me. I was starting to doubt my own sanity. Does she know where I live?"

"I don't think so. I think she's limited her activities to the downtown area. And it shouldn't happen again. I've had a long talk with her."

"Thanks. Listen, do you know anything about Judge Ferry? I've never appeared before him, but the lawyers in 100 seemed to think we'll get a good trial here."

"I've heard he's pro-prosecution and a tough sentencer."

"All I know is what I read in his bio in the *Daily Journal.* He's an ex–federal prosecutor. He's been on the Super Court bench less than five years. Sometimes those United States attorneys can be a little too white-bread for my taste."

"You make it sound like a bad thing." Lee was laughing.

We had been ordered to be in Department 108, Judge Ferry's court, at ten sharp and had about twenty minutes to go. A floral dress came into view. It was the defendant's mother, this time in the company of J. T. Sloats and the client. The trio lumbered by, pointedly ignoring our presence, and took a position on another bench on the opposite side of the hallway.

"Excuse me." It was the bailiff from 108. "His Honor wanted me to check to see if all parties are present on the Norton case. If so, he'd like to get started a little early. His morning calendar took less time than expected."

As soon as we were inside the courtroom, Judge Ferry asked Ms. Sloats and me to join him in chambers. "I see 100 has sent me an assault, attempt-murder case," the judge began.

"More like a simple battery, if you ask me," Ms. Sloats snapped.

"Really?" Judge Ferry sounded intrigued. "Please tell me about it. Perhaps we can resolve the case without a trial."

Ordinarily, this would be just what I wanted to hear from a judge. My preference is always to attempt to resolve matters by way of plea and sentence negotiation and to avoid the trauma and uncertainty of a jury trial. But the time for negotiation was long past. I had already weathered an acrimonious and unproductive pretrial conference in my home court. I had spent hundreds of hours preparing myself and my witnesses for trial. Even the judge in Department 100 had attempted to broker a plea bargain, but to no avail.

I didn't want to waste more time jawing with Ms. Sloats. Plus I really wanted to be further away from her physically. The far end of counsel table would be bad enough, but the close proximity of the judge's chambers was taking its toll. Didn't the judge smell it? *Eau de Sloats* had pervaded his chambers.

The judge wore an impassive expression. I took note of his bony face, small eyes, lipless mouth, and thin nose. Perhaps his sense of smell was mercifully impaired by those narrow little nostrils? His hands were neatly folded in his lap and his head was craned forward. He appeared almost entranced by my opponent's words.

To my amazement, Ms. Sloats was actually pitching the simple battery idea. I let her talk for a while without interruption. If she wanted to provide me with a preview of the defense case, I wanted to listen. If I understood her correctly, they were going to argue that the defendant only struck the victim once, and then only in self-defense. The horrific injuries sustained by the victim were not caused by the defendant. Someone else must have inflicted those injuries after the defendant left the scene.

What a thoroughly absurd position to take. So why was the judge nodding his head in apparent agreement?

"Tell me this, Ms. Sloats," His Honor said. "Does your young client have a criminal record?" Where was this going? Had the judge accepted the defense version of the facts? And why wasn't he asking the deputy D.A. about the accused's criminal record? And why had he characterized the defendant as "young"? My hinky feeling was coming back.

"Excuse me, Your Honor," I interrupted. "I'd like to share the People's understanding of the facts with you before we discuss a negotiated plea."

His Honor nodded his assent and I briefly outlined the facts of the case, including the extent of the injuries. It seemed to me that Judge Ferry was not nearly as transfixed by my presentation as he had been by my opponent's. Although I felt my rendition of the facts was compelling, the judge's eyes kept straying around the room. I found myself peering in the same direction.

Well, well, well. His Honor was clearly a man who held himself in high esteem. On every wall there were photographs, charcoal drawings, acrylics, and watercolors. Ferry's chambers were a virtual art gallery and the subject matter was remarkably consistent—every work of art depicted the Honorable R. Jay Ferry. There he was in a line drawing, pontificating from a lectern. Over here His Nibs could be found portrayed in pastels, luxuriantly enrobed and wielding a mean-looking gavel.

The chambers conference was going nowhere. It soon became clear that Ms. Sloats was looking for a dismissal but would settle for a misdemeanor plea and a probationary sentence. To my utter amazement, His Honor did not seem affronted by this suggestion. So much for his pro-prosecution reputation.

"Your Honor," I said, exasperation putting an edge on my voice, "this is a felony case with a probable state prison sentence. I'd be willing to take a plea to the assault charge with the GBI allegation and have the attempt-murder charge dismissed. My position on sentencing would be to recommend putting over the disposition until we can have the benefit of a 1203.03 [pronounced 'twelve-oh-three-oh-three'] diagnostic study."

Generally I don't favor sending a defendant out for a ninety-day diagnostic study. In the vast majority of cases, the court and counsel don't need the assistance of the state prison officials in determining whether or not a convicted felon is a suitable candidate for incarceration at the state level. In this case, however, we were confronted with an unusual situation—a defendant with no prior record charged with a truly heinous crime. And Judge Ferry was acting like probation was a real option. I figured a 1203.03 report recommending a state prison sentence might serve to tighten those loose judicial screws.

Ms. Sloats told us her client would have none of it. Apparently our chambers conference had served to harden the defense position. Now she was saying that Norton was disinclined to plead to anything, not even a misdemeanor. The judge shrugged his slight shoulders and instructed his clerk to call for a panel. The trial of *People v. Robert Norton* was finally getting under way, close to a year and a half after the crime had been committed.

I felt compelled to bring up a potentially touchy point. "Your Honor, before we begin jury selection, I would like the court's guidance on how much the jury may be told about the reasons for the victim's unavailability."

"What do you mean?" Ferry seemed honestly perplexed.

"I don't think they need to be told a thing!" Ms. Sloats weighed in.

"I've gone ahead and prepared a possible stipulation," I continued, ignoring Ms. Sloats's mindless comment. "Obviously, the jury will wonder where the victim is. This is not a homicide case, and we don't want our jurors drawing improper or prejudicial conclusions based on the victim's absence."

"Good point," His Honor said.

"Since when is a prosecutor concerned about protecting a defendant from prejudice?" Ms. Sloats sniped.

"Since the moment I took my oath as a deputy," I snapped back. "Plus, when I convict someone, I like the crook to stay convicted! I don't want to see any reversible error in any case I touch, okay?"

"I'll have none of that type of colloquy, Ms. Batt," His Honor said primly.

I immediately apologized although I felt it was Sloats who deserved the reprimand. For a split second I wanted to shriek, "She started it!" like an angry child. Sloats was definitely pushing my buttons.

I vowed to control myself and produced copies of my typed stipulation for the judge and defense counsel, who both spent what I thought was an inordinate time reading the thing. Here's what it said:

> The named victim in this case, Jesús Ramírez, is deceased. Although there may be testimony presented that Mr. Ramírez never completely recovered from the injuries he sustained as a result of the crimes allegedly perpetrated by the defendant, the People are not attempting to prove that the actions of the defendant resulted in the death of Mr. Ramírez.
>
> If such evidence of Mr. Ramírez's injuries is presented, it may be considered by you only as it relates to the charges and special allegations against the defendant as stated in the Information.
>
> You are not to speculate as to the nature, manner or cause of Mr. Ramírez's death. The fact that Mr. Ramírez is dead cannot be used by you as evidence of the defendant's guilt in this case.

"Well," His Honor finally said, "this seems okay to me. Counsel?"
"I guess it's all right," Sloats admitted grudgingly.

A Good-Looking Jury

Lee and I both stood and faced the back of the courtroom as our jury panel filed in. They looked great: well dressed, racially mixed, varying ages, and—most important—they looked alive. They were smiling and conversing with each other. I glanced at Lee, who smiled broadly. We were off to a good start.

Judge Ferry had a unique way of conducting the voir dire process. Typically, twelve individuals are called from the audience by the clerk, seated in the box, and questioned. When a potential juror is excused, another member of the venire is asked to take that person's seat. Some judges like to use what we call a "six-pack" system where six additional potential jurors are seated in the box at the outset. The benefit is that everyone knows who the next juror will be. Many times attorneys will feel they might as well stop while they're ahead—that the six potential jurors look worse than what they've got.

For reasons unknown to me, Judge Ferry had created his own special jury selection system, which he dubbed the "twenty-four pack." Not only was it a dumb name, it was a dumb system. His method involved cramming twenty-four folks into the jury box. Obviously, they all couldn't fit, so additional chairs were brought in and the area between counsel table and the witness box was packed with dutiful but uncomfortable potential jurors.

Because the deputy D.A. sits closest to the jury box in any courtroom, Judge Ferry's cozy configuration helped to create an immediate rapport between the jurors and me. Some of the potential jurors were only a foot or two away from where Lee and I were sitting. They could see my library of nine large green three-ring binders filled with, no doubt, important and compelling evidence to which they would soon be privy. Even though I thought this was a stupid system, I had no intention of complaining.

Jury selection proceeded quickly, at least at my end of counsel table. All the potential jurors looked good to me. Their answers to the standard inquiries, as well as to the few esoteric questions permitted by the court, were reassuring. Not only did they look good, they sounded good: thought-

ful, articulate, serious. With the exception of one young man whose ac-
quaintance with the English language seemed remote, I challenged not
a single juror, not for cause nor peremptorily.

Things were not going quite so smoothly on the other side of counsel table. Where Lee and I took a split second to confer and agree on
each juror, Sloats and Norton took what seemed like an eternity. I noted
with some satisfaction that this delay had a pronounced effect on our
judge. He played with his pencil, wiped his glasses repeatedly, examined
his manicure, and cleared his throat. This fidgeting did nothing to speed
up the process.

The prosecution kept accepting the jury "as presently constituted"
while the defense found fault with one juror after another. In addition to
causing judicial consternation, this lopsided process was having an effect
on the jury panel, an effect that could only be beneficial to the prosecution. The repeated acceptance of the continually changing jury panel
bespeaks confidence — confidence in the evidence to be presented and
confidence in the jurors who will hear the evidence. Concomitantly,
the repeated rejection of one panelist after another sends the contrary
message.

The morning ground slowly on. Judge Ferry broke for lunch, allot-
ting merely an hour, in an attempt to achieve what we call judicial economy. This maneuver failed to have a salutary effect. Thanks to Ms.
Sloats's sluggish pace, the afternoon session was characterized by the
same mind-numbing tedium as the morning session. I kept track of the
number of peremptory challenges the defense had expended and, according to my notes, we were reaching the end. The defense had used
its last.

Once again, I passed for cause and accepted the jury as constituted.
To my utter amazement, Ms. Sloats asked the court to "thank and excuse" yet another juror. His Honor did not react, so I rose to my feet and
asked that we be allowed to approach the bench.

"Is that necessary, Ms. Batt?" Ferry snarled. "We need to move matters along!"

Don't yell at me, I felt like saying, I'm not the one who's moving at a snail's pace and using more than my legal allotment of challenges. Instead I said, "Yes, it is necessary." I could have brought the defense error to the judge's attention in open court but I try to be polite.

At sidebar I informed the court of my calculations. He called the court clerk up to the bench to confirm that what I was saying was accurate. Ms. Sloats started sputtering. It wasn't fair. She should be allowed to kick this last juror who, no doubt, would be prejudiced against her client if kept on the panel. Someone should have told her that she had used all of her peremptories. His Honor seemed at a loss.

"I'll stipulate that the juror in question may be excused," I said. His Honor's pinched expression softened for a moment—score a couple of brownie points for the prosecution, I thought—but Sloats had a suspicious look on her face.

Perhaps she had noticed that the next potential juror was an uncommonly handsome Italian man who had been giving me broad smiles throughout the day. Nonetheless, Sloats was stuck between the proverbial rock and hard place, and Mr. Carlo Barzini became Juror Number Twelve.

THE PEOPLE'S CASE

Not to appear immodest, but the prosecution's case in chief went very well. After a short and straightforward opening statement, in which I had embedded some key words such as "vigilante" and "diminutive victim," I got down to business. A regiment of Stalwarts marched on and off the stand, followed by a platoon of medical and law enforcement personnel, led by the brilliant and dashing Dr. Gregory Miller.

Judge Ferry was not thrilled that I insisted on calling each and every member of the Stalwarts who had been out on patrol on the night in question. He called Ms. Sloats and me up to the bench and suggested that if defense counsel didn't register an objection soon, he would make and sustain his own and put a stop to what he called my "unnecessary parade of witnesses."

I calmly explained that I was not, and had no intention of, eliciting "cumulative" testimony, something that would be objectionable. I told His Honor that I would be happy to make an offer of proof regarding what each witness's testimony would be. That seemed to thrill Judge Ferry even less. He made a gesture akin to brushing some form of detritus off the bench, which Ms. Sloats and I interpreted to mean that we should return to our places at counsel table.

My "parade of witnesses" continued uninterrupted. It was important that the jury understand that I was giving them everything and trusting them to be able to sift out the essential facts from the evidence presented. If I had not called all these witnesses to the stand, a good defense attorney could make it appear that I was hiding something.

A witness may be called by either side. Although a truthful witness will give the same testimony whether it is elicited by the prosecution or the defense, the jury's perception of the evidence may be colored by the context in which they hear the testimony.

The only glitch in my case in chief involved Lloyd Linden. A hearing, outside the presence of the jury, was held to determine whether or not I would be allowed to present the evidence involving Norton's behavior toward the tagger and the transvestites. This testimony was critical to proving the intent element on the attempt-murder charge.

The defense attorney screamed that it would be "unfair" to her client if the jury heard this evidence. I argued that it was admissible under Section 1101(b). Unfortunately for the prosecution, the court relied upon another Evidence Code section. It was one of Judge Ferry's personal favorites — Section 352.

Section 352 provides that the court has the discretion to exclude evidence if its probative value is substantially outweighed by the probability that its admission will confuse, mislead, or prejudice the jury or unduly consume court time. The undue consumption of court time was the hook on which His Honor hung his decision.

My chances of convicting Norton on the attempt-murder charge were now Slim and None, and Slim had just pulled a groin, as the expression goes. I remonstrated with the judge that he was placing a premium on judicial economy at the expense of giving both sides a fair trial.

"I have had just about enough out of you, Ms. Batt" was His Honor's retort. Ferry spit out the sentence as if each word nauseated him.

I was beginning to think this guy didn't like me. For a split second I toyed with the idea of taking a writ, but I knew it would be a waste of time. Although the equities were on my side, there was not a chance that the writ would be granted. In this area of the law, the trial court is given wide latitude and unfettered discretion. I would have to show an abuse of discretion in order to prevail.

My strategy included calling Jim Weaver and Cameron Hill as People's witnesses. I reasoned that if the defendant's presence impeded either of them from giving truthful testimony, I could always "Green" them. This is legal shorthand for the eponymous case allowing impeachment by use of prior contradictory or inconsistent statements. Fortunately, no Greening was necessary. Both Cameron and Jim testified in complete conformance with their previous statements. Neither one looked too happy about it, but each doggedly answered the questions posed.

Ms. Sloats's efforts on cross-examination proved worse than futile. Several prosecution witnesses took umbrage at her accusatory tone. Jim Weaver was one of them. From her questions, the implication was clear: if Norton did not inflict these horrendous injuries, someone else must have. Since Weaver was the last one to take a close look at the "drug dealer," perhaps Weaver struck the punishing blows?

I could have interposed an objection—many of the questions were argumentative—but I chose not to. The more Sloats pushed, the more Weaver stood his ground. Wasn't it true that Weaver had a similar flashlight? No, it was not. Wasn't it a fact that the drug dealer was merely stunned when Weaver saw him on the pavement? Oh-oh, I thought, here it comes. One of the cardinal rules of trial advocacy is Do Not Ask a Question Unless You Know What the Answer Will Be.

"No, he was not 'stunned,'" Jim fairly shouted. "His head was bashed in, okay?"

Okay with me, I thought. It doesn't get much better than the defendant's good buddy laying out the accused in open court. The witness had not been quite so graphic on direct examination. Sloats took a long time to ask her next question. She couldn't end her cross-examination on such a sour note, but what was a safe area for inquiry?

"Isn't it true that you spent over an hour with the detective and the D.A. on this case?"

"Something like that."

"And isn't it true that they told you how to testify in this case?"

"Yes, they did."

"I thought so!" Ms. Sloats stated smugly as she wedged her substantial frame back into her chair at counsel table.

"Redirect?" His Honor asked.

"Thank you," I responded to the court, and then asked: "What exactly did Detective Benson and I tell you regarding how to testify?"

"You both said the same thing. Just tell the truth."

ICING ON THE CAKE

When I first read the police reports in the case, I had decided that, if the case went to trial, Jean-Luc would be my final witness. After all, he was the closest thing to a hero in this story, and I always like to end with a strong witness. Now, in the wake of Weaver's performance, Jean-Luc's testimony would be icing on the cake.

The direct examination went well. Jean-Luc related his observations clearly and vividly. I allowed myself a quick glance at the jury. They were alert and focused, even after spending close to two weeks in the jury box and hearing from so many other witnesses. I wondered what Sloats would try on cross-examination. Would she also accuse Jean-Luc of being the true culprit?

It turned out that Ms. Sloats had something special in store for Jean-Luc. Wasn't it true that Jean-Luc found Robert Norton to be an attractive man? Jean-Luc graciously agreed: yes, Robert was an attractive man. Wasn't it also true that Jean-Luc had made "a pass" at Robert, had been politely but firmly rebuffed, and was now testifying against the defendant for revenge?

The look on our witness's face was one of shock and anger. There was a long moment of complete silence in the courtroom while Jean-Luc stared at Ms. Sloats. Then Mr. Jean-Luc St. Pierre rose slowly to his feet in the witness box and turned directly to the jury.

"I am a gay man," he announced in a voice that filled the courtroom, "and I am not in the least ashamed to say so. I also have AIDs and have been fighting the effects of this cruel disease for several years. Quite frankly, I have not had the desire to make a pass, as you call it, at anyone for quite some time. And I have never, in my entire life, ever made any type of overture to any straight man. What an outrageous accusation! I am a thoroughly civilized man. I would never stoop to such boorish behavior!"

Jean-Luc glared at Ms. Sloats and then resumed his seat in the witness box. There was another long moment of silence, broken finally by His Honor.

"Ms. Sloats?"

"Your Honor?"

"Do you have another question?"

"Oh. No, no. Nothing further."

"Ms. Batt?"

"No further questions, thank you. With the receipt into evidence of all previously marked exhibits, the People would rest."

"Finally," I thought I heard Judge Ferry mutter under his breath.

Mystery Witness

I had assumed that, since I had called every witness I could think of in my case in chief, the defense would have only one witness to call and that would be the defendant himself. I was wrong.

We had recessed for lunch, and when court resumed in the afternoon, Ms. Sloats gave her opening statement. To my delight, she outlined a preposterous defense. In effect it was two defenses melded awkwardly together. First, it was self-defense against a vicious, knife-wielding, drugged-out dope dealer. And second, it was the ever-popular SODDI defense, i.e., Some Other Dude Did It.

Ms. Sloats informed our jury that there would be an "unimpeachable, independent eyewitness" who would confirm the validity of these two somewhat contradictory defenses. I resisted the impulse to leap to my feet and object during Ms. Sloats's presentation.

What on earth was she talking about? If she had an eyewitness, who was this person? As soon as she concluded her opening remarks, I asked if counsel might approach the bench. I got the standard sour expression coupled with a brief nod of the judicial head.

"What is it now?" His Honor wanted to know as soon as we had re-assembled at sidebar.

"Your Honor, this is the first I hear of an alleged eyewitness. I have received no reciprocal discovery —"

Judge Ferry cut me off and turned his unpleasant gaze on defense counsel. "Is this true?"

"I just found out about this witness myself," Sloats protested.

"Your Honor," I said, "the People object. This is a clear discovery violation. Unless counsel can explain to the court's satisfaction why we are learning of a hitherto undisclosed witness at this late stage in the proceedings, sanctions should be imposed. Either the defense should be barred from calling this individual as a witness or, at the very least, the People should be allowed a continuance in order to conduct our own investigation."

"We'll take our afternoon recess a bit early," the judge advised the jury and then asked Ms. Sloats and me to join him in chambers.

"Tell me about this new witness." His Honor turned to Ms. Sloats.

"Well, his name is Arthur Waterman and I have his address here somewhere," Sloats replied and began dredging in her massive briefcase. The judge and I watched as she removed a collection of items including two Diet Coke cans (one of which was open and not entirely empty), a partially eaten ham sandwich of indeterminate age, a wad of old news-papers, and what appeared to be an assortment of bills and other per-sonal correspondence.

"Your Honor," I interposed while Sloats continued to plumb the depths of her briefcase, "at a minimum, I'm going to need the witness's full name, date of birth, address, and phone number. If any statements by the witness have been memorialized, I would request copies."

"Ms. Sloats, are you able to provide this information?"

"Date of birth?" Sloats responded distractedly.

"I'll need that information to run Waterman's rap sheet," I ex-plained.

"He has no criminal record!" Sloats roared indignantly.

"We're getting nowhere," Judge Ferry observed. For once I found myself in complete agreement with the court.

"I am going to allow the defense to call this witness, but I'm going to give the prosecution the afternoon to prepare their cross-examination. I'm asking you, Ms. Sloats, to provide whatever information you have on this new witness as soon as possible. I'll excuse the jury and we will be in recess until tomorrow morning. And I trust there will be no further de-lays of this nature." The judge glowered at both of us.

As soon as we were back in the courtroom, I filled Lee in on what was happening.

"Sloats was ready to call this mystery witness to the stand, so he must be out in the hallway or somewhere close by," I said in an undertone. Lee winked at me and left the courtroom.

After court adjourned, I returned to my office to await Lee's call. I spent the time returning phone calls, reading my mail and e-mail, and looking over my closing argument. I added a few refinements based on how the testimony had played out in court. Within the hour, Lee's call came through.

"You can call me Columbo!"

"You sound very satisfied with yourself. What have you got?"

"Everything you need to take this guy apart in court. First of all, it's Waterson, not Waterman. DOB is 8-3-68 and he does have a record. It's a felony record for embezzlement plus he's got a couple DUI convictions. And here's the best part—guess where this guy lives?"

"Hmmm. Next door to the defendant?"

"How did you know? Did Sloats call?"

"Nope. Haven't heard from her and don't expect to. I just figured that this 'new' witness had to be someone the defendant knows. Probably owes Norton a favor and our boy decided this was the time to collect."

"Are you psychic? I ran Waterson through all the criminal databases and then, just for fun, I looked for him in the civil registry of actions. One of his drunk driving cases resulted in a civil lawsuit for damages. It went to trial and Waterson beat the case. I know you can guess who the critical defense witness was."

"Robert Norton?"

"Bingo!"

"Well, so much for the unimpeachable, independent eyewitness the jury has been promised."

WARMING UP

At a quarter of ten the next morning Ms. Sloats trundled over to where Lee and I were waiting in the hallway outside Department 108. Even at that hour, she looked grimy and was emitting her typical foul odor.

"Here!" Sloats said, and thrust an equally grimy piece of paper at me. My worthy opponent then stalked off down the hall. On the paper was an untidy scrawl that read:

Arthur Waterson. Date of Birth: 1968.
Residence: Los Angeles, California.

"Well, at least she got his name right and the year of his birth," Lee said, looking over my shoulder. She started laughing and then stopped abruptly when she saw the expression on my face.

"I was just thinking," I said in response to her questioning look, "about all the deputy D.A.s who might be blindsided by someone like J. T. Sloats."

So much of what makes a prosecution successful involves the diligence of the prosecutor and the investigating officer. Some deputies are quick to blame the jury when they fail to secure a conviction, but I've never seen it that way. If it's a righteous case, and the D.A. and the detective are diligent in putting it together, the jury will convict.

"I can't thank you enough for all the work you've done on this trial, Lee. And it wasn't even your case."

"Well, it sure is now. And I don't mind working my ass off for you — I know it's appreciated."

And, thanks to Detective Benson, I was able to demolish Mr. Arthur Waterson on cross-examination. His direct testimony, standing alone, might have conjured up a speck of reasonable doubt. His story was simple. He had been riding his motorcycle on Seward when he observed the defendant and a slightly smaller man facing each other on the sidewalk. It was clear to Waterson that the smaller man was the aggressor. He had an object, possibly a knife, in his left hand and was circling the defendant. The defendant was unarmed and had taken a "defensive posture."

On cross I established that Waterson was a convicted felon and that his crime involved moral turpitude. I also established that he lived next door to the defendant and had resided there for almost three years, that the defendant had been a witness for him in a civil case, and that he was here on behalf of the defendant to offer whatever help he could.

Regarding his recollections of the night in question, he wasn't sure whether he had been traveling north or south on Seward. He had been wearing a helmet because the law requires it, but it did not impede his vision. He had not been drinking and was completely sober and wide awake. He knew what he saw. The little guy was attacking Robert, no doubt about it.

If he learned that the "little guy" was right-handed, would that change his testimony regarding in which hand he remembered seeing the object? *No. Well, maybe.*

Was he sure he saw an object? *Yes.*

Could it have been a gun as opposed to a knife? *Yes.*

Was it shiny? *No.*

Why would he speculate that it was possibly a knife? *Don't know. Maybe someone mentioned that the drug dealer had a knife.*

Who mentioned that the victim was a drug dealer? *Don't know. Maybe read about it in one of the local papers.*

Didn't he realize when he read the article that he was possibly an important witness? *No. Well, maybe.*

Did he contact the police? *No.*

When his neighbor Norton was arrested, he must have contacted the police then to let them know they were making a mistake? *No.*

Why not? *Didn't want to get involved.*

What about Norton—did he have a weapon that night? *Oh, no. Definitely not. His hands were open. Like he was showing the drug dealer that he had nothing, no money, no weapon.*

His palms were open? *Yes.*

If he learned that Norton admitted having a large flashlight and striking the man with it, would that change his testimony? *No. Well, maybe.*

It was like flogging a dead horse, shooting fish in a barrel, taking candy from a baby—I could have gone on, but why? I had made my point and anything more would be mean-spirited. Jurors rarely enjoy seeing a witness degraded and demeaned.

The Best Part

Sloats attempted, unsuccessfully in my view, to rehabilitate Waterson on redirect.

"She shot herself in the foot with that witness," Lee whispered in my ear. I nodded my head in agreement.

Their only hope now rested with the defendant himself. Could he convince just one juror that he acted in self-defense and/or that someone else came upon the stunned victim and gave him the coup de grace? If he could get just one person to believe that, then he could hang the jury.

Norton's performance on direct examination was impeccable; he was soft-spoken, polite, and articulate. And in marked contrast to his lawyer, Norton's grooming was beyond reproach. His well-scrubbed face emerged from the starched collar of a pale blue shirt. His dark blue suit was freshly pressed for the occasion and his black loafers sported a spit shine. A red tie and an American-flag lapel pin completed the ensemble, sending the unequivocal message that he was one of the good guys, a real American.

The testimony was just as Sloats had outlined in her opening statement. Yes, he had struck the drug dealer, but not on the head. He only hit him once, a couple of times at most. And only on the back and shoulder area. And only in self-defense. After all, the drug dealer had attacked him first with a knife. Then, when the drug dealer was down on the sidewalk, and only to scare him and keep him from attacking further, Norton pounded the pavement with his flashlight.

When he left the scene, the drug dealer was uninjured. Just stunned. Or playing 'possum. Someone else must have come by later and delivered the blows to his head. The witnesses who say otherwise are confused or have had their testimony molded by the police and prosecution.

The initial police work on the case had been perfunctory, to put it politely. I was frustrated that the only piece of physical evidence booked by the responding officers was the flashlight. It would have been nice to have Norton's other gear, as he called it, to show the jury.

To my delight and amazement, Sloats produced a large sack and began extracting items: a pair of boots, a jacket, a belt, a baseball cap. I offered no objection and these items were received into evidence as Defendant's A through D. The defense then rested its case.

It was 11:30 in the morning and, contrary to his typical method of wringing every minute of court time out of each day, His Honor turned to me solicitously and asked if I would like to begin my cross-examination after the noon recess. Probably has a lunch date, I thought.

"Thank you, Your Honor," I responded, "but the People are prepared to go forward now." I didn't want the defense version of the case to have time to sink in during the lunch hour, and I was impatient to begin what I think is the best part of any criminal case—cross-examination of the accused.

His Honor gave me a sour look but nodded his head in acquiescence. I was on my feet.

First of all I wanted to wipe that self-satisfied look off the defendant's face. The jury needed to see what Norton looked like on the night of the crime. It was time to put Defendant's A through D to good use. After a few questions designed to establish the defendant's eagerness to rid his beloved hometown of the burgeoning criminal element, I shifted my focus to the defense exhibits.

Q. Was there a particular reason why you chose to wear a hat on a warm summer night?

A. The reason why I wore a hat at night is because I never wear a hat except on patrol. That way it makes it more difficult for the criminals who see me in the daytime to identify me as a member of the Stalwarts. I don't want to be an easy target.

Q. So the hat is part of the clothing you wore while on patrol at night in an attempt to camouflage yourself so that you would look different during the day, is that right?

A. I wouldn't use the word "camouflage."

Q. Did you use the hat to obscure your face?

A. No, you can clearly see my face with the cap. I can put it on and show you that it does not obscure my face.

Q. Please do. Please put it on just as you wore it on that night.

A. All right.

Q. Could I ask you to put the belt on, as well, to show us how that works?

A. Okay.

Q. Did you use this belt to hold various items such as the flashlight?

A. Yes.

Q. Could you demonstrate how the flashlight fits onto the belt?

A. Like this.

Q. Defense B, this olive drab jacket, could you put this on as well?

A. [Witness complies.]

Q. We might as well be thorough. Could you take a moment to slip off your loafers and put on these boots, Defense D?

A. Okay.

The transformation was complete. The refined, mild-mannered Dr. Jekyll had mutated before our eyes into the evil, menacing Mr. Hyde! Good time for the lunch break, I thought, and, as if I had telegraphed the message, Judge Ferry broke in:

"Ladies and gentlemen, be back at 1:30 sharp. Remember the admonition. Do not form any opinions or discuss this case or the subject matter of this case with anyone. Have a nice lunch."

"That was a good morning's work." Lee beamed at me on our way back to my office. "You're a pretty good trial lawyer, you know."

"Well, don't sound so surprised, Lee."

In general, I use every minute of my lunch hour when I'm in trial. There always seems to be something more to do before going back into court. This time was different. I couldn't wait for the minutes to pass. I was ready. It was time for me to attack the key area of the defense case.

When court reconvened, I started with questions concerning the relative positions and actions of the victim and the defendant when the physical encounter took place. When you know a witness is lying, an effective way to demonstrate this for the jury is to pose very detailed, highly specific questions.

Naturally, Norton remembered quite vividly what had *actually* happened that night. My cross-examination obliged him to block out his memory and make up an alternate version on the spot. This is not an easy task, even for an intelligent, well-rehearsed witness.

Robert Norton ended up describing a ludicrous scenario. The smaller man, whom he insisted on calling "the drug dealer," was leaning forward with his knees bent, holding the knife like a tennis racket, and attempting to stab the defendant with an upward motion.

Q. He was shorter than you, and he was hunched down, so that made him even shorter, is that right?

A. Yes. Well, he was taller than you are.

Q. Most are. But, in any event, it was at this point that you struck him in the back?

A. Yes.

Q. Now, he's coming at you with a knife extended toward your belly, is that right?

A. Yes.

Q. How far away from him are you at that point?

A. Three feet.

Q. And did you have to extend yourself to strike that first blow?

A. Yes.

Q. Would it be fair to say that the thing closest to you at this point was the knife?

A. Yes.

Q. The tip of the knife blade was the thing closest to you?

A. [Witness nods.]

Q. The next closest thing was his hand, is that correct?

A. Uh, yeah. Yes.

Q. The next closest thing was his arm and then his head, his neck, and his shoulder?

A. Uh.

Q. Is that correct?

A. Yes. Yes.

Q. So you had to extend your reach, past his hand, his arm, his head, in order to hit him on his back?

A. Yes. Okay. Yes.

Things got even better as my questions forced Norton to scramble for plausible answers. The victim had been found in a prone position on the sidewalk, with his head facing northeast near the wall of the warehouse and his feet pointing in a southwest direction, closer to the curb. This position was consistent with my theory of the case—that the defendant had come up behind the victim, struck him down with a single, powerful blow to the back of the head, and then repeatedly pounded the right side of the victim's cranium.

Norton had testified that "the drug dealer" had somehow "spun around" after being struck in the back and, in a series of motions defying the laws of physics, had ended up in the position in which he had been found.

Then, apparently realizing that he was contradicting the second part of his defense, i.e., that someone else did it, Norton quickly amended his testimony to state: "But he probably moved after I left and then was attacked by someone else."

Before Norton could go any further, I turned to the judge and asked that the defendant's last remarks be stricken from the record. There was no question pending, and his comments were both speculative and self-serving. The court was obliged to grant my motion and admonish the jury to disregard what they'd just heard.

How satisfying. The defendant's desperation was almost palpable. I moved quickly to another line of inquiry, the flashlight. As you may recall, the police reports indicated that it had been recovered from the defendant's sink. This was a point not to be overlooked.

Did the defendant habitually store his flashlight in the kitchen sink? *No.*

What was it doing in the sink? *Well, it had to be washed.*

And why was that? *Well, it had something on it.*

And was that "something" the blood and brains of the victim? *Of course not! [bristling with indignation].*

What was it? *Well, it was spit.*

Spit? *Well, worse than spit. It was a loogie. It was a great big glob of phlegm.*

What color was this substance? *Uh, sort of yellow and reddish-brown.*

The point had been made. I caught a couple of jurors shaking their heads.

My final questions for the defendant revolved around the fundamental dichotomy in his defense, or defenses if you prefer. On the one hand, he was in fear for his life and thus felt justified in using deadly force. On the other hand, he inexplicably did not do so; rather, some other person must have inflicted the devastating injuries after the defendant left the scene.

Norton seemed happy to return to his favorite topic—how terrified he was of the knife-wielding drug dealer. Of course, he was in fear for his life. He believed he would be stabbed or slashed to death if he didn't act to save himself.

So you hit Mr. Ramírez just as hard as you could? *[Long pause.]* With all your might? *Well, maybe not as hard as I could. But pretty hard.*

And only twice? *Yes.*

And both times in exactly the same place on the victim's back? *On the drug dealer's back or shoulder area.*

But in exactly the same place both times? *Yes.*

Did you hear the emergency room doctor testify that there were no injuries to the victim's back or shoulder area? [*Long pause.*] Not even bruising? *Yes.*

And you were unable to disarm the alleged assailant? *That's right.*

And when you turned your back on him, the victim was still armed? *Yes.*

And only "stunned" or "playing 'possum"? *I don't know what you mean.*

Those were your words that you used to describe the condition in which you left Mr. Ramírez, isn't that right? *Yes.*

So, you turned your back on a violent man with a knife who was attempting to kill you, even though you had been unable to either disarm him or incapacitate him? [*Really long pause.*]

No further questions.

GIVING IT TO THE JURY

We were in the home stretch now. Exhibits had been received into evidence. Both sides had rested. It was time for the attorneys to argue and the judge to instruct. Before closing arguments were to begin, Ms. Sloats and I met with Judge Ferry to discuss the jury instructions.

To my utter amazement, the judge suggested instructing the jury on simple battery. Although we were in chambers, I had the urge to leap to my feet and shriek *objection!* Instead I asked, as politely as I could, why the court thought the evidence supported such an instruction.

"I think it's quite clear, Ms. Batt," His Honor responded in an imperious tone. "If the jury concludes that Mr. Norton failed to prove he acted in self-defense but finds that he, nonetheless, struck the two blows to the victim's back, then we are talking about battery."

There was no reasoning with Judge Ferry on this point. Although Ms. Sloats had not requested an instruction on misdemeanor battery, she was pleased to sit back and let the judge help her out. In the end, the judge decided to instruct on the charged offenses as well as all possible lesser-included crimes.

It is essential for the lawyers to know how the jury will be instructed before they give their closing statements. Based on how Judge Ferry would instruct, I knew I needed to make some last-minute changes to my argument. I decided to use visual aids to help get my point across. The prosecution's position was simple. Our interpretation of the facts was reasonable and the defendant's explanations were unreasonable.

My first chart addressed Norton's claim of self-defense.

DEFENSE #1: SELF-DEFENSE

"Attacked by knife-wielding drug dealer, forced to use flashlight to defend self"

REASONABLE	UNREASONABLE
• Run for position of safety	• Pursue man who has knife
• Call for help	• Don't call for help
• Strike only in response	• Strike first
• Stop when danger ceases	• Strike more blows
• Have some injuries	• Have no injuries
• Preserve evidence	• Destroy evidence
• Disarm assailant	• Turn back on armed man
• Tell bystanders of knife	• Tell no one at scene
• Stay at scene	• Go home quickly
• Call police ASAP	• Wait to be arrested
• Show "knife" to police	• Leave "knife" at scene
• Exhibit some remorse	• Remain remorseless

Charts, diagrams, maps, photographs, and other physical evidence can help a trial lawyer to speak without continual reference to written notes. In my case, there is another benefit. I hate being imprisoned behind a lectern. There are two reasons: it calls attention to my height (or lack thereof), and it creates a barrier between the jury and me.

Even in courtrooms where the judge insists that lawyers stand behind the lectern (and you know Ferry was one of those), the use of charts is always a permissible reason to step out from behind that troublesome piece of furniture.

I made another chart to demonstrate the absurdity of the defendant's second defense, that Some Other Dude Did It.

DEFENSE #2: ALIBI

"It wasn't me—some other person beat the victim after I left"

REASONABLE	UNREASONABLE
• Different weapon used by other person	• Similar weapon used
• Victim leaves scene if only stunned	• Victim unable to leave
• Victim in different position on pavement	• Victim in same position
• Victim found elsewhere	• Victim found there
• Witnesses to second attack	• No witnesses
• Injuries to victim's back	• Only head injuries
• Time elapsed before second attack	• No time for second attack
• Defendant shows some remorse	• Defendant remorseless

I admit I harped on the defendant's lack of remorse. It was something I found personally repugnant, and I hoped the jury would agree with me. Ms. Sloats argued vehemently that her client was a peace-loving, civic-minded young man who had acted as any reasonable person would in a life-threatening situation.

Sloats argued that the victim's unconscious body was found at a location other than the one where Norton had struck him down. All right, it was on the same street. And on the same side of the same street. But it was a different location. Thus proving the point that the victim was able to get up and move on before being attacked by the other person.

To this end, Ms. Sloats produced the largest photographs I had ever seen used in a courtroom. They were life-size shots of the east side of Seward between Santa Monica and Lexington, the next street north. She taped these exhibits to the courtroom walls, creating a monstrous mural.

What was the point of this? Sloats launched into an incomprehensible harangue about loading zones and parking meters and other "landmarks" to prove that Ramírez must have moved after his encounter with Norton. She compared her photographs with the "puny" eight-and-a-half-by-eleven pictures the prosecution had introduced into evidence. I suppose the implication was that the prosecution had somehow hidden the truth from the jury by using smaller than life-size exhibits.

Sloats was not troubled by the fact that the prosecution's photographs were taken at the time of the crime and were admitted into evidence as exhibits in the case, while her mural consisted of photographs taken almost a year and a half after the events in question. I did not object.

The more Sloats talked, the more desperate she sounded. She was sweating profusely, and I was sure the jurors' ears were not the only organs being assaulted.

My closing remarks were to the point:

"The defendant pursued the victim and struck him down using this flashlight. Once the victim was on the pavement, the defendant struck him several more times in the head, causing the severe injuries the doctors have described.

"There was no knife. No one saw a knife and no knife was recovered. Mr. Norton never said anything about a knife at the time of his encounter with Mr. Ramírez. The defendant had no injuries—not so much as a scratch.

"Without evidence that a knife ever existed, the self-defense claim is going nowhere. So Mr. Norton gives you a whole other defense—someone else did it. To that end, the defense attempts to confuse location and time.

"They want to confuse you with parking meters, loading zones, driveways, light poles, and foliage. They want you to think it took longer than fifteen minutes for Jean-Luc to return to the scene. They want to put the defendant as far away from the blood on the pavement as they can. A loading zone sign becomes a significant landmark. Just as blood on the flashlight becomes a glob of brown phlegm.

"Finally, they want you to think so little of the victim that when you realize that the defendant is guilty, you won't want to convict him. After all, removing Ramírez from the streets was almost a public service.

"This little fellow was an obnoxious drunk, possibly possessing or selling marijuana. He looked unkempt. He had acted crazy earlier in the evening. He represented everything that was wrong with Hollywood.

"In fact, although the prosecution need not prove motive, this may well have been the defendant's motive. Here was someone who symbolized everything Mr. Norton hated. And he was a little guy. The defendant could be a real hero, he could pound this guy into the pavement and walk away, and no one would object.

"Mr. Norton counted on the Stalwarts going home and doing nothing—and that almost happened. He didn't count on Jean-Luc having an attack of conscience or curiosity and going back. He didn't count on Jean-Luc telling Chris Fox and Chris calling the paramedics and the police. He didn't count on the medical evidence telling the story of what had really happened.

"Now the defendant is counting on you, ladies and gentlemen, or just one of you, to look the other way. The court will instruct you on the law, and you have already promised that you will follow it. If you can find one instruction that says that Jesús Ramírez is not deserving of the protections of our laws, then acquit. But if you follow the law and your oath as jurors, you will convict the defendant as charged."

I sat down and Judge Ferry launched into the instructions, after which he entrusted the jury to his bailiff. The jurors rose from their seats and filed into the jury room to commence their deliberations. I offered up a small prayer—let Carlo Barzini be the foreman.

THE VERDICT

It took four very long days for the jury to return with a verdict. During that time some of my fellow prosecutors who had been following the progress of the case subjected me to a grueling cross-examination. What had I done to confuse the jury? What evidence had I omitted? What argument had I failed to make?

None of their questions were as searching and recondite as the ones I asked myself. I had done my very best. The jurors all seemed intelligent and thoroughly engaged in the process. Was I so close to the case that I failed to see something? I took complete responsibility for the outcome, whatever it would be, but, with each passing day, I felt less confident that it would be a guilty verdict. And I kept plaguing myself with the same question. In what way had I failed?

When the call came that the jury had a verdict, there was no time to reach Detective Benson. I grabbed my file and took the elevator down to Department 108.

J. T. Sloats and Robert Norton were already seated at counsel table and the perpetually florally frocked mother was sitting in the back of the courtroom. They must have been waiting out in the hallway. Waiting in the hallway every day for four days? As soon as I had taken my seat at counsel table, the court clerk buzzed the judge and he took the bench.

The jury was then invited into the courtroom, and the judge asked if a verdict had been reached. I had to smile when Mr. Carlo Barzini rose to his feet as the foreman of the jury and presented the bailiff with the signed verdict forms. The bailiff handed the forms to the judge, who with a deliberately impassive expression examined each page. The forms were then handed to the court clerk, who intoned:

"Title of Court and Cause. We, the jury in the above-entitled case, as to Count One in the Information, the crime of Attempt Murder in violation of Sections 664 and 187 of the Penal Code, find the defendant, Robert Norton, NOT GUILTY."

I held my breath. I looked at the people in the jury box. Their faces betrayed nothing. They were as impassive as Judge Ferry. The clerk continued:

"We, the jury in the above-entitled case, as to Count Two in the Information, the crime of Assault by Means of Force Likely to Produce Great Bodily Injury and with a Deadly Weapon, to wit: a flashlight, in violation of Section 245(a)(1) of the Penal Code, find the defendant, Robert Norton, GUILTY. We further find the Special Allegation that the defendant, Robert Norton, during the commission of this offense, intentionally inflicted Great Bodily Injury on the victim, one Jesús Ramírez, in violation of Section 12022.7 of the Penal Code, to be TRUE. So say you one, so say you all?"

The jurors responded "Yes" in unison and I breathed an audible sigh of relief. The judge thanked the jury for their service and excused them. He advised them that they were now free to discuss the case with anyone, including the attorneys, and if they wished to remain in the hallway, the attorneys would be out momentarily. After the jurors departed, Ferry set the date for sentencing.

That hinky feeling was returning. I knew this was a state prison case, but I also knew that I could not rely on Judge Ferry to see things my way. As I had prior to the trial, I suggested a Section 1203.03 diagnostic study.

"No need," the judge retorted. "I've heard the evidence and I know what this case is worth. It took the People almost two years to bring this case to trial and it felt like we spent another two years in trial. The sentencing will take place in two weeks. Period."

When Ms. Sloats and I emerged from the courtroom, the entire jury panel was there to greet us. Sloats gave them a sweeping and disdainful look. Norton and his mother then appeared and the triumvirate marched off together.

Mr. Barzini, still in the role of foreman, spoke on behalf of the group.

"We wanted to apologize for taking so long to reach a verdict, but we really struggled over the attempt-murder charge. When we took our first ballot, there was complete agreement on the assault charge and the great bodily injury allegation. No problem. We were unanimous that you had proved those things. But, Ms. Batt, we all wanted you to know that we think you did a great job, but you just didn't prove the attempt murder. We believe he did it, of course. But we think you didn't prove it beyond a reasonable doubt. Sorry about that."

"No need to apologize. I think you're right," I responded.

"You do?" another juror asked in amazement.

I explained how difficult a charge of attempt murder is to prove and complimented the jurors on doing a fine job.

"What happens to Norton now?" another juror wanted to know.

I told them about the sentencing hearing and what options were open to the judge.

"Can we attend the hearing?" Mr. Barzini asked.

"That would be a first," I said. "While there is no legal or procedural reason to prevent you from attending, most jurors are happy that their service is over and don't want to spend another day in the courthouse if they don't have to. But if any of you want to attend, you would be welcome to do so. Now that your jury service is concluded, each of you is like any other member of the public. And the courts are open to the public."

As soon as I got back to my office, I called Lee with the good news. She had been assigned to a double homicide case and was overwhelmed with work but promised to be at the sentencing hearing if possible. I then called John Winston, Victoria Cathcart, and Jean-Luc St. Pierre. They were all relieved, but concerned that Judge Ferry might not sentence Norton to state prison. I had to admit that I shared their concern.

Victoria promised to do her part. All her many contacts would be notified and encouraged to attend the sentencing. John had made arrangements to bring Jesús's family to California so they could attend the sentencing. Jean-Luc would be at the hearing, along with most of the Stalwarts. We hoped that with a courtroom full of intensely interested onlookers, His Honor would do the right thing.

And there was one thing left for me to do in the two weeks I had before the sentencing hearing. Like Lee, I had other cases pressing in on me, but I had to complete this one. Unfortunately, many prosecutors think their work is done once the jury has brought back a verdict. They neglect to view the sentencing hearing as an integral part of the criminal justice process, and frequently this works to their detriment. In any case where the sentence is contested, I write a sentencing memorandum to the court.

A good sentencing memorandum should take the court through the calculus of aggravating and mitigating factors that the trial judge is mandated to consider in arriving at a just sentence. In Norton's case, my memo addressed the initial determination of probation versus state prison and demonstrated why a state prison sentence was appropriate. I then focused on why the high term was the most appropriate state prison sentence to impose. You might think such a memo unnecessary in a case where the defendant bashed in the head of an unarmed man and left his victim to bleed to death on the pavement . . . but I had that hinky feeling again.

THE SENTENCE

The day for Norton's sentencing had arrived. I entered Department 108 for what I hoped would be the last time—not just on this case but in my career as a prosecutor. I had decided that, if I ever were sent to Judge Ferry's court again, I would lay paper on him.

I was early and, looking around the courtroom, I was amazed to see that every seat was already taken. The Stalwarts were out in force: I nodded to Victoria, Aram, Dixie, Jean-Luc, the Georges, Lloyd and Shirley Linden, Larry and Susan Goldfarb, Rachel Stern and Donna Ritter, and other members of the group I recognized by face only.

John Winston was seated on the other side of the courtroom with a group of people I knew must be the Ramírez family. They looked like something out of a Gorman painting—humble yet self-possessed, beautiful yet unaffected. I went over to them and was introduced to the uncle, the father, the mother, and a younger sister.

"*Gracias,*" Jesús's mother whispered, taking my hand briefly.

"*De nada,*" I responded, the full import of the phrase resonating painfully. I saw her eyes fill with tears and realized that I, too, was on the verge of crying. I turned away.

The media were well represented. In addition to the local Hollywood press, the beat reporters from the *Los Angeles Times* and the *Daily Journal* and a commentator from one of the local news radio stations were in attendance. The jury box was empty, but its recent occupants were all in court. A smiling Carlo Barzini waved at me. I nodded in response and scanned the courtroom one more time before taking my seat at counsel table. Amazing. Even Jim Weaver and Cameron Hill were in the audience, and they weren't under subpoena.

I took out my notes in order to review them one last time. I wanted my remarks to be brief but compelling, and I didn't want to belabor the points I'd already made in my memorandum. Lee Benson slid into the chair beside me, a little out of breath.

"Didn't think I'd miss the show, did you?"

"Thanks for being here."

"What's wrong? You look worried."

"I don't know. I've got that hinky feeling again."

A loud banging noise announced the arrival of attorney Sloats (briefcase slamming into swinging door), followed by Robert Norton (in dark suit) and mother (in garish floral attire). It was almost comedic but I didn't feel like laughing.

"Where's the judge?" Lee wanted to know. "Isn't he usually on the bench putting every nanosecond of court time to good use?"

Minutes passed. The audience became restless, their whispers growing louder and louder until the bailiff felt obliged to ask for quiet. More minutes passed and the court clerk, looking concerned, got up from her desk and disappeared into chambers. More minutes passed.

Suddenly the clerk reappeared, followed immediately by Judge Ferry, who hurriedly took his place on the bench. The bailiff was taken off guard and was only able to blurt "Come to order!" rather than the more elaborate and pompous opening that His Honor preferred.

"Calling the case of the People versus Robert Norton. The record will reflect that all parties are present. We are here for the probation and sentencing hearing. I have reviewed the court file as well as the sentencing memorandum filed by the People. I have decided to follow Ms. Batt's suggestion and have a diagnostic study prepared in this case. The bailiff is directed to take the defendant into custody for transportation to Chino State Prison pursuant to Penal Code Section 1203.03. We will set a new date for sentencing ninety days hence. If the report can be completed earlier, the sentencing date will be advanced. Time waived for sentencing?"

Ms. Sloats answered in the affirmative, the court's question being a virtual formality.

"Your Honor," I interposed, "members of the victim's family have traveled here from Mexico and would like an opportunity to address the court."

"They may do so at the next court date. We are in recess." Ferry disappeared off the bench.

There was a moment of dead silence, and then the entire courtroom erupted in confused chatter. The bailiff put a brawny arm around Norton's shoulders and guided him to the lockup door. As the handcuffs closed on his fleshy wrists, the reality of the situation suddenly registered with Norton.

"Noooo! Noooo! Mother, do something!" he wailed.

The bailiff nudged Norton through the door and then closed it behind them. We could hear Norton's muffled screams fading away. The mother, also slow to appreciate what had just happened, stood up abruptly and began howling. Before things could get any crazier, the bailiff called for backup and the courtroom was cleared of all spectators.

"Lee, we're screwed," I said as I picked up my file and we headed out into the hallway.

"Why do you say that? Didn't Ferry just do exactly what you had asked him to?"

"Yes, but for all the wrong reasons."

I explained to Lee that Ferry was determined to give Norton probation. But, to his dismay, the judge found his courtroom had been packed with witnesses, jurors, civic leaders, close relatives of the victim, and — most significant — members of the media. For Ferry to impose such a light sentence in such a heavy case with such an audience would be political suicide. He couldn't continue the sentencing without some sort of reason, so he latched onto the diagnostic study as an excuse.

"Marissa, this is a state prison case," Lee declared.

"You don't have to convince me. What I'm saying is that Ferry will manage to continue the sentencing until nobody cares anymore, and then he will give Norton probation."

"I hope you're wrong about this."

I wasn't wrong. It took about sixty days for the diagnostic study to be completed. On the sixty-first day, a somewhat slimmer Robert Norton was hauled back into Department 108. Ferry was probably calling Chino on a daily basis to hurry along the report. God forbid his favorite defendant should spend a day more than necessary in state prison.

The report was a blistering denouncement of Norton as a vicious, remorseless, narcissistic, overbearing individual subject to uncontrollable rages. The authors noted that Norton had finally admitted that he had lied on the witness stand and that Ramírez had been unarmed.

The report concluded by stating that "Norton's volatility, lack of moral integrity and complete absence of remorse combine to make him a walking time bomb. As such, he constitutes a serious threat to the safety and security of the community. The diagnostic staff are in unanimous agreement and therefore recommend that Robert Norton be remanded to the Department of Corrections."

This time the courtroom was about half full of spectators. Members of the Ramírez family were not in attendance, as John could not afford to pay their travel expenses and lodging for a second trip. Jesús's mother had written a letter to the court, which John had translated and was prepared to read. The only juror present for this second hearing was Carlo Barzini, who had sworn he would see the case through to the very end. All the reporters had lost interest except for my friend Jon Goodman of KNX radio, who was there as a personal favor. I was pleased to see that Victoria Cathcart, Jean-Luc, and a handful of Stalwarts had made the trip.

"With a report like this, Ferry is going to have to send our boy to the joint," Lee assured me.

"It's not happening, Lee. Ferry will come up with some excuse."

Sometimes I hate it when I'm right. Ferry continued the case again, this time to allow Ms. Sloats time to hire her own psychologist or psychiatrist to prepare a report on Norton's suitability for probation. Of course, Sloats hadn't asked for a continuance and the idea of hiring her own shrink would never have occurred to her.

On the third date set for Norton's sentencing, the courtroom was almost empty. Victoria Cathcart and John Winston were there. Jean-Luc could not afford to take any more time off from work but had called me that morning with words of encouragement. True to his word, Carlo was there to see it through. He gave me a big smile and a thumbs-up signal from his seat in the back of the courtroom. And, despite her demanding caseload, Lee Benson was sitting right next to me at counsel table. No relatives of the victim. No civic leaders. No members of the media.

The unholy trinity of Sloats, Norton, and Norton's mother arrived with a new addition to the defense team. Dr. Seymour Breck was not a member of the court-approved panel of forensic psychiatrists and psychologists. In fact, he had no training in forensics. He had not read any of the police reports or transcripts in this case. Nor had he spoken with a single witness. He had not attempted to contact the prosecutor. In fact, the idea of doing so had never occurred to him. He had received all his information from the best source—the defendant himself. As far as Dr. Breck was concerned, everything else was just hearsay.

Dr. Breck's report described Robert Norton in glowing terms. (Big surprise.) Norton was a mild-mannered man who wouldn't hurt anyone. He had only acted in self-defense when his life was threatened. The time spent in the penitentiary had deeply traumatized him. What had happened to him was a travesty.

Rather than merely submitting Breck's report, Sloats insisted on calling him as a witness. Ordinarily, Judge Ferry would not have tolerated such redundancy, such a waste of precious court time. But, in the context of the Norton case, His Honor was eager to hear from Dr. Breck. It was okay with me; at least I'd have the opportunity to cross-examine the doctor.

As soon as the doctor had concluded his testimony—which in every way mirrored his written report—I rose to begin my cross-examination. I was going to destroy this quack. His lack of forensic training alone made him close to worthless as a witness. Plus all his conclusions were based exclusively on the defendant's lies. Before I could ask my first question, Judge Ferry cut me off.

"You have exactly five minutes to convince me that I should not grant probation in this case. You can use that time any way you like. You may question the doctor or you may use the time to argue. It's up to you." This pronouncement was accompanied by a lipless smile. I was stunned. We had just wasted close to an hour listening to Dr. Breck paraphrase his written report. And I was to have no more than five minutes to present the People's position.

I chose to argue and argue I did. I argued my heart out for five minutes. These were my last words to the court:

"Your Honor, I have prosecuted violent criminals for over twenty years. In that time I have never seen a case involving injuries of this magnitude in which the victim survived. Admittedly, Mr. Ramírez died sixteen months after the attack. Your Honor, the nature of this case—the particular viciousness of the attack and the severity of the injuries—mandates a state prison commitment."

I ended my argument by reading John's translation of Mrs. Ramírez's letter: "Jesús was my firstborn child. He was always a good boy and did his best to help his family. That is why he traveled to the United States. When he came home to us, I thought I would die. My beautiful son had been turned into something not even human. A monster. On the outside. But inside, still my sweet son. Jesús was the sun and the moon to me, and all the stars in the sky. Jesús was my heart. My heart is gone."

I sank back into my chair at counsel table.

"Great argument," Lee whispered in my ear.

"Not great enough," I whispered back.

The absence of the press emboldened Ferry.

"I find there are many mitigating factors in this case," he began, "not least among them the fact that Mr. Norton was attempting to clean up the streets of Hollywood. He was helping his community defend itself against the criminal elements. Mr. Ramírez was, no doubt, under the influence of some substance and was behaving in a fashion where he was creating a disturbance and calling attention to himself. Now, Mr. Norton did act out and lose his temper for a moment. But I believe that losing one's temper for a brief moment in an altercation on the street should not require me to ignore the many years of law-abiding conduct and service to his community that Mr. Norton has performed."

With that, His Honor sentenced Robert Norton to probation.

A REFLECTION

About a month after the sentencing, I got a call from the Georges.

"We're having a party—a little get-together—next Saturday, and we'd love for you to attend," George said.

"And if the date doesn't work for you, we'll pick another," Jorge cut in. "After all, you're our guest of honor."

"I tell him all the time not to sound so desperate. It's simply not attractive," George complained.

"Oh, don't mind him, he's such a fussy queen. You'll come, right?"

"I wouldn't miss it. What can I bring?"

"Just yourself and Detective Benson if you think she'd like to come."

The evening had a magical quality. It was now late May, and the weather was so mild that the party was held outside on the patio. A full moon reflected in the swimming pool, candles flickered, and the amber lanterns cast a warm glow on a lavish buffet table. There were kabobs and sushi, salads and knishes, cakes and pies. Dixie had contributed her famous fried chicken, and the Lindens had made lobster rolls, a Nova Scotia delicacy. Apparently many of the Stalwarts were good cooks.

"This is a great group," Victoria decreed, resting on a lounge chair with her plate piled high.

"The greatest member of our group is Jean-Luc," Lloyd stated matter-of-factly.

"You must really like my jambalaya!"

"I'm serious, Jean-Luc. You were the only one who went back. You saved a life."

"I wish I could have done more."

"We all do the best we can," John Winston said. He had brought Victoria a drink and was now sitting next to her. I had never noticed before what a handsome couple they made.

"Lloyd is right, you are the man!" Chris Fox chimed in.

Jean-Luc looked embarrassed and uncomfortable. He made his way over to where I was sitting by the pool.

"I'd like to talk to you alone, Marissa. There are some things that are bothering me."

We walked to the pool house and Jean-Luc invited me into his home. Wall sconces illuminated a red tile floor, whitewashed shuttered windows, colorful throw rugs, a futon bed, and, dominating the room, a Buddhist shrine.

I walked over to the altar, which consisted of a wooden cabinet on a low table. The cabinet is called a butsudan. The butsudan's double doors were open, and inside was the Gohonzon, the True Object of Devotion, a scroll on which is depicted the enlightened life of the Buddha.

I got down on my knees, pressed my palms together, and chanted, "*Nam-Myoho-Renge-Kyo, Nam-Myoho-Renge-Kyo, Nam-Myoho-Renge-Kyo.*"

"You're a Buddhist!"

"Yes, Jean-Luc. I've been practicing for many years. You said something was bothering you."

"Several things. They all have to do with the case. With Robert. And with Jesús. I mean, no one stopped Robert. His two friends were close enough to do something. But they just stood there. Then everyone just went home. I did, too. And now Jesús is dead. And the trial, that bothers me a lot. If there had been any justice at all, Robert would be locked up now. I know I don't sound like a very good Buddhist, but that judge was a complete asshole."

"Jean-Luc, we know that everything is governed by the Mystic Law of Cause and Effect. Jesús made the causes to suffer these terrible effects in this lifetime. It was a devastating tragedy but, from a Buddhist perspective, it was a karmic debt that had to be paid."

"All right. But what about Robert? He made a terrible cause, and the effect was he got probation. How fair is that?"

"Jean-Luc, you know that the Law of Cause and Effect is very strict. Like the law of gravity, it operates whether or not people know about it or believe in it. Just as the lotus flower blooms and seeds simultaneously, the latent effect is born at the same instant the internal cause is made. It may not manifest itself immediately, but the effect exists in a dormant condition until activated by some external cause. We both need to have faith in the Mystic Law."

"Sometimes Buddhism sounds so scientific."

"Some say Buddhism is the Unification Theory of Physics."

"I'm still troubled that Robert is out on probation."

"I am, too. In one sense, this can only be described as an injustice. But we both know that, from a Buddhist perspective, justice is always done. If not in this lifetime, then in the next."

EPILOGUE

The Melting Man

It is with uncanny symmetry that my career in the D.A.'s office has come full circle. More than a quarter of a century ago, as a second-year law student, I took a practical course as a district attorney intern. My professor assigned me to a small courthouse on Regent Street in Inglewood. It was there, as a certified law student, that I put on my first preliminary hearing, tried my first jury trial, and was berated by the first of many chauvinist judges for being female and having the temerity to think that I could practice law.

This particular Inglewood municipal judge took issue with my very appearance, his primary complaint being my hair. I was right in the middle of arguing a rather subtle point of law when His Honor, palms pressed toward me in an act of silent entreaty, asked that I, and I alone, approach the bench.

If you have read the preceding stories with care, a little red flag should have sprouted in the rich soil of your fertile mind. Yes, a prosecutor should never, ever, have an ex parte communication with a judge on any matter before the court, and His Honor was asking me to do just that.

I was flabbergasted. And true to the consensus of the Brotherhood of Forensic Psychologists, I was caught in a Flight or Fight paralysis. I looked helplessly at the deputy public defender on the opposing side of the table. He'd been around for at least a year, a highly experienced lawyer in the context in which I was operating.

"What do I do?" I mouthed silently. To my dismay it looked like my Worthy Opponent was about to break out in gales of laughter. As it was, he bent over and made a sound halfway between a hearty guffaw and a hacking smoker's cough. What a cretin, I thought. But then he straightened his torso, turned toward me, and hissed loudly, "Do what the judge says."

A thousand unpleasant thoughts crowded my brain on the mile-long walk up to the sidebar. Had I said something so inordinately stupid that the judge felt he needed to correct me right now and, in order to help me save face, he was going to tell me what an imbecile I was off the record and without the public defender as a witness? Or maybe it was something so ghastly that he would never want me in his courtroom again, and he would be calling my professor as soon as he got his righteous self off the bench to tell him that I deserved an F in the class?

I was at sidebar. His Honor peered at me over his frameless half-glasses.

"I can't have you in my courtroom anymore," he began.

I failed to control an audible gasp of horror. He *was* kicking me out of his courtroom.

"What have I done?" I stammered, perhaps a little too loudly for our sidebar conference.

"It's your hair," His Honor informed me, in a tone no better modulated. "It's simply too curly," he went on, to my complete astonishment.

"I beg your pardon?" My voice sounded a little like a squawk this time.

"I said, it's too curly. I mean, for God's sake, you have these little golden-brown ringlets all over your head."

"But, it's natural. I mean, I don't curl it. That's just the way it is."

"Well, I find it to be unacceptable. It's simply too—uh—too distracting. You know, for a courtroom setting."

"Sorry," I mumbled, unconsciously twirling one of those distracting ringlets around my forefinger.

His Honor sighed after a brief pause. "All right, you may remain in my court, but you must do something about your curly hair. Maybe if you used a headband or put it in a ponytail or something."

"I'll do my very best. Thank you, Your Honor." I couldn't think of anything else to say and I had already learned, even at that tender age, that it's always a good idea to thank the judge, even if he's just put the screws to you.

My very best was rollers the size of tin cans and lots of hair gel. The straight look would last, on a nonhumid day, until midmorning when my 'do would do what it always did and start to go back, as we say in South-Central. By afternoon, the dread ringlets would have returned. And when I say dread, I do not mean dred. I'll have you know that I never allowed my hair to lock. Braids yes, dreds no. It was my personal concession to the rigid conformity favored by the L.A. D.A.'s office.

So there you have a little vignette of Life as a Female Certified Law Student in Inglewood in 1972. "A window in time that memory enframes," as my beloved Judge Ringer, who was also a poet, once said.

As I write this, I am once again assigned to the Inglewood courthouse. It's the same little two-story building on Regent Street with the same grimy gray and black checkered linoleum floors and the same lack of potable water. But now, in its present iteration as part of the Thurgood Marshall Justice Center, instead of housing four courtrooms devoted to felony preliminary hearings and misdemeanor jury trials involving adult defendants, it has three courtrooms devoted to juvenile delinquency cases. One of the courtrooms has been turned into a waiting room for the young miscreants and their families—there are too many of them to wait in the hallways.

When I was first transferred from the hustle and bustle of the downtown Criminal Courts Building to the relatively low-keyed and slow-paced juvenile justice assignment in Inglewood, I thought I would lose my mind. With no jury trials for juveniles, and the nature of most juvenile crimes being typically less factually complex than adult prosecutions,

I needed less time for preparation. A confounding factor contributing to my overall boredom was the glacial pace of the proceedings in these three courtrooms.

There was one judge—admittedly a poststroke impairment was probably the cause—who spoke so slowly that it could not be imitated. That slow. By paying my dues with many months spent in the slower two courtrooms, and by reminding everyone of my seniority, and, ultimately, by virtue of the arrival on the scene of a new and improved boss, I was transferred to the courtroom of the sweetest, smartest, and fastest judge in the building. Yesss!

But I was still bored. The big problem here was not the judge but rather what to do while waiting for the various defense attorneys to arrive on the scene, read their files (if they remembered to bring them), and either persuade their respective clients to admit (our cutesy way of saying plead guilty) or go to trial.

I had studied the other courtroom personnel in an attempt to see how they managed the situation. In one courtroom the court reporter did crossword puzzles all day long. In another the bailiff attended to his rather complicated social life—on the county phone. I had noticed that two of the court clerks appeared transfixed by something on their respective computer screens. After a short time I found out why: they were engaged in an ongoing chess tournament against one another—on the local area network.

Well, I tried the crosswords for a while. Still bored. Then I graduated to reading novels. At first I worried that the judge might think this behavior disrespectful, but I guess seeing his reporter doing crosswords day after day had inured him to such conduct. I reread a number of the classics. Not boring, but I still had that sense of anxiety felt only by a true type-A personality. I needed to be multitasking.

So I'm sitting in the courtroom of the sweetest, smartest, fastest bench officer and one of my noncivilian (that's cop) witnesses leans over the jury box (that's where all the law enforcement witnesses like to sit so they're not right next to the minors and their police-hating families in the audience) and says:

"Hey, what are you so busily typing on your laptop? Are you writing the next best-seller?"

"That is my plan."

"No kidding?"

"No kidding."

"Uh, what's it about?"

"It's about a couple of cases I handled when I was working downtown. It's about three cases, to be precise."

"What were they about?"

"Well, one involved an arson, rape, attempt murder with multiple defendants and multiple victims. One was a homosexual rape case. And one was a bludgeoning of an unarmed man on the streets of Hollywood. But they all are about the strength of the human spirit and my faith that justice is always done, whether or not we see it in the courtroom."

"No kidding."

"No kidding."

"So listen, I was involved in an interesting case one time. I was just a rookie, working 77th. They radioed for all the rookies to roll to the crime scene. You see something as weird as this once in a career. We called it the Case of the Melting Man."

"What was it about?"

"You wouldn't believe it. While this man is asleep, this woman pours some boiling acid or something on the poor guy's face and on his dick—I mean, his genitals. Sorry, ma'am."

"It wasn't acid. It was Red Devil Lye. Happened over on Myrtle Street, didn't it?"

"Yeah. It did. How did you know?"

"I prosecuted the case."

"No kidding!"

"No kidding. Small world, huh?"

"Tell me more about it. All I remember is seeing that poor guy rolling around, butt-naked, on his front lawn. What ever happened to him?"

"Well, he was a mover. He drove moving vans for a living. He had done it for years, ever since he got out of the Marines. He never regained his eyesight, but the company took him back anyway. They gave him a new job wrapping breakables. Same pay. Turned out, he was very good at it."

"What about his, you know, his gonads?"

"Same as his eyes. Basically burnt off by the boiling lye. Put him completely out of commission sexually. Even had to sit down to pee."

"Oh jeez." My friend the cop looked queasy.

"We filed two charges on his wife—aggravated mayhem and assault with caustic chemicals causing great bodily injury."

"So it was his wife that did it. What happened to her?"

"In a certain way, that's the more interesting part of the story. She pled not guilty and we went to trial. She was represented by one of my favorite public defenders, a guy named Stu Mintzer, who has since retired. We tried the case to a jury and it hung up, eleven to one.

"The one holdout was an older white woman. For some reason she identified with our defendant. I asked her what the problem was, where I had failed to make my case. She said I had proved beyond a reasonable that the defendant had committed the crimes charged, but that she still couldn't vote to convict. Why not, I asked. She said she just knew that the victim had done something horrible to deserve such an attack. She just knew it.

"So, Stu and I were stuck retrying the case. We decided to do it right away and get it over with. Nobody likes a retrial. We were back in court within a week and about to call for another jury panel when Stu approaches me. He says his client wants to talk to me, alone. That's an ethical no-no.

"I told Stu I'd be willing to talk to his client, but only if he were present as well. He tells me that his client doesn't want him there, that she wants to talk to me privately. I was curious, but I needed to protect myself, so I put the whole thing on the record and got the judge to warn the defendant against talking to me. She was undeterred. So I talked with her privately.

"She had a question. She wanted to know if I hated her. I assured her that I did not hate her at all but that I was appalled by the heinous nature of her crime. She then asked me what I thought she should do. I was astounded. A defendant asking her prosecutor for advice. Well, I told her.

"I told her she should plead guilty as charged and that I would argue that she should spend the maximum number of years in the state prison. She didn't even blink. I told her that she presented a danger to others. That no matter what she thought her husband had done—she was convinced that he was cheating on her—that no matter what she thought, her actions were vicious and demonstrated a callousness toward human life that was horrifying. I told her that she needed both rehabilitation and punishment and that I thought she should be locked up for as long as the law allowed.

"She nodded slowly and we reentered the courtroom. I had been talking to her in the lockup. The bail set had been too high for her to bail out. Anyway, we go back on the record and she pleads guilty and the judge maxes her out."

"No kidding."

"No kidding."

"You know, maybe you should put this story in your book."

"Maybe I will."

APPENDIX

Twenty-five Rules for Giving Effective Testimony

1. If you can answer a question with a yes or no, do so.

2. Say "yes" or "no." Do not nod or shake your head or mumble "uh-huh" or "uh-uh."

3. Do not volunteer any information that is not requested.

4. Keep all your answers short and to the point.

5. Speak in complete sentences.

6. Answer in a loud, clear voice.

7. Look at whoever is doing the questioning, whether it is the prosecutor, the defense attorney, or the judge. Do not look at me when the defense attorney is questioning you.

8. Do not stare at the defendant; it will only distract you. Look at the defendant only when asked to identify him.

9. Focus all your concentration into listening to the questions and answering them accurately.

10. Be sure the questioner has finished the question before you answer.

11. On the other hand, do not pause too long before answering; it will look like you are making up the answer.

12. Do not speak unless there is a question pending.

13. If you do not understand a question, ask to have it rephrased.

14. Do not, under any circumstances, answer a question you don't understand.

15. No one expects you to remember every detail. If you do not remember or do not know something, say so.

16. However, do not say you do not remember something just because it is painful or embarrassing to discuss.

17. As much as possible, try to remember and repeat the exact words the defendant used when you are asked what he said.

18. When asked questions about time, distance, height, weight, and age, estimates are acceptable. Don't be more specific than you feel is honest.

19. Do not apologize for your testimony. Avoid prefacing your answer with such comments as "I guess" or "I don't really remember, but —".

20. The defense attorney may ask questions that end with "isn't that true?" Do not agree with him if it is not true.

21. The defense attorney may ask offensive questions. Do not get angry. Remember that it is not a personal attack against you.

22. If you find yourself getting upset or tearful, do not hesitate to ask the judge for a moment. If you need a break to use the restroom, ask the judge; don't sit there and suffer.

23. Direct examination will usually proceed in chronological order. Cross-examination will generally jump from topic to topic in no apparent order. Do not let this confuse you.

24. The defense attorney may show you written statements, police reports, or transcripts of prior testimony in an attempt to impeach
you. You should not feel obliged to conform your testimony to such
prior statements. If there are discrepancies, you should be prepared
to explain them.

25. The judge may propound questions. It doesn't mean he has a problem with your testimony, it just means he's awake.